Communicat

A Guide for Health Work

Richard Bolstad with Margot Hamblett,
Te Hata Ohlson, and Jan Hardie

Longman Paul

Longman Paul Limited
46 Hillside Road, Auckland 10,
New Zealand

Associated companies throughout the world.

First published 1992
Reprinted 1994, 1996

ISBN 0 582 85967 0

Produced by Longman Paul Ltd
Printed in Malaysia
through Longman Malaysia, GPS
Typeset in Cheltenham Light 10/12 pt
WP/01

We use **paper from sustainable forestry**

Contents

Foreword vi

Part One: Basics of Communication 1

CHAPTER 1: Getting in Contact 3

- Introducing Yourself 4
- Warmup 12
- Culture and Meeting 18

CHAPTER 2: Just a State of Mind 23

- Anchoring Yourself to the State of Your Choice 24
- The Social Roots of Self-Esteem 36
- Parent, Adult, and Child States 46

CHAPTER 3: The Context of Communication 55

- Approaching Others 56
- Spot the Difference 60
- The General Impression 66
- Just Thinking 72

CHAPTER 4: Problem Solving 83

- Problem Ownership 84
- Setting Goals and Solving Problems 89
- Learning 95

Part Two: Caring for Others 99

CHAPTER 5: Hearing Someone Else Fully 101

- Rescue, Persecution, or Help? 102
- The Listening Attitude 109
- Reflective Listening 115

CHAPTER 6: Helping Someone Change 125

- The Helping Process 126
- Skills of Helping 139

Part Three: Meeting Your Own Needs Along With Others' 153

CHAPTER 7: Assertive Communication 155

- Assertiveness 156
- I Messages 166

CHAPTER 8: Resolving Conflicts 183

- What is Conflict? 184
- Power over Others 190
- Conflict Resolution 197

CHAPTER 9: Values 209

CHAPTER 10: Group Communication 221

- What Happens in Groups 222
- Helping a Group Reach Agreement 229

CHAPTER 11: Conclusions 241

- Saying Goodbye 242
- Putting the Pieces Together 250

A Farewell 259

Index to Exercises 261

Index 267

He Tauparapara

Tini whetu ki te Rangi
Ko nga whakaaro hou taka haere
Ki Papatuanuku
Hei kakano mo nga aitanga
Whakatupu, whakarapu
Ka werohia
Ka whakapoutamahia
Ka tu te tangata
Mana motuhake.

Just as there are multitudes of stars in Father sky,
so there are new thoughts roaming Mother earth:
—seeds for descendants growing and searching.
By challenging; they progress until they are able
to stand tall in their own uniqueness.

Te Hata Ohlson

Richard Bolstad and Margot Hamblett have lived for many years in a non-authoritarian family, where they reap the benefits of the skills taught in this book. They live with their children, Francis, Jacob, Jessie, and Tom (aged 12 to 19). They enjoy learning to live together, and passing on the skills to others. Both Richard and Margot have taught communication skills to a wide range of caregivers, including parents, teachers, naturopaths and counsellors. Richard is a nurse (R.Cp.N.), teacher (Dip. Tchg. Tert.), psychotherapist (N.Z.A.P.), herbalist (Dip. Herb.), and N.L.P. Master Practitioner (I.S.N.L.P.). Margot has a B.A. in Psychology, and has worked as a social worker, counsellor, and teacher. She is an N.L.P. Master Practitioner. Together with Bryan Royds and Lynn Timpany they run the National Training Institute for N.L.P. (Aotearea/New Zealand).

Te Hata Ohlson and Jan Hardie have been in a bicultural relationship for nearly twenty years. Jan is 41. Te Hata is 46. Te Hata's children are now 25 and 23, and Jan and Te Hata's daughters are 16 and 13 years old. Both Jan and Te Hata are from a teaching/education background. They have both been involved with broadcasting; Te Hata as frontperson for 'After School' and 'You And Your Child', Jan with the Children's Television Foundation and as a member of the Broadcasting Standards Authority. Both were patrons of the Treasures Baby Club. They have shared with many the ways of communicating across race, gender, and class differences.

FOREWORD

Communication: a beginning

In a way, your reading this foreword is like a meeting between you the reader and myself the writer. In that sense, it's important that I welcome you to this book. I'm sure you'll discover that what you have in front of you is not just an opportunity to learn how to communicate better when you are helping others. This is a book which will be almost impossible to read without learning how to *enjoy* your life more, discovering new ways to make your dreams become realities, and becoming more fully who *you* are. I am sure because I know how my own life has changed over the last fifteen years as I have discovered the things you'll read about here.

When someone claims to teach 'communication skills', or writes a book about how people get on with each other, I'm always curious to know how *they* get on with others. If they're going to help me, can they do it themselves? And anyway, what do they mean by 'good communication'? Well, the reason I have written this book is first and foremost because I treasure life with my family, because I enjoy my friendships with the people I work with and others, and because I so much appreciate the human interaction that my job requires. Even more, each day I wake up looking forward to excitement, relaxation, love, and a sense of abundance. To me these are the most important successes I could ask for, and I have a very genuine sense of gratitude — and sometimes even of amazement — as I think of them. Gratitude because I know that it is not luck that has led me to them, but the *skills* explained in this book.

I have had the opportunity to train as a nurse, as a teacher, and as a psychotherapist; to be a parent and a marital partner. What you are about to read here is the *heart* of what I learned in each of those places. You too may have chosen to work in one of the caring professions or in a helping role. In that case I know something of your underlying affection for people and your willingness to meet others' needs as well as your own. You probably have wondered how you can keep that caring and openness alive in the day-to-day realities of the years ahead. In this book we will learn how to ensure it not only stays alive, but *flowers*.

That means that you won't be learning tricks to manipulate others, or theories that have to be ignored so you can survive in the real world. You *will* be learning how to make contact with others in their own way, how to see what people mean and present yourself so that they can see what you mean, how to help both yourself and others set goals and actually achieve the kind of success that *really* counts, how to stick up for your own rights and explain your opinions without putting others down, even how to help a group function fluently. As we go, you'll learn to celebrate the diversity of people, based on qualities such as culture and gender.

Obviously, all this will help in your job. You could even choose to use this as 'just' a textbook. But then, why sell yourself short? You deserve to enjoy the fruits of good communication *throughout* your life. So why not take the time right *now* to get a sense of what it would be like to have those skills I mentioned above *as fully as you want*. This is something you can do especially well if you actually create an image in your mind of what your life will look like once you've learned the skills discussed in this book. You can imagine yourself with these abilities — picturing where you work and what you do, who you live with and how, the way you behave and how others respond to you. Make that picture as big and as bright as you need, and tell yourself just how worthwhile it is for you to learn to communicate. *Now*, just for a moment, put this book down and actually take the time to imagine that future you, *before* you go on to the next sentence.

As you did that, you begin to feel some of the sense of delight that is there for you when you read this book. Now you'll be able to read playfully, enjoying the journey; but seriously as well, knowing the incredible potential you have. You'll be able to experiment; trying things out, disagreeing with us when it suits you, and still taking out exactly what *you* need to create that future you've imagined.

Because I wanted this book to have a personal style. I have used the first person ('I' and 'me') throughout. Many of the examples are experiences from my own life. However, I am not the only author of this book. My partner Margot Hamblett wrote the sections relating to women's issues, and suggested numerous important changes.

Te Hata Ohlson and Jan Hardie reviewed all sections of our work, also providing material on cultural difference and Maoritanga. I believe the four of us have co-operated in the spirit which you'll learn about as you read on. The richness of this book comes from our collective experience.

Richard Bolstad
1992

Margot and I would like to dedicate the book to Francis, Jacob, Jessie, and Tom.

PART ONE

Basics of Communication

CHAPTER 1

Getting in Contact

KEY CONCEPTS:

Developing realistic beliefs about meeting people

Group warmup and group contracts

Effects of culture: Maori and Pakeha welcomes

Introducing Yourself

Objective: to be able to initiate and maintain a 2-minute conversation with someone you've just met.

STARTING OUT

In 1964, Psychologist Carl Rogers agreed to be filmed in a half-hour counselling session with a woman named Gloria. During these brief 30 minutes, he simply sat down and talked with this woman, whom he had never met before. And yet, Gloria kept in contact by mail with Dr Rogers for the next eight years, maintaining that those minutes had profoundly affected her life.

What was the magic which enabled Carl Rogers to have such an impact on his clients? It was what counsellors have since come to call *rapport*, a sense of mutual understanding and 'at-one-ness' which close friends often experience routinely. Can it be learned? Absolutely! *You* can have that same extraordinary effect. Over the next three chapters you'll learn the structure of rapport. We'll begin by collecting some important ideas about how to *start* a conversation or a relationhip with people. Later in the book we'll revisit these 'choices for talk' and explain them in detail. So for now, you don't have to be an expert in these methods. The aim is merely to have enough ideas so you can start a conversation or meet someone new.

An introduction is not 'just' an introduction. A great deal of research shows that the first four minutes with someone are crucial. Therefore, I encourage you to make sure you've read my 'Foreword'; it's your introduction to me.

THE NEED FOR MEETING

If you work in a helping role, especially, you'll want to be able to meet people in ways that immediately convey welcoming and quickly create rapport. A health professional, for example, is often required to be interacting at an intimate, private level with clients only minutes after meeting them. He or she needs to build high quality communication quickly.

And yet for many people, to achieve any form of communication is difficult. I worked as a counsellor with the phone-in line Mensline after it was set up in 1987. In our first year, we discovered that the most common complaint men rang us about was loneliness. Some of these men did not know where to meet people or what to say to begin a conversation with a stranger. But others were married men. Having someone in the house is not a guarantee of good communication! If you have ever been at a party where you know only one or two people, you'll be aware that it's quite possible to be lonely in a crowd.

BELIEFS ABOUT INTRODUCTIONS

Everything we study in this book will be useful as you set out to meet people, but for now the following is crucial: what you say to *yourself* before you meet someone, and what you say to *them* when you do meet. Most people who *don't* make contact with others have some unpleasant beliefs about what will happen if they *do*. They quite often tell themselves that:

1 People want to be left alone. They don't want to talk to me.
2 If I approach someone who doesn't want to talk to me, a disaster will happen.
3 Most other people are totally confident and totally in charge in social meeting situations. They will therefore be able to watch me and hear what I say from a critical perspective.
4 If someone is able to notice what I'm doing and mentally criticises it, a disaster will happen.

New Beliefs

Sounds familiar? The best one could say about these beliefs is that they make some fairly big assumptions about people we don't even know yet. If you have shared these assumptions, you might like to remind yourself of more realistic beliefs such as:

1 Although *sometimes* people do want to be left alone, more often they enjoy meeting others.
2 If I approach someone who doesn't want to talk to me, I can easily back off and find someone else to meet, knowing I have given myself an extra opportunity to practise introducing myself.
3 *Most* people are much more aware of their own needs and of working out what *they* will say when they meet me, rather than theorising about me.
4 If someone *is* aware of what I'm doing and even disapproves of it, this can actually be an interesting chance to meet this person at a new level.

You will certainly feel different about meeting people depending on which set of beliefs you tell yourself.

Map and Territory

The fact that people can have such widely different beliefs about the same situations reminds us of a very basic principle in communication. What people *believe* is happening in a situation, their internal feelings, images and the way they talk to themselves, is not the same as the actual situation. Put in other words, *the map in your head is not the territory*. People get information from the territory they live in, through their eyes, ears, nose, tongue, skin, and so on. Then they organise that information into their own internal map of the world. A person locked in jail may have a real-life problem meeting people. Their territory is limited. The problem most of us have though, is that our *map* of the territory is limited. It's not what *happens* that holds us back, but our *beliefs* about what happens.

EXERCISE 1.1

Aim — to recognise the way beliefs (or 'maps') change the way we feel about and respond to situations.

Imagine that the situation you are in is that you are waiting in class for your group leader/teacher to appear. She is now half an hour late. Divide into five small groups and each group read only one of the following beliefs. Assume that you accept *that* belief about the situation you are in, and discuss in your small group how you *feel* in this situation.

Belief for group one: You've noticed that the teacher seems to be taking a very casual attitude lately, and you suspect she may have not bothered to turn up. Find a word to describe how you feel about her not having arrived.

Belief for group two: You saw the teacher in town on her bike before, and think she may have had an accident. Find a word to describe how you feel about her not having arrived.

Belief for group three: You seem to recall that the teacher gave you this session off. You have turned up unnecessarily. Find a word to describe how you feel in this situation.

Belief for group four: You can't quite remember what the arrangements were for this session. Perhaps you were to meet somewhere else today, or perhaps this session was cancelled. You're not sure what you believe about this. Find a word to describe how you feel about the teacher not having arrived.

Belief for group five: You've developed the impression that your teacher is rather shy, and finding it difficult to cope with the sessions. Find a word to describe how you feel about her not having arrived.

Now, get together in a whole group and share your words to describe the feelings you had in that same situation. Were they the same? If not, how would this have affected your actions if the teacher did turn up then?

Most people are not aware that every 'situation' they are in is actually an internally generated map of the real world events. In order to understand this, we always create our own model or image of what actually exists.

Practice

Giving yourself the opportunity to meet people will enable you to form a whole new map of what that's like, and you can *feel* differently about it as a result. If simply talking is difficult for you, you can experiment several times over the next week with:

— smiling and saying 'Hello' to people you pass in your work or study situation.

— phone a library, a citizens' advice bureau, a movie theatre, or a department store to ask for information about their services.

— making brief, safe conversational statements in a place where you need to wait with others (a bus stop, a supermarket queue, a movie theatre line, a waiting room, etc.). A comment about the situation is fine (for example, in a supermarket, 'Seems to take longer and longer doesn't it. Do you know what is the quietest time here?', in a movie theatre queue, 'Well, there are plenty of people here. Have you heard what the movie's like?'). In such situations, some people may be surprised enough not to respond, but in most cases you will get an encouraging reply.

WHAT TO SAY

What people actually say in a beginning conversation will vary of course. But the most powerful and engaging comments fit into three basic categories. It helps to be able to:

1 Say things about yourself

a *Introduce yourself*: 'Hello, my name's . . . .'

b *Ask for what you want*: 'May I sit here?', 'What's happened at the meeting so far?', 'I was trying to find the cafetaria before. Do you know where it is?'

c *Say something about how you are right now*: 'I've just started my course and don't know anyone here.', 'I've been studying all day and really need a break.'

2 Say things about the other person

a *Ask about them*: 'Where are you from?', 'What kind of work do you do?', 'How has your day been?'

b *Offer assistance when needed*: 'I'm just getting a cup of tea. Can I get you anything?', 'Here, let me help you with that.'

c *Acknowledge what the other person has said*: 'Sounds like you had a good day.', 'So you're new here too.'

d *Offer genuine compliments* (These may be followed by a question to make them easier to reply to): 'That's a nice jacket, where did you get it?', 'You seem to know your way around here well. Have you been here for a while?'

3 Say things about shared experiences

For example, 'I see you're doing the same course as me.', 'It has been incredibly hot lately hasn't it.', 'Did you watch that programme on body language on TV last night?'

The point is not to memorise all these topics, but to read through them now and choose which options *you* would like to be able to add to your choices. Then you can practise them. Good communication is about giving yourself more effective choices.

Three Meetings

As you read this introductory dialogue between a nurse and patient, you can check which of the topics the nurse uses to initiate conversation.

Nurse (entering room and pulling back the curtain): Good morning Mrs Upton. I'm Jo Adamson. I'll be looking after you today.

Mrs Upton: Oh, Good morning.

Nurse (seeing Mrs Upton attempting to sit up in bed and moving to assist): Can I help you with that pillow?

Mrs Upton: Thank you. I feel so frail having to be moved around like this.

Nurse: It is hard to get used to isn't it. Luckily it's just for a few days until the incision heals. How are you sleeping?

Mrs Upton: Oh, alright I guess. I find the ward very warm you know.

Nurse: Yes, so do I. Does it mean you don't get to sleep till late, or do you have a sort of restless night?

Mrs Upton: Oh no, I'm getting to sleep. But I still feel tired in the morning when I wake, and I think that's the heat. So last night I got the nurse to open that window there. I hope that's alright.

Nurse: Certainly. Good for you. It helps me to do my job better when you're able to tell me what you need. Well, I'll be back to take you for your shower after breakfast. Okay?

In this next example, someone is initiating a conversation in a more traditional meeting place: a hotel.

Robin: Hello. I'd like to join you for a drink if that's okay.

Gina: Ah. Sure.

Robin: My name's Robin.

Gina (*nods, then points to herself*): Gina.

Robin: I've just started a welding course at the Polytech this month. What do you do with yourself, Gina?

Gina: Well, I work as a cleaner in a department store. It's okay, but it doesn't leave me much time in the evenings.

Robin: I'm glad to have caught you on an evening off then.

Gina (*laughing*): You haven't 'caught me' yet. Anyway, I don't usually bother going out, but tonight I just felt like a break.

One thing both these conversations have in common is their simplicity. It's really not necessary to have a lot of fancy lines to start talking to someone. You only need a few basic ideas. Here is how Dr Carl Rogers began that extraordinary conversation which Gloria felt changed her life. Notice again that same simplicity, as he uses similar comments from the three categories we listed above:

Carl Rogers: Good morning.

Gloria: How are you Doctor?

Carl Rogers (*overlapping her comment*): I'm Doctor Rogers. You must be Gloria.

Gloria: Yes I am.

Carl Rogers: Won't you have this chair. (*They sit down.*) Well now; we have half an hour together, and I really don't know what we'll be able to make of it, but I hope you can make something of it. I'd be glad to know whatever concerns you.

Gloria: Well, I'm . . . Right now I'm nervous; but I feel more comfortable the way you're talking in a low voice, and I don't feel like you'll be so harsh on me. But, ah . . .

Carl Rogers: I hear the tremor in your voice, so I'm aware. . .

Gloria: Ah, well the main thing I want to talk to you about is: I'm just newly divorced. . .

Gloria draws our attention, even in these first few comments, to another important part of meeting people, when she says 'I feel more comfortable the way you're talking in a low voice'. As you develop your ability to initiate a conversation, you'll want to know more than just, 'What do I say?' You'll be curious about how you say it. And that's exactly what we go on to deal with in Chapter Two.

EXERCISE 1.2

Aim — to investigate different ways of initiating conversations.

1 Begin by having everyone walking around the room, weaving in and out of the others, attempting to walk into any empty spaces they see. Once everyone is moving, have them greet each person they meet with a smile. After a minute or so, have them greet each person with 'Hello'. After another couple of minutes have people greet each other by shaking hands or by touching elbow to elbow.
2 Next, have people find someone else (preferably someone they don't know well) and sit down in pairs with them. Each person then takes 2.5 minutes to introduce themselves to the other in their pair by talking about 'what they hope to get out of attending this course'.
3 Have people change partners and pair off again, this time introducing themselves by talking for 2.5 minutes each about 'The most significant positive experience they've had recently'.
4 Change partners and introduce themselves by talking about 'Who I am as a person'.
5 (Optional) Other topics for pairs could include 'the person I get on best with', or 'the ways in which you and I are similar or different', or 'the movie I most enjoyed'.
6 Get together in the large group and share:
— which activity or topic was most helpful in getting to know the person you were with?
— what other topics do you need to discuss to get to know someone well?
— how would you need to modify the list of topics if you were thinking about meeting people in your professional situation?
7 (Optional) Choose the most popular topic, and have each person introduce themself to the whole group by saying a few sentences about it.

EXERCISE 1.3

Aim — to recognise how beliefs about people we meet affect our meeting.

1 Get people into pairs. In each pair, the participants take turns making statements to each other beginning with the words, 'It's obvious to me that . . .', and describing something they have *seen* or *heard* of their partner (e.g. 'It's obvious to me that you are wearing a red jersey.').
2 Next, participants take turns making statements that begin, 'I guess that . . .', and describe something they could guess about the other person based on what they've *seen* or *heard* (e.g. I guess you're feeling tired.')
3 Then participants make statements beginning, 'I guess you can tell . . .', and describe things they think the other person knows about them (e.g. 'I guess you can tell that I'm aged about twenty.')
4 Finally, participants make statements beginning, 'I *hope* you can tell . . .', and describe what they would *like* the other person to know about them (e.g. 'I hope you can tell that I'm interested in getting to know you.')
5 Discuss, in the pairs, what this exercise was like.
6 Come back to the main group and discuss the following:
— were people's guesses always correct?
— if not, in what ways did their guesses vary from reality?
— how might this affect our meeting people?
— what effect did making these statements now, in your pairs, have on your feeling of closeness to the other person in your pair?

Warmup

Objective: to be able to describe the need for warmup to a group, and suggest at least four specific activities to meet this need.

WHAT IS WARMUP?

In 1980, I attended a 'Leadership Skills Laboratory' course run by George Sweet, Margaret Merton, and Anne Kilgour at Lincoln College. I had only met a couple of the course participants before, and I had no idea what to expect from the course except what information the enrolment form provided. After only five days though, I felt as if each person in the group was dear to me, and there were tears in my eyes as I prepared to leave. Furthermore, I had made a commitment to change almost every relationship in my life, based on the principles that the course taught. I had formed a friendship with George which was to be the basis of a whole career change. And I had learned some of the most central concepts which I now share with you in this book.

It's interesting to ask what makes a group work so well together that people's lives can be changed by it over as brief a time as five days. In fact, how do people who have never met before get to feel like 'a group'? The answer is *warmup*. If your job involves working in a group (with clients *or* with colleagues), if you ever plan to live in a group (such as a family), then the process of warmup is essential for you to understand.

TWO QUESTIONS

To understand the meaning of the term 'warmup', let me remind you what it's like at first to be part of a group. Think of some group you've joined (perhaps when you started a new school, or a new job). At such a time, people have two sets of questions paramount in their minds. The first is, '*Who* is here? Will they like me?', and 'Will I like them?' The second is, '*What* will we do here? What are the rules?', and 'What will I get out of it?' People, joining any group put a lot of energy into trying to find the answers to these sets of questions. If they find satisfactory answers to the first set (the 'who' questions) they develop a sense of *cohesion*. The group feels 'together'.

People see each other as likeable, and come to trust each other. If they find satisfactory answers to the second set (the 'what' questions) they develop a sense of *contract*. The group knows what to expect from their time together, and they are committed to using that time effectively to get the things they value from being together. Therefore, cohesion and contract are what make people feel *warmed up* to being in a group.

Answering the Two Questions

It's not a good idea to leave it to chance whether people get satisfactory answers to these questions. When group members don't feel connected to each other or don't know what to expect from their time together, they often give up. Also, they may keep trying to sound out the situation, make links to others and see what's going on *while* the group is trying to do its task.

It makes more sense to set aside time at the start of a group to actually answer both sets of questions. Time to introduce people; time to discuss what will be going on in the group and what its aims are. Once this has been done, the rest of the group's task will get done much quicker. If you plan to help a group work well, it is most important that you arrange some time to discuss these issues. It may be as simple as having a meal together and discussing it. Or it may involve doing some of the following specific exercises.

EXERCISE 1.4

Aim — to learn each others' names and begin creating a sense of group cohesion.

A series of choices for groups:

1 **Introducing a friend**: People are asked to get into pairs (perhaps on the basis of finding someone of a similar height, or by turning to the person beside them), and take four minutes to learn each others' names and *reasons for coming to the course*. They then return to sitting in a circle, and (in no particular order) introduce their partners to the group. The partner may correct or add information as they are introduced.

2 **Adjective and name**: Group members choose an adjective which begins with the same letter as their name (e.g. 'Able Adam', 'Intelligent Imelda') and take turns introducing themselves to the group by this adjective and name. Each person attempts to recite all the names created so far, and then add their own. Examples of adjectives are: adaptable, accepting, bold, boisterous, calm,

carefree, dependable, determined, energetic, elegant, friendly, fair, gentle, giving, happy, helpful, imaginative, intelligent, jovial, jaunty, kind, keen, lively, loving, merry, mature, notable, nice, observant, organised, playful, powerful, quick, questioning, relaxed, reliable, satisfied, sociable, trustworthy, thoughtful, understanding, upright, visionary, valuable, warm, wise, xenophilic (means liking strangers), youthful, yummy, zestful, zealous.

3 **Cushion toss**: In this activity, someone begins by tossing a small cushion to someone else in the group, calling out that person's name as they do so (at first people will choose to toss to those whose names they recall. Later they can try for those they are less certain of. After everyone has had 2–3 turns, most of the names will be known). The person catching the cushion says, 'Thank you . . .', supplying the name of the person who threw it to them, and then calls out the name of the person they are throwing it to.

4 **Map of New Zealand**: People are invited to stand on an imaginary map of New Zealand, placing themselves either where they come from, or somewhere in the country they feel most connected to. (This requires a large floor space. Distort geography as appropriate, e.g. putting Australia nearby if needed.) Each person then talks about where they are standing and why.

5 **Circle activities**: If you have at least ten people, there are many introductory activities that can be done in a group, standing first in a circle. For example:

— hold hands and close your eyes; then attempt to form a square and then a triangle, each time without talking or opening your eyes until you 'sense' you have the right shape.

— everyone turn to the right and give the person in front of them a shoulder massage (if you're not sure how, check what the person behind you is doing).

— still facing the person on your right, move the circle in tighter, and all sit down on the knees of the person behind you (the bigger the group and the tighter the circle, the easier this task).

The circle is a common cultural symbol of togetherness, and these activities emphasise that symbolism.

6 '**Everyone who . . .**'. This is a kind of co-operative musical chairs. Seat everyone on chairs in a circle (facing inward), and remove one chair, so that one person is standing in the centre. This person then makes a statement beginning, 'Everyone who . . .', and describing some quality that at least some group members will have in common (for example, 'Everyone who is wearing something blue.', or 'Everyone who had toast for breakfast this morning.') All the people that this statement is true for must then stand up and quickly try and sit down in a different chair to the one they have just been in. The person in the centre is also aiming to sit

in a chair at this time. If they succeed, a new person is in the centre ready to think up the next 'Everyone who . . .' statement.

7 Many of the other group activities described further in the book (for example, the Trust Toss described in Chapter 2) are good for building cohesion too.

EXERCISE 1.5

Aim — to create a sense of contract about how the group sessions are run.

1 Explain the idea of a group contract as a list of agreements about *how* we will work together (rather than *what* we will learn). Examples could be given to emphasise the advantages of this, e.g. the value of having some understanding about confidentiality, so people feel safe to discuss how they've used communication skills in their life without having the world told about it.

2 People get into pairs to discuss what they would like included in such a contract.

3 The group leader collects ideas from the pairs, writing them up on the whiteboard or a sheet of paper. At this time do not debate or clarify them; simply collect ideas to consider later. Add your own ideas too.

4 The group goes through the list of ideas one by one, checking (a) do they understand what is meant by each one — the person who suggested it can explain, and (b) do they agree with it. Attempt to reach agreement and leave for later any that cannot be agreed on.

5 The group checks who is responsible for ensuring that this list of agreements is being put into practice. Except for a very few matters (e.g. making sure the class gets through the course outline), the whole group can be encouraged to be collectively responsible for keeping the contract working.

6 Either the sheet of paper on which the list was written is kept and brought to future sessions, or a copy is written out and photocopied for all group members.

A GROUP WARMS UP

How did this warmup process work at the Leadership Skills Laboratory I mentioned earlier? We began with cups of tea and coffee, and sat in a circle for introductions. The three leaders introduced themselves first, after which the participants did the same. Next, the group divided into three smaller sections, each of which planned a 30-minute introductory event 'to introduce us to one another to commence the life of the group'. Each section then ran its introductory event with the whole group.

After this, we got into pairs to discuss our expectations and goals for the course. When we returned to the main group, we collected these and discussed guidelines or standards for working together. The leaders suggested:
— work in the here and now
— speak for yourself
— stick to feelings
— make statements not questions
— confidentiality.
The group agreed with these and added:
— remain flexible about these guidelines
— respect and support the feelings of others
— be responsible for ourselves
— encourage experimental behaviour.

The Playgroup
As we take another example of a group's first meeting, check for yourself how this particular group is meeting its needs for *cohesion* and *contract.*

Sharon (a mother with a 3-year-old son, Jamie, and a 1-year-old daughter, Joanne) was invited by her friend Annette to come over on a Tuesday afternoon, and discuss setting up a playgroup for local parents. There were five parents at that first get together, and Annette had made hot drinks and scones. A woman who was part of another playground started the discussion. She began by checking that everyone knew each others' names. There was one person whose name Sharon was unsure of, so they reintroduced themselves. The woman went on to explain how her playground had run, and that led to a discussion about the best times to run it. They decided on Mondays, 1pm to 2.30pm, which gave two of them time to get back for school-age kids. Someone asked what they would do about 'discipline', and it was agreed that individual parents would try and supervise their own children, at first anyway. Because Annette's house had the biggest main room, it was proposed to keep the group meeting there for now. Before leaving, people made a list of the toys they could bring, and Sharon offered to bake a cake for the first session.

Importance of Contract

Every group which survives *has* a contract of some sort. It may be written down, agreed upon verbally, or merely worked out based on 'what we've always done'. But it exists. Discussing the 'rules' openly gives people a chance to design the very best agreement for all involved. Without open discussion, each person must *guess* the rules from the reactions they get to their actions.

This results in group members 'testing out' a new teacher to find his or her limits, for example. In some groups the rules will be developed by one person or subgroup, or even by an outside agency. But research confirms the fairly obvious fact that people are much more committed to rules they participate in making. Remember, for a rule to work it not only has to be written down or announced, it also has to be put into action by each person there. We'll discuss this point further in Chapter 8.

Culture and Meeting

Objective: to understand the main differences in procedures for meeting people, between the two main cultures in Aotearoa/New Zealand.

THE EFFECT OF CULTURE

'Culture' is the word for the total way of life of a people, including all their beliefs, values, ways of behaving, language, and so on. Obviously, then, good communication requires an understanding of culture. No matter how good a communicator I may be, if you move me half way round the world and put me in a totally different cultural setting, I'll have difficulty. It's like trying to play rugby football with a netball rulebook.

As a counsellor, I have worked with many people who don't feel very good about their communication skills. One such man came to see me because of increasing arguments with the woman he lived with. He sat by me, looking down at the floor and explaining that one of his biggest failings was his inability to make eye contact with people. Also, when he and his partner argued, he somehow was unable to get across to her that he wanted to apologise. No matter how he demonstrated his sadness, sitting close to her and trying to do things for her, she didn't get the message. And the things they argued about really puzzled him. For example, when they went to her parents' place for the weekend, she wanted to ring up beforehand and sort out what food they would bring. He felt humiliated by this — it seemed rather petty and rude. Surely they should just take whatever they could, and things would work out.

Different, Not Bad

Was this man a poor communicator? No, he was an excellent communicator. Then why was he having so much trouble? And why did he *believe* he was no good at communicating? Because he was playing rugby with the netball rulebook. *His* way of communicating worked perfectly in the family he grew up in, because that family was Maori. It did not work with his partner because she was from a European-based culture: a culture where people value 'looking you in the eye' rather than looking down to indicate politeness; where people talk about their feelings rather than expressing them (at a funeral, for example, she might say, 'I'm so sorry' rather than simply weep and hold someone); where people negotiate the arrangements for hospitality rather than giving a koha (gift). Both ways of life work perfectly. And it's quite possible for people to live together even when they grew up in different cultures ... providing they understand the difference and know who they are.

Problems begin when we assume one culture is better than others, or more normal. The next step towards difficulties is to pretend that cultures don't exist, and everyone is 'the same'. It's as if someone said, 'There's no difference between netball and rugby. The reason why you're losing the game is because you're no good at sports (or too lazy to try). You'll have to learn *our* rules better.' The fact is that there *are* differences. And in the last 30 years, communications experts have begun to document the details of cultural difference (details that many people from minority cultures knew all along).

As I listened to this man describing each of his communication 'failures', I affirmed for him that his responses sounded perfectly sane and skilled *and* that they were very much as I understood Maori responses to be. After half an hour or so he was glowing with a new sense of understanding, and working out how he could contact a Maori counsellor to explore this further. We spent the last quarter of an hour rehearsing his process of explaining this to his partner in a way that would be respectful of her.

MAORI AND PAKEHA

Every time someone tells me that, 'Most so-called Maoris aren't really Maori at all; they don't speak the language'. I remember that man and what he taught me. Because *he* didn't have all the Maori words to explain what was happening to him either. He didn't even think of himself as Maori at first. And why would he, after twelve years in a school system where culture was never even discussed? But none of that changed the fact that, culturally, his responses were understandably most easily from a Maori perspective.

What can we call the European originated culture in New Zealand, so we can discuss it and affirm *its* worth, just as this man came to affirm his being Maori? The word I prefer to use for my own culture (my ancestors came from Wales, Norway, and other parts of Europe) is Pakeha. I like this word because it reminds me that I am a New Zealander, not a European. I know it was developed at a time of friendship between European explorers and Maori, and used by the British when they wrote Te Tiriti o Waitangi. Its most likely origin is the older Maori word 'Pakehakeha' ('imaginary beings resembling people with fair skins', according to H.W. Williams *A Dictionary of the Maori Language*). If you'd rather find another word then please do, but in this book I'll use Pakeha to refer to my own culture.

The Welcome

In their book *Talking Past Each Other*, Joan Metge and Patricia Kinloch discuss the different responses Maori, Samoan, and Pakeha people have to situations of meeting. These points are crucial for us to understand in this chapter as we think about how we meet people. Because both Maori and Samoans stress the importance of formal welcomes including speeches of welcome, they often feel *unwelcomed* in Pakeha introductions which emphasise the importance of dispensing with formality. In the Maori setting, a formal welcome involves a succession of steps in which the emotional distance between tangata whenua (hosts) and manuhiri (guests) is reduced. Movement past the gate to the marae (the space in front of the meeting house) is initiated by women from each group giving the call (karanga). This may be followed by a chant waving the visitors on (the powhiri). Next, there are exchanges of speeches and greetings (whaikorero and mihi), each of which is embellished by a song (waiata). A gift (koha) is given by the visitors (manuhiri), and they are then invited forward to make physical contact and press noses together (hongi) with the local people (tangata whenua). The ceremony is concluded with the sharing of food. Each step in this process has a correct protocol related to its deeper spiritual significance.

Informal Welcome

After the formal welcome, an informal welcome, or mihimihi, will often occur, inside the wharenui or at another appropriate space. Here, people may stand, one at a time, introducing themselves by stating their links to:
— maunga (mountain)
— awa (river/lake/harbour)
— waka (ancestral, ocean travelling 'canoe')
— iwi (tribe)
— hapu (subtribe)
— marae
— whare tupuna (ancestral house)
and mentioning:
— their own name
— parents' names
— childrens' names

— own occupations and interests
— something about the occasion and their expectations.

This speech will usually conclude with a waiata, song, or poem. From a Maori perspective, important aspects of such meetings are:

1 The physical closeness between speaker and audience, and the use of touch,
2 The open, nonthreatening, warm atmosphere with a total acceptance of each person, and
3 The use of much non-verbal language such as nods of the head, and eyebrow gestures. These are discussed more fully in Chapter 3.

Individual Meetings

In meeting individually, say Metge and Kinloch, both Maori and Samoans focus their questions on where the person has come from (immediately and more long term in ancestry). They avoid asking directly, 'Who are you?' (tantamount to asking 'Who do you think you are?'), but instead ask, 'Where are you from?'

The process of a meeting or group session in Maori and Samoan terms usually begins with karakia (prayers), and food is eaten *after* the formal proceedings, not before or during them.

In contrast, Pakeha gatherings often emphasise informality by mixing eating and discussion, and expecting people to make individual contact with others if they want, rather than routinely greeting them. At many meetings, the reverse is true once formal discussions begin. Whereas Maori might debate an issue relatively freely within the meeting house (whare-nui), Pakeha meetings often follow a complex protocol of motions, amendments and points of order.

Basic Humanity

As we ask how these differences came about, we are reminded of the basic unity of humankind. Every culture has formed its own unique answers to such questions as, 'How do people meet and come to feel close to each other?', 'What can be done about the fact that strangers often see the world through different eyes?', and 'How do we create the conditions which all human beings need for sustenance, such as love?' These questions are put in English here, but there is a universality to them. Only the answers vary. And with such urgent questions, can we really afford not to welcome that variety of answers?

SUMMARY

Every relationship has a beginning, and in this chapter we have learned how to make those beginnings work for you. We considered *the importance of positive internal beliefs* when you are getting the confidence to meet people. In several examples you saw *how people begin conversations* by talking about (a) How they are and what they want, (b) How the other person is and what they want, and (c) shared experiences.

Particularly when people meet as a group, the appropriate process depends on the cultural setting. *Pakeha group introductions* often emphasise informality and individual approaches. *Maori welcomes* often use a sense of increasingly less formal steps, gone through in a group. These steps include speeches of greeting (mihi), usually embellished with waiata.

In any group, the successful results of the first meeting are a sense of *contract* (understanding what will happen in the group) and *cohesion* (feeling closer to the people who are there). Creating this sense of contract and cohesion is known as *warmup*.

References & Further Reading

Bach, G.R. and Deutsch, R.M. (1970) *Pairing*, Avon Books, New York.

Bolstad, R. (1989) 'Breaking the Ice', in *Tutor* 37, January 1989, Tutor Education Centre, Wellington.

Clanchy, M. (1986) *Sometimes It's Difficult to Say 'Hello'*, Hyland House, Melbourne.

Johnson, D.W. (1972) *Reaching Out*, Prentice Hall, Englewood Cliffs, New Jersey.

Metge, J. and Kinloch, P. (1984) *Talking Past Each Other*, Victoria University Press, Wellington.

Rogers, C. (1965) in Shostrum, E. (ed), *Three Approaches to Psychotherapy* (film number 1), Pyschological Films, Orange, California.

Stevens, J.O. (1971) *Awareness: Exploring Experimenting Experiencing*, Real People Press, Moab, Utah.

Tauroa, H. and Tauroa, P. (1986) *Te Marae*, Reed Methuen, Auckland.

Zimbardo, P. (1981) *Shyness*, Pan Books, London.

Zunin, L. and Zunin, N. (1972) *Contact: The First Four Minutes*, Ballantine Books, New York.

CHAPTER 2

Just a State of Mind

KEY CONCEPTS:

Visualisation, affirmation, and body position

Changing internal states: relaxation

Maoritanga, Maori, and Pakeha esteem

Women's and men's issues

Parent/adult/child ego states

Anchoring Yourself to The State of Your Choice

Objective: to be able to use visualisation, affirmation, postural change, and anchoring to produce a desired internal state.

STATE

A few months ago, I noticed something puzzling about marking students' assignments. I discovered that on certain mornings, I woke up eager to get into the job, realising that it would only take me a few hours and looking forward to the satisfaction of completing it well. My body felt full of energy and I had the same sense of eager curiosity I sometimes get reading a new novel. On other mornings, I woke up feeling totally different. I'd look across at the mountain of assignments to mark: there they were, and here I was. My body felt tired, and I knew that getting started wasn't going to help, because even after, say, half an hour of work, there'd still be a mountain of assignments to do. I'd think of all the other things I could achieve easier in that half hour, and start doing one, avoiding the assignments again.

How can the *same* task feel so totally different from one day to the next? The answers are all about how we get ourselves from one *state* of mind to another. What state of mind you're in is the single most important factor deciding how well you relate to others. For example, remember the last time you fell 'in love'. Actually put the book down for a moment and think back to a time when you first realised you were in love with someone. Do you remember how that felt? There may have been a pounding in your chest, or butterflies in your tummy. Chances are you woke up that day charged with energy. Perhaps you were more affectionate with others around you, touching them a little more, smiling more. Probably the whole world literally looked brighter to you, and you may have been particularly aware of the beauty of the flowers, or the way birds sing in the trees. You may have taken time out to watch the sunset, or savoured the smells of blossoms or autumn leaves. If you can't recall a time like this for yourself, I'm sure you can remember noticing the difference when someone else around you was 'in love'.

Research on the 'Love' state

Researchers at the Menninger foundation, in Kansas, USA, studied people who reported being 'in love'. They found they had reduced levels of lactic acid in their blood (lactic acid is a byproduct of muscle use: it gives that aching feeling after exercise). The people studied had higher levels of endorphins (chemicals which are the body's natural painkillers) and higher levels of immunoglobulins (their white blood cells were protecting them better from infection). So these people weren't just *imagining* that they felt good. Their bodies were *naturally* less tired, more comfortable, and healthier than usual. They were in a different *state*.

Defining State

A state is the total neurophysiological pattern you have at a particular time (all the things going on in your mind and body at that moment). Love is a state, and so are confidence, relaxation, self-esteem, creativity, and most of the other things you've ever wanted to experience. As you know, people can go through the same events and yet be in a totally different state. You and I may listen to the same speaker and find that, while I enter a state of boredom, you enter a state of fascination. What causes one of us to experience the state called boredom and another the state called fascination, then, is something going on *inside* each of us.

Have you ever wished something could feel more interesting, could look more exciting, but you don't know how to get *out* of the state you're in? In this chapter you'll learn how to do just that. It won't be just 'positive thinking' — you'll learn how to produce *real* change. And it won't require a lot of hard work or telling yourself off — it will happen naturally. Too good to be true? Read on.

State: Map and Territory

The idea of state is another way of saying that *The Map Is Not The Territory* (see Chapter 1). The 'in love' people the Menninger Foundation studied were living in the same world as everyone else in Kansas that year. Their different state of mind meant that they had a different *map* of the territory. In this case their map showed them where to look to see sunsets and spring flowers, where to hear the music of the birds, and how to feel the beating of their own heart. It was their internal representation of the world which enabled them to find these things. Someone with a different internal representation would have found different things. Similarly, what enabled me to feel enthusiastic about marking assignments one morning, and overwhelmed another morning, was the different way I represented the situation to myself.

Vision

For me, a very important part of my 'map' is the internal pictures I make about what I'm doing (for you it may be more important how you talk to yourself, or the sensations you get in your body). On the mornings I felt 'overwhelmed' by my work, I created a picture of myself struggling through the assignments. It was a *still* picture, which didn't give me much feeling of achievement, and I could see all the work still to do, motionless beside me. I even saw the picture as rather dark and gloomy. On the mornings I felt 'enthusiastic' about my work, I created a movie of myself doing the assignments, completing them, and smiling as I congratulated myself on getting the job done. The picture was *bright* and *fast-moving*. I only had to play that movie through a couple of times to start feeling really eager to get started.

Once I understood the difference, I was able to get myself into the state of enthusiasm easily, *every* time. It didn't take any work, it just meant using the natural way of motivating myself which I had already developed. For most people, imagining themselves doing the thing they want, finishing it, and *enjoying* the results is a powerful motivator. Usually it works even better than imagining all the bad things that could happen if you didn't get the job done. And it certainly works better than just imagining yourself stuck halfway through the job. But don't take my word for it. Watch next time you feel really enthusiastic about doing something, and see what kind of things you picture. When you eagerly bake a cake, for instance, do you see the mixture lying still in the bowl, or do you imagine how it will look finished, and then sense how you'll feel as you and others enjoy it?

How Visualising Works

The reason these pictures make a difference is that your mind responds to the pictures in your head as if they were real. Therefore, two people with different visual images will have different states of mind, and will behave as if they are in different situations. Making pictures which work for you is called 'visualisation'.

Some people say they can't see things in this way. That's okay. It works if you just pretend to see things. Actually, even people who are very good at imagining *don't* see things exactly as intensely as real life (if they do, we usually encourage them to get psychiatric help!). Your 'subconscious' knows how to visualise, and that's all you need. Take the way you found your way home yesterday. Did you need to carry a piece of paper with your address written on it, or did you just recognise which house was yours? To recognise your house amongst all those others means having a *really good* subconscious picture of what it looks like. If you can visualise yourself achieving tasks even half that clearly, it'll work fine!

Self Talk

Another important part of how people's maps help them to move from one state to another is how they talk to themselves — I mentioned in Chapter 1 that different beliefs will make people *feel* differently as they meet others. Usually, people find that talking to themselves about how well they're doing, or hearing someone else's voice telling them that they've done well, creates a positive state. Telling yourself all the things that are wrong with you, and talking to yourself about how things might go badly, is generally not as much fun. Most people get enough of that while they are young to last them a lifetime. Telling yourself you are lovable, intelligent, capable, and in other ways a worthwhile human being is called self-affirmation or self-validation. If it's not culturally appropriate for you to tell *yourself* this, then imagine hearing the voice of someone who loves you and wishes you well saying the affirmations to you. This is a way of accepting and valuing their love for you.

Choosing Your Voice

How you hear the voice saying these things is very important too. Saying, 'I am lovable and capable' in a high, tense, trembling internal voice is not nearly so convincing as saying it in a warm, calm, relaxed tone. In fact, the tone, speed, and loudness of the voice may be *more* important than the actual words. You'll understand this if you've ever had insomnia. Most people who can't get to sleep lie there talking to themselves about how they need to get to sleep, how they'll be in trouble the next day, and so on. But even worse, they usually *shout frantically* at themselves. No wonder they don't sleep with all that racket going on inside their head! Try saying the same thing in a slow, quiet, sleepy voice (with even a yawn occasionally) and you'll be able to tell the difference right away. It's like visualisation. Your mind reacts as if the sounds inside your head are *real*. Another example, for instance, if you've got a critical voice inside your head telling you off, you could have it say the same words in Donald Duck's voice, or to the theme music of your favourite comedy TV programme. Again, your mind will respond to the *way* the words are said, as if they were really being said that way. If you're going to have voices telling you off, it's only logical to make them a little lighthearted.

Posture

A third way people can change *state* naturally and easily is by use of body posture and movement. Like visualisation and affirmation, this is something you've probably done before. By learning *how* you do these well (the pictures, words, and postures that work *for you*), you can do them well whenever you need to, almost effortlessly. What do you think would happen if you hunched your shoulders over, hung your head down, breathed slowly with an occasional sigh, and moved very slowly . . . for the next *half an hour*? That's right. Probably you'd feel less energetic; quite possibly you'd feel depressed. (You could make sure of it by only seeing vague, gloomy, still images, and by telling yourself off for being so 'hopeless'.) The same thing works for states you'd *like* to create.

Confidence

You don't need to *force* yourself to feel different. Simply change your posture with an attitude of 'I might as well be in this posture as the other'. Let's try it with 'confidence'. Remember a time when you felt extremely confident. It may have been a time when you were by yourself, or with others who liked you; it may have been a time when you were doing something you knew you could do well, or a time when you felt sure you *could* do something. Whatever it is, take the time to find such a memory now, before you read on.

And now, as you remember that time, sit or stand in the exact position you were in as you were confident. Be aware of your back, of your arms and legs, of your breathing. (You can increase the sensation by *seeing* the things you could see on that occasion, and by *talking* — to yourself or aloud — and listening to the subtle change in your tone of voice). Being in this position will help you to access your own natural ability to be confident.

After all, it's no surprise that the way your body is will affect the way you feel. Ever had a warm bath or shower and washed your hair to get to feel better? Ever done some challenging exercise and felt more awake afterwards? Ever laid down after a hard day and begun to feel more relaxed? The sensations you give yourself physically affect your emotions, just as visualisation and affirmation do. Insurance companies have found that people who are kissed goodbye each morning by their spouse have less accidents — even when the kiss was simply a 'routine measure'. The sensation affects the person's state.

Breathing

In his book *The Psychobiology of Mind Body Healing*, Ernest Lawrence Rossi details many of the ways our body has been shown to affect the mind. Even the way you breathe through your nose is related to your state of mind. In an alert and active state, right-handed people breathe more fully through the right nostril. At this time, EEG recordings of the brainwaves show more activity in the dominant half of the brain. In a very relaxed state, right-handed people breathe through the left nostril. During relaxation, the brainwaves show more activity in the nondominant side of the brain. Even more amazing, simply blocking the left nostril (by pressing the side of your nose) will make *right-handed* people more alert. Blocking the right nostril relaxes them (all these findings are reversed for left-handed people). Which nostril you breathe through changes your brainwave pattern *and* your state of mind! Give it a five-minute trial *now* while you read this book. You couldn't ask for an easier way to relax at night and wake up in the morning.

Anchors

Changing your breathing is only one of a number of easy ways to change your state of mind within five minutes. Consider another experience we have all had. You're listening to the radio and a song is played you haven't heard for several years. As you hear it, the *feeling* of what it was like all those years ago comes back to you, and you begin to recall details of what was happening then. Another example: you're going past a dentist's office, and as the door opens you catch a whiff of antiseptic. Even though you're not getting treatment, your heart begins to pound and you feel a twinge of anxiety, checking your mouth and wondering if you need any fillings. A third situation: there's a place you visited many times when you were younger, where you had many happy experiences. Now you visit it again and just sit there, like you used to, looking around at the scene you recall from those times. As you do so, you're surprised by the feelings of pleasant nostalgia that flood over you. You can almost hear the voices of those who were there, and feel like doing again the things you once did here.

In each of these situations a dramatic change in state occurs, which did not require any 'effort' to make it happen. And in each case, there is some 'stimulus'. When you *see*, *hear*, *feel*, *taste*, or *smell* that stimulus, the *whole* state begins to reoccur all by itself. The *song* on the radio is a stimulus first present when you were in a certain state; the *smell* of the dentist's office was a stimulus first present when you were in an anxious state; and the *scene* of your earlier visits is a stimulus first present when you were in a happy state.

Anchoring

Using a stimulus from an earlier time when you were in a certain state, to recreate that state now is called *anchoring*. Anchoring is happening all the time. The only way you can read these words is by the way each particular group of letters anchors you to a meaning you associated it with earlier.

Probably if I say the word 'anchor', for example, you can hear how those letters are meant to sound, and see a picture of what an anchor looks like. You may even have a feeling associated with those letters.

The most famous use of anchoring is in Dr Ivan Pavlov's experiment with hungry dogs. Every time Pavlov fed his dogs, he rang a bell. Soon he found that only ringing the bell caused the dogs to salivate, to go into the state of readiness to eat. There's not a great demand for getting people to salivate by ringing a bell. But there *is* a demand for enabling people to relax, to feel confident, to feel caring towards each other, to be creative, and so on. Let's say you would like to *feel relaxed while communicating with people.* Luckily, you probably have a time each day when you *are* relaxed already. Choose a time when you are very relaxed (perhaps in the time just before you fall asleep?), and try the following: At that time each day press your left thumb and forefinger together and say to yourself in a calm voice 'Relaxed and Confident'. (There's nothing magic about pressing your thumb and forefinger together, it just happens to be something you're only likely to do in this state, so it probably doesn't have any contradictory states already anchored to it.) After only two or three days, you'll be able to approach **someone**, press your thumb and forefinger together in just the same way, say 'Relaxed and Confident' to yourself in the same calm voice . . . and you *will* relax. The more you use this technique, the more powerful it will get.

Ensuring Anchors Work

Anchoring should be absolutely effortless, so if it doesn't 'work', simply check that (a) you were actually in the desired state when you 'set' the anchor, (b) the anchor doesn't occur in other contradictory situations, and (c) you recreated the anchor just as it was originally. Then repeat the anchoring process.

When you are communicating with others, especially as a helping professional working with clients, your state of mind is crucial. Confidence, relaxation, alertness, caring, and creativity are amongst the many important states you will be able to create using the techniques outlined in this section. These techniques for altering state include:

1 Visualising in the way *you* most successfully create the desired state (e.g. seeing yourself in a bright, life-size movie showing the success of your endeavour).
2 Affirming yourself and talking to yourself in a voice appropriate to the desired state.
3 Assuming a posture and breathing style appropriate to the desired state.
4 Using a stimulus associated with the desired state, to anchor you into it.

EXERCISE 2.1

Aim — to use postural change to create a state of trust. (Trust Fall)

1 This exercise can be done in groups of between six and twelve people, and is easiest done by having the group leader demonstrate it first. Have the other members of the group form a fairly close circle round a central person. The central person stands up with arms folded or held by their sides, keeping their legs straight, and standing in the same spot throughout the activity. Those around the circle raise their hands, palms facing the central person, ready to catch them as they fall. This may be easier if the people in the circle brace themselves by putting one foot back a little.

2 The central person closes their eyes and, keeping their body straight, falls backward to be caught by those in the circle. The circle then passes them *gently* around or across to be caught by others. It is **most** important not to drop the central person, and to be *in* close enough to ensure they feel safe (you may start right up close and move back a little as they indicate). The sense of trust which this exercise generates is related to the sense of *caring* with which people are handled.

3 Discuss how the exercise went, accepting each person's own experience rather than comparing or evaluating it as 'good' or 'bad'.

EXERCISE 2.2

Aim — to use visual imagery to create a state of raised self-esteem. (Visual Swish)

1 Have each person think of a situation in which they often behave in a way they'd like to change, due to low self-esteem (we might define self-esteem as the ability to like yourself, so 'low self-esteem' means not liking yourself; judging, blaming, or rejecting yourself). The kind of behaviour people might want to change includes smoking, overeating, avoiding people, criticising others, getting nervous, and so on. Once they've chosen the behaviour they want to change, have them check what they always *see* just *before* the behaviour starts (for example, a smoker may see their hand holding a cigarette; someone who gets nervous may see a group of people waiting for them to speak). They need to find something their mind can use as a *cue* that this is the time when this exercise will have its effect. Have them 'see' this cue situation

(as they see it in the real situation) as clearly as they can. This is the 'cue picture'.

2 Next, get everyone to clear their mind and create an imaginary picture of *themself* as they would look when they were confident, happy with themself, and full of skills, and new ways to act. This picture should be such that, by just looking at that new self, they could tell that that person no longer has any need to change the behaviour (just as, for example, when looking at a confident skier, you would know from their whole posture, and so on, that they don't need skiing lessons). Have people check that, as they look at that new self, there is no part of them that objects to them becoming the person in their picture. If they are uncertain in any way, they can ask the 'uncertain' parts of them to change the picture slightly, so it 'feels right'. I'll call this picture of the person with all these new choices the 'resourceful picture'.

3 Have people see a *big bright* square image of the cue picture in front of them, with a *small dark* square image of the resourceful picture in it's centre. Explain that, on instruction, they are going to see these pictures change over. The small resource picture will flood out to fill up the whole screen and brighten up at the *same time* as the cue picture shrinks and darkens to insignificance. If this seems complex, assure them that they can do it just as well 'subconsciously' by *pretending* to see it all.

4 Have them swap images at a signal from you (perhaps saying the word 'swish' and gesturing with your hand), as quickly as they can. Once they can see the big, bright resource picture, have them *clear the screen* ready to start again. Repeat this process six times, starting each time with the cue picture as the big picture, and ending with the resource picture as big and bright, always clearing the screen between times.

5 Have them get into pairs and re-imagine the situation where the behaviour *used to* happen, to see if they can detect any subtle changes in what they see or how they feel.

EXERCISE 2.3

Aim — to use tone of voice and anchoring to create a state of relaxation.

1 In this exercise, the group leader reads out a series of instructions to help the group to remember times when they have been very relaxed. Begin reading these out in your ordinary talking voice, but *gradually* slow down and lower the tone of your voice so you are talking in a relaxed, at ease way. Read words printed in emphasis just *slightly* more emphatically.

While you are reading, the group members will follow these suggestions and remember the situations. At certain points in the instructions, they will be told to 'anchor' their memory. This means, for the purpose of this exercise, to press their left thumb and forefinger together (thus anchoring what they are remembering to the sensation of that hand position). This should be explained before beginning. Group members should be seated, with their eyes open or closed as it suits them.

2 Here are the instructions to be read out (any ambiguity is intended):

'I'd like you to choose from your memory a time when you were completely safe and relaxed . . . a time when you may have been at home in your room . . . or on holiday somewhere . . . or in a place that is special to you . . . and remember what it is like to be relaxed now . . .' (pause ten seconds). 'And as you recall a time . . . perhaps even just coming home from work and resting so fully that you drift off . . . I'd like you to notice what you could see at that time . . . because often there is something you *can see* that really reminds you of how easy it is to *relax* . . . which may be the deep blue of a sky . . . or the colour of the walls . . . or some particular thing that reminds you of how you *slow down* . . . even if it's just the way your eyes defocus a little and blur round the edges as you get that sense of ease . . . when it really doesn't seem important to focus on anything in particular . . . except to notice what you see that reminds you of being relaxed . . . and *anchor* it by pressing your finger and thumb together now . . . so you can go on to ask yourself what you could hear as you relaxed in that place . . . which may be just that silence . . . like the quietness in this room, which any unexpected noises remind you of . . . or may be the sounds of nature . . . or of the things which are so much a part of that place where you relax . . . or even just the way that, as you relax, the sounds around you have a slightly different, even echo-like quality . . . like the sound of my voice now . . . as you *anchor the sounds* of relaxation by pressing your finger and thumb together again now . . . leaving you ready to recall the position you were sitting or lying in then . . . and how your body feels as it is relaxed now . . . because you are relaxing now, are you not . . . ? And often as you begin to relax you may be aware of the discomforts in your body . . . just like when you put your feet up and feel the tension drain out of your legs . . . which is part of your blood flowing easier . . . like the warmth of your cheeks as the blood flows easier to the outside of your body . . . and the gradual slowing down of your breathing . . . which happens when you are at ease . . . so that as you are aware of the feeling of being relaxed you can *anchor that feeling* by pressing your finger and thumb together again now . . .' (pause four seconds* then begin, gradually speeding voice up again) 'and knowing that you have that sense of relaxation stored with that anchor, begin to remember where you are here, now, in this group. In your own time, open your eyes fully (you may want to blink them and focus again), stretch your arms, and listen to the normal sounds of the room, as you come back to being fully here and ready to talk.'

3 Discuss how this was, in pairs, and then in the group.

4 At a later date, have people test their anchors by pressing their finger and thumb together. As you explain that you want them to do this, use the same tone of voice you used while reading the relaxation exercise.

EXERCISE 2.4

Aim — to observe how your state of mind naturally changes.

1 Allow half an hour for this exercise. Have group members sit with their backs straight and their legs uncrossed (or crossed in such a way as to balance the left/right sensations — e.g. 'sitting crosslegged' or in a yoga posture). Have them close their eyes and pay attention to their internal state; including all the images, internal or external sounds, and sensations they are aware of. This is not a time to try and *change* these experiences, but simply to observe as one might listen to excellent music, watch a beautiful sunset, or experience a warm bath. There is no need to choose one thought above another, to search for a particular state, or to theorise about or organise one's mind. This is simply a process of being *with* whatever state of mind occurs, being *aware* of it, *observing* it with fascination. There is no particular aim, and no one sensation, state, or thought is more important than any other. This is an experiment to discover what actually occurs over the 30 minutes.

2 After 30 minutes, have everyone open their eyes, return to external reality, and share what happened in pairs. Discussion might include:

a What states of mind did you enter?

b Were you able to simply be aware, or did you find yourself thinking about and trying to change what occurred, i.e. making yourself as an *observer* separate from the state you were observing? (Notice that this is how internal conflict occurs: one state opposes another state, tries to alter, or stop it.)

c If you were able to be aware, did you find that your state of mind changed naturally (e.g. calming down) without any technique?

---

* *If you are using this relaxation process as a prelude to another exercise, move on to the next exercise from this asterisked point, instead of bringing the group back to the room.*

The Social Roots of Self-Esteem

Objective: to be able to identify the social processes which create different states of self-esteem for people of different culture or gender.

SELF-ESTEEM AND SOCIETY

Self-esteem is a state of mind where a person is able to appreciate or like themself. Psychologist Carl Rogers considered it the most important state of all. His research showed that, whatever the problems people have when they come to a counsellor for help, the one thing they have in common is low self-esteem. Whatever else happens when counselling is successful, the one thing you can be sure about is that the person has more self-esteem.

In the last section you learned some of the ways you can build your own self-esteem (e.g. through affirmation, visualisation, and anchoring). To change your own state of mind gives you the freedom to respond to people in the way you would like to, despite any outside influences.

Of course, there *are* outside influences on your state of mind. They include your childhood experiences (which will be discussed in Parent, Adult, and Child States, pp. 46–54) as well as the influence of the world around you today. Below follows an example of how the social world around us affects people's state of mind.

UNEMPLOYMENT

Charles Waldegrave and Rosalyn Coventry quote research, from several countries, about the social effect of unemployment. Every time unemployment rises by 1 per cent, there are 6 per cent more people who need psychiatric treatment, 4 per cent more people who commit suicide, 4 per cent more people who end up in prison, and 6 per cent more people who murder someone. Amongst the people who are unemployed, more bronchitis will occur, more heart disease, more skin disease, and more stomach ulcers.

Does unemployment influence people's state of mind? Without a doubt. Does it affect their communication? Yes, drastically! Our main focus in this book is what the individual can do to improve communication. But in this part of the book I will discuss some of the ways society as a whole affects people's self-esteem and their ability to communicate. *Note*: where New Zealand statistics are given, unless otherwise noted, these come from the book *Poor New Zealand* by Waldergrave and Coventry (1987).

MAORI IN PAKEHA SOCIETY

In 1986, 30 per cent of admissions to Oakley Psychiatric Hospital came from the 12 per cent of the population who were Maori. The Maori suicide rate has increased six times in the last 20 years. What is happening in our society to damage Maori esteem like this?

Part of the answer, I believe, is the anger which many Pakeha direct at Maori. Once, while I was biking to work, I passed a man with the slogan 'Speak English or Die!' written on his tee-shirt. I felt frightened and I speak English fairly well! What effect was this man having on immigrants to New Zealand, who had difficulty with English, or on Maori, whose language will only survive if it can be spoken regularly here in its home country? Research shows that applicants with a Maori name will be offered 20 per cent less job interviews than similarly trained people with an English name. Real estate agents will offer them less properties to consider in 83.9 per cent of cases, and they will be accepted as tenants for flats less often than other people. Whatever you may think are the reasons for these responses, the fact is, they are bound to have a major effect on Maori.

Mana Maori

In different cultures, people find different ways to feel good about themselves (individually *or* as a group) and to have a sense of identity (of knowing who they are). In many European based cultures, one of the first

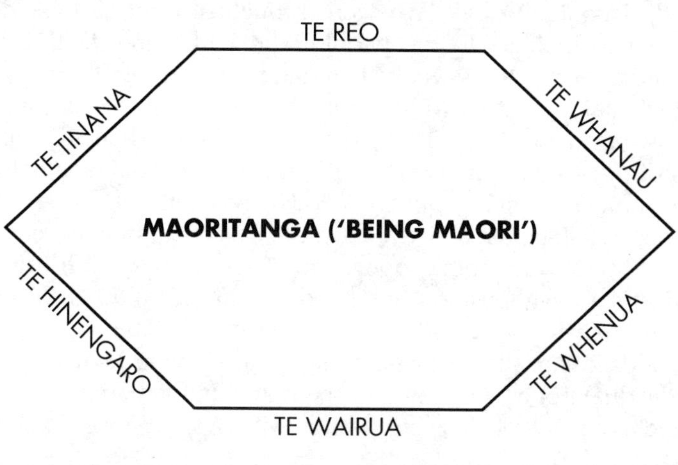

things one person asks another is, 'What do you do for a job?' Much of the sense of identity in these cultures comes from work. The model (see p. 37) and explanation of the origin of Maori identity is given by Te Hata Ohlson:

For Maori, Mana, or esteem (rather than *self*-esteem) is gained by one's relationship to all these six elements. As an individual, a Maori's esteem is based on how he/she can effectively complement and add to the whole. The areas are:

1 *Te reo* — the language of one's own tribe, together with a knowledge of tribal protocol, whakapapa, lore and culture.

2 *Te whanau* — the family, which could include relations other than immediate family, e.g. aunties, uncles, cousins, grandparents. Kinship ties.

3 *Te whenua* — the land and environment, and its relationship as kin, through papatuanuku (mother earth). Maori families buried the placenta, birth cord, and afterbirth in a special place at their kainga or home ground.'Whenua' also means 'placenta', 'umbilical cord' and 'afterbirth'.

4 *Te wairua* — wairua is spirit, including the human spirit. This is linked to Mauri or life force, ihi (strength/confidence), and mana (esteem).

5 *Te hinengaro* — emotions and thoughts.

6 *Te tinana* — the physical being, i.e. body.

Individual and Group Esteem

Te Hata Ohlson's description emphasises the importance to Maori of one's *relationship* to larger wholes. On the contrary, in Pakeha culture it is often assumed that esteem can be achieved by celebrating one's personal successes. Joan Metge describes how Pat King went to see a Pakeha counsellor at Marriage Guidance. The counsellor suggested she build up her self-esteem by making a list of the things she was good at. King explained, 'I couldn't do it. We were brought up not to look down on anyone, but to look up to the people who had mana, to the kuia and koroua, and above all to be whakaiti, not to push yourself.'

To be whakaiti (modest, with humility) is not the same, Metge explains, as being whakamaa (a word which implies shame, shyness, withdrawal, and loss of mana). She quotes Anaru Penrose: 'Whakamaa is not *taking* a lowly position, it is being *put* in a lowly position. One does not seek whakamaa. Whakaiti is a lowly position that one might seek, adopt, incorporate into your philosophy, but a lowly position of honour. Whakamaa is a lowly position of dishonour.' In fact, then, the modesty or humility of whakaiti is an important part of esteem for Maori.

Metge adds, 'Whakaiti goes with being secure in your identity, not simply as an individual but as a link in a descent line and a member of a descent group, and as a result of close association with older relatives in childhood.'

This is the part of the challenge of building esteem, in *Maori* terms, which the Pakeha counsellor was unable to pick up. It involves reforging the links with all six elements of Maoritanga. Esteem does not exist in a vacuum. It can only be built successfully on the basis of a person's own cultural values.

Sources of Pakeha Identity

The situation of Pakeha is rather different. Even if someone were to wear a tee-shirt saying 'Speak Maori or die!', it could not have the effect on me, as a Pakeha, that 'Speak English or die!' has on Maori people. After all, my language is spoken 99 per cent of the time on TV, in parliament, in our schools, and in the streets. It is a fairly safe bet that English will survive.

Nonetheless, many Pakeha do feel uncertain about who they are. As we learn about the injustices involved in the colonisation of New Zealand/Aotearoa, we as Pakeha search for ways to respond without being paralysed by guilt. In our search, we often ask, 'Who are our people anyway?', and 'Why are we here?'

Richard's Ancestors

My own ancestors came to Aotearoa from Wales, Norway, Ireland, and England. In each case, they were escaping the poverty of Europe and hoping for a more egalitarian society where they could own their own land. Hans Hansen and Christiane Pedersdatter (who took the name 'Bolstad' after leaving Norway in 1872) were leaving their feudal life as farm labourers for a section in the new 'town' of Norsewood. Within a few years they had lost their struggle with the totara forest and were once more labouring on other people's land. Forty years later, my mother's father, Richard Watkins, left for the new colony 'down under'. Like so many other settlers, his dreams of self-sufficiency had eventually to fit into the restraints of a suburban quarter acre section.

It was the Treaty of Waitangi which enabled these people to settle here. The Maori tribes accepted earlier settlements, trusting the Pakeha would honour our side of this deal. The Bolstads, for example, were given a formal welcome by Paora Rerepo and Ngati Kahungunu. But the land companies, in their eagerness to sell, were less carefull about the treaty. Thomas Chapman and Mary Ann Hicks, ancestors of mine who arrived at the Nelson settlement in 1842, found that much of the promised land there had never even been bought from Ngati Toa. Within a year, the determination of the New Zealand Company officials to enforce the illegal subdivision of Nelson land had resulted in the first battle between settlers and Maori, at Wairau.

Maori, Pakeha and the Treaty

I believe my ancestors made the best choices they could, to find a better life for themselves and their families. But they, of all people, could have understood how important land can be to a people's self-esteem. I share my forebears' dream of a fairer society. Now, 150 years later, I think it's time to recognise that this fairness has to include a respect for the Maori people's special relationship with their land. This special relationship is acknowledged clearly in Te Tiriti o Waitangi. I consider it important to my self-esteem as a Pakeha, that we honour our side of that deal.

WOMEN'S REALITY

There are similar issues when we consider self-esteem for men and for women. 75 per cent of all drugs for psychiatric symptoms, sold in New Zealand, go to women. Twice as many women as men present with psychiatric problems in the health system.

We don't have to look far to find social sources for the lower self-esteem of women. One is the attitude that has been called 'sexism'. Just as racism is present when one culture assumes its superiority and is able to implement this; so sexism involves one sex (usually men) assuming a belief in their own superiority and acting to put this into practise. This includes:

- Unequal sharing of decision-making power. In 1986, research by the Ministry of Women's Affairs showed that only 13 per cent of members of Parliament, 14 per cent of local body councillors, and 9 per cent of Mayors were women.
- Unequal sharing of resources. Even when women's work is paid for (which it isn't in the case of housework for example) the 1986 census showed women's average incomes were half that of men ($7 641 compared with $15 104).
- Unequal sharing of work. The New Zealand National Council of Women Research in 1984 found only 14 per cent of married women were able to share the housework with their husband.
- Men's violence against women. According to David Shapcott's research, 30–40 per cent of New Zealand men say that under certain circumstances they would rape a woman.
- Pressure on women to conform to a very narrow ideal of attractiveness. One aspect of this usually unattainable standard is body shape. A study of nursing students in Wellington revealed that 43.6 per cent are caught in a cycle of dieting and binging, as they struggle to reach the 'ideal' shape. 6.6 per cent of them have a life-threatening eating disorder such as anorexia nervosa (where the refusal to eat sometimes leads to death from starvation) and bulimia nervosa (binge-purge syndrome, where

massive overeating, sometimes followed by vomiting or laxative use, can result in death from kidney, heart, or stomach damage). A survey of 100 Auckland 15- and 16-year-old women showed that only 9 per cent were in *any* sense medically overweight, but 68 per cent wanted to be thinner.

Sexism in Language

Sexism is also expressed in the way men and women talk with each other. This produces some rather subtle assaults on women's self-esteem, which will be discussed in more detail.

In the English language, even the words we use assume male superiority (Maori, on the other hand, is an example of a language virtually free of sexism). In English, the average person can be called the '*Man* in the street', and the achievements of our species are the achievements of '*Man*kind'. A very sexually active man is a 'stud' (complimentary) while a very sexually active woman is a 'slut' (insulting). 'Sissy' (from the word sister) is an insult, while 'buddy' (from the word brother) is a compliment. 'Being a man' means acting strong (complimentary) while 'behaving like a woman' means being ridiculously weak (insulting).

One of the challenges of effective communication, then, is to find ways of talking which are *inclusive*, rather than male centred: to avoid saying 'he' when we mean to include any person, to avoid saying 'man' when we mean to include all people. Using inclusive language supports *everyone's* self-esteem, and that is the first step towards successful relationships.

Women's Talk — Men's Talk

Research shows some important differences between the ways that women and men talk in groups. Reviewing the research about this, Baird notes that studies have shown the following:

MEN	WOMEN
Start conversations more	Respond to others' conversation more
Talk about the task or goal more	Talk about social relationships more
Give more information	Express warmth and helpfulness more
Talk more and use more words	Say less as men talk more
Interrupt people more often	Avoid unpleasant conversations more

Talk about themselves more	Talk about others more
Make more statements about what is	Use more questions
Describe 'objective' facts more	Express personal opinions as opinions

Response to the Two Styles

Women opposed to sexism have had two types of response to this difference in conversational style. One response (epitomised by Anne Wilson Schaeffs book *Women's Reality*) has been to affirm 'women's talk' as part of an emerging *female* way of relating to the world. The other (represented in books such as *Desire: the Politics of Sexuality*, Ann Snitow, Christine Stansell, and Sharon Thompson (eds)) has been to call for an end to the division between 'female' and 'male' ways of relating.

Both groups agree that there are some ways men and women relate which damage women's self-esteem. These include what Anne Wilson Schaeff calls 'peacekeeping talk'. In peacekeeping talk, women are careful not to rock the boat. Hoekelman notes that peacekeeping talk is common when female nurses deal with male doctors. She calls it 'the doctor-nurse game'.

The Doctor-Nurse Game

Here is an example quoted by Loland Menikheim: A doctor re-prescribed librium (a tranquilliser) for one of his patients. After thanking the doctor for the drug prescriptions, the nurse added, 'Oh, Doctor, I forgot to tell you that the night nurse reported that Mrs M. was nauseated after each librium. Did you want to write a new order?' The doctor, who had forgotten the night nurse's report, then replied, 'Yes, thanks Trudy. I did want to change the order'. Notice how the nurse's comments fit precisely with the research about women's style of talking. Instead of stating her disagreement with the doctor, she asks a question and suggests he has made the decision. She thus comes across as helpful and non–threatening, and appears to be simply responding to his comments.

Menikheim points out how similar 'peacekeeping talk', used by women such as housewives and secretaries, preserves the pattern of male control. Women's wisdom, skill, and contribution to society is covered up in this process, and women are deprived of opportunities to feel good about themselves. And yet when women do not co-operate with the game they are viewed as rude, aggressive, and domineering.

Men's Changing Identity

Chapter 8 discusses alternative ways for individuals to co-operate, without one person using their power over the other. For now it's also important to realise that men's control of conversations and of society is not just a personal issue. It is a social issue, and the solutions need to involve major changes in the way we raise children, present men and women in the media, structure our government, and so on. What do men think about all this? Are they eager to protect their power; to go on playing the doctor-nurse game? I don't think so. Ken McMaster and Peter Swain use the analogy of a bully to describe men's tendency to control others. They say, 'We have met and worked with many men who have the strength to take on the challenge and explore the bully in themselves. These men are clear that the rules and roles of being a bully no longer fit. It hinders them from being co-operative, nurturing, sensitive towards and caring for their partners, family children and friends. We haven't yet met a man who deep down enjoys being a bully. Many of the men we meet are afraid of themselves and feel guilty about how they are within their families. They know at heart that there must be a different way.' McMaster and Swain say that they are 'challenging all men to join us in stopping men's violence to women; and we ask, are you man enough?'

It's a new definition of 'being a man' that such people promote. One which asks men to find their self-esteem not from power over others, but from a greater power — over their own lives.

EXERCISE 2.5

Aim — to affirm the significance of group members' ancestry and sense of place.

Give members 1–2 weeks' warning, so they can research their ancestry. Members who are adopted may like to research their adoptive family or their birth family, depending on circumstances. Some people, of course, simply may not be able to collect much information.

1 Have the group get into pairs and discuss:
  a Who were your ancestors and where did they come from?
  b What customs and values do you imagine your ancestors had which are still part of your life today?
2 Change partners and discuss:
  a What places in New Zealand have your family lived?
  b What parts of New Zealand are special to you and why?
3 Have each person choose one place in New Zealand which is special to them. Create an imaginary map of the country, spread out on the floor, and have people stand where their special place is. Share with the group where each person is standing and why.
4 Have people sit down again, and ask them to take time to write down individually some of the customs and values they have experienced in their family, and in the culture they are a part of.

(Values simply means things that are important to you; perhaps things such as family support, individual rights, respect, freedom, equality.)

5 Have people check the list to see which things are precious to them. Which customs or values are important enough that they be passed on to their children and to future New Zealanders. Discuss in pairs, and then collect ideas from the group.

EXERCISE 2.6

Aim — to affirm group members' sense of gender identity.

1 Divide the class into two groups (if there are men and women, try to include both in each group). Give each group a felt pen and a sheet of newsprint. One group is instructed to think of all the women they know, and list characteristics they have in common. The other group is to do the same with men they know.

2 Report back and discuss:

a What are the main differences?

b What would you expect to happen if a group of people with the characteristics listed for women and a group of people with the characteristics listed for men tried to work together?

c Which group (from the lists you have here) appears to have the best self-esteem?

3 Give group members time to think back through their life and find an action of theirs which (a) they feel proud of, and (b) they could only have done as a person of their gender. Such actions could include being a son or daughter, a mother or father; being a supportive same sex friend; being involved in a helpful way with a group or class where only people of their sex were members, and so on. Ensure people have plenty of time to fully recall such an action. Have them find a word to describe the personal characteristic they demonstrated at that time.

4 Share these words. (You may want to make two new lists from them, or to invite people to share the events themselves.)

EXERCISE 2.7

Aim — to help group members understand the social origins of body image, and affirm their own body (adapted from Hutchinson (1985)).

1 Have each person privately list six individuals from their past or present life, who have probably had an influence on how they feel about their body.
2 Invite people to relax, and close their eyes, then tune in to the way they think and feel about their body.
3 Repeat the following instructions six times: 'Imagine that one of those six people comes into the room now and walks around you .... Watch what that person looks at and hear what they would say about your body, if you asked them .... Check how what they say has affected your feeling about your own body .... Ask yourself whether there is anything you have swallowed from their comments which you would like to spit out .... If there is, actually imagine yourself spitting it out, and hear yourself saying something strongly positive about the aspect of your body concerned. Take time to ensure you have done this if you needed to ...'.
4 Have people share in pairs what this was like, and then report back to the group. Questions might include:
a In what ways was your body image affected?
b How easy was it to reject comments you didn't want to swallow?

Parent, Adult, and Child States

Objective: to be able to define the parent, adult and child *ego states* in transactional analysis (T.A.) terminology.

SOME PUZZLING STATES

After waiting ten minutes from the arranged starting time, the tutor stood up and proceeded to tell his class what he thought about their arriving late for his session. He moved quickly, walking backwards and forwards in front of the room, and emphasising each sentence with a wave of his index finger. He spoke loudly, his face reddened and his forehead creased, his eyes staring fixedly at each of the latecomers in turn. 'I'm fed up with this sort of behaviour', he explained. 'It's about time you people started behaving a bit more responsibly. You certainly won't be able to carry on like this once you're in the workforce.'

At that point, John — one of the students — resolved that he was not going to say anything in that day's class. He looked steadily down at the ground, sitting back in his chair with his arms folded. He held his mouth tightly shut, with the corners of his lips downturned, and sighed every so often. Beside him, Liz was clenching her hands tightly to her chair and leaning forward. Her forehead was also creased towards the centre; and every so often she breathed in and opened her mouth to speak, but then stopped herself and sat back. 'He never gives us any chance to explain', she told John later, 'I shouldn't have bothered coming at all! I can't learn this stuff anyway.'

The states of mind that the tutor, John, and Liz are in are common enough. John and Liz have felt that way several times before in their life. In fact, they first learned to respond that way when they were children. Their tutor has experienced his state before too, and the first time he experienced it was probably when someone *else* (a parent or a primary school teacher) was in that state and told *him* off.

BERNE'S MODEL

Eric Berne (1910-1970) developed a way of categorising people's states of mind as:

a Responding to here and now events using your actual abilities: the Adult Ego-state.
b Responding in the way you did as a child: The Child Ego-state.
c Responding in ways you've copied from parents or parent-figures: the Parent Ego-state.

This is the way Berne diagrams it:

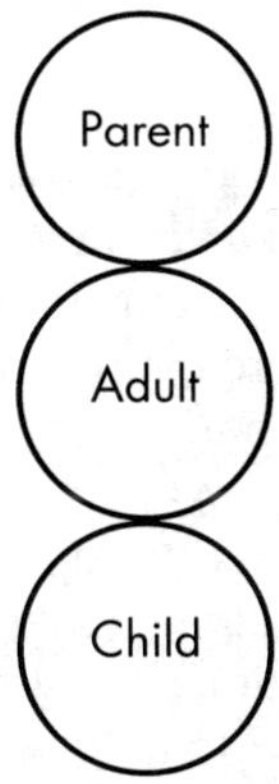

Memory

In 1951, neurosurgeon Dr Wilder Penfield showed that when particular places in the side areas of a person's brain are stimulated with an electrode, the person will *re-experience* a situation from their memory. They will see, hear, feel, taste, and smell the experience as it originally occurred, complete with the emotions they had then. Like a video recorder, our brain stores the memory of everything that has happened to us, along with the state we were in at that time. The 'Parent' and 'Child' ego-states, as described by Berne, are the result of a person replaying these video tapes and responding as if the original situations are occurring now. In such cases, actual experiences from childhood are shaping our current state of mind.

Each of these 'ego-states' has certain feelings, ways of thinking and ways of behaving that consistently go together. When the tutor described above is in his Parent ego-state and wanting to tell someone about a difficulty he has, he consistently *feels* angry, *thinks* about the way the other persons' actions will cause them problems, and *behaves* as he did above (shouting, waving his finger at people, and so on). When John is in his Child ego-state and someone else is asking him to change, he consistently *feels* helpless and resentful, *thinks* about how pointless it is to say anything, and *behaves* accordingly (not speaking, avoiding looking up, and sighing). At this time, neither of these people is actually responding to what is happening here and now. The tutor probably knows some much better ways to get people to change than shouting and waving his finger, and if he was in his *Adult* ego-state he could use them. John probably isn't helpless, and if *he* was in his Adult ego-state he might even help himself by finding useful things to say. He might feel anxious as he took that risk, but he wouldn't feel helpless.

Remembered States and Crises

This is a powerful part of how people respond to crises. For example, Bertil Jacobsen of Sweden's Karolinska Institute studied hundreds of cases of suicide, and found that suicide is four times more likely when a person's *birth* was by breech delivery, forceps delivery, or caused lack of oxygen. Under stress, someone who has had a very early brush with death tends to go back to *that* Child ego-state. What happens to us in our childhood, especially our very early childhood, *is* important. The work of psychotherapy often involves helping people to heal from events which happened very early in life. At times a psychotherapist has the person re-experience the hurting child state, to achieve this healing.

Psychotherapist Arthur Janov claims about therapy with suicidal people 'those who relive the near death experience in and around birth seem to finally resolve that fixation on death and suicide'. The person can then respond in an adult way to their actual life.

Using Each State

Does this mean it's always a bad idea to be in your Parent or Child ego-state, and always best to be in the Adult state? Certainly not. There are times when it's quite appropriate to respond in a similar way to your parents. 'Watch out for that car!', you might call out as your friend steps onto the road. The words come automatically without you having to think how to react to the here and now; you may well be in your Parent ego-state. Getting someone a hot lemon drink and breakfast in bed when they have the flu may also be Parent state behaviour. In the same way, it's *sometimes* quite sensible to respond just as you did when a child. Saying 'Sorry' when you bump into someone in a busy department store is probably an automatic response that you learned as a child, but it generally helps people feel better. Being able to 'let your hair down' and join in fully with a spontaneous game your friends are playing is also a use of the Child state.

So much of the richness of life comes from being able to fully re-experience child states. Sigmund Freud stated 'happiness is a childhood wish fullfilled'. Even reading this book may, if you think back, be connected to your own hopes and dreams as a child. Perhaps, as a young child, you imagined working in a job caring for others, and reading this book is part of that dream coming to life now. Perhaps you wished for very special, loving relationships, and your growth towards those led you here. Whatever the source, when you remember the sense of curiosity, excitement, fascination which you had as that child, it enriches you now.

Excluded and Contaminated States

Actually, not being able to use one of the three ego states is more of a problem, according to Eric Berne. People who 'exclude' their Parent state (and so have no ready-made rules) may make great criminals but poor friends. People who 'exclude' their Child state, on the contrary, will be fairly responsible, but not much fun to be with. And to exclude your Adult state means to have no responses to here and now reality at all — to be 'crazy', in fact. A healthy person, in Berne's terms, can move freely from state to state as it suits the situation. They can also tell which state they're in. Having an *excluded* state is only one kind of unhealthy structure. Even more common (as in our example classroom situation above) is for a person to think they are responding in an Adult way to the here and now situation, while actually behaving in a Parent or Child way.

Liz (one of the students in our original example) tells John 'I can't learn this stuff anyway'. As she says this, her Adult thinking is *contaminated* by a belief she first developed in childhood. In Chapter 1, we listed several Child contaminated beliefs people often hold about meeting others, and then supplied Adult alternatives. Just as serious are Parent *contaminated* states where someone mistakes Parental slogans for Adult reality (slogans such as 'All students are lazy', 'People can't be trusted', or 'Give someone an inch and they'll take a mile').

The tutor in our story probably believed he was giving some sound Adult-to-Adult advice to his class, while actually speaking out of his Parent. He may then have been quite surprised to get back a Child response from some students.

Here's how Berne diagrams such contamination:

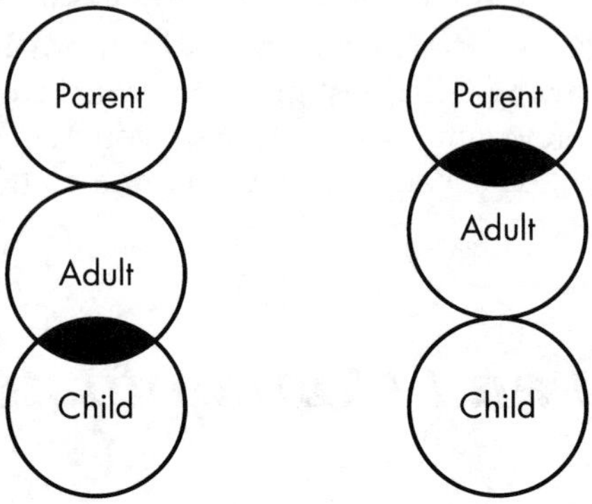

Child Contamination (e.g. Liz)

Parent Contamination (e.g. The Tutor)

Transactions

When two people talk to each other (perhaps one person saying 'Hello' to the other, and the other person replying) we can also use Berne's diagrams to demonstrate what happens. For example:

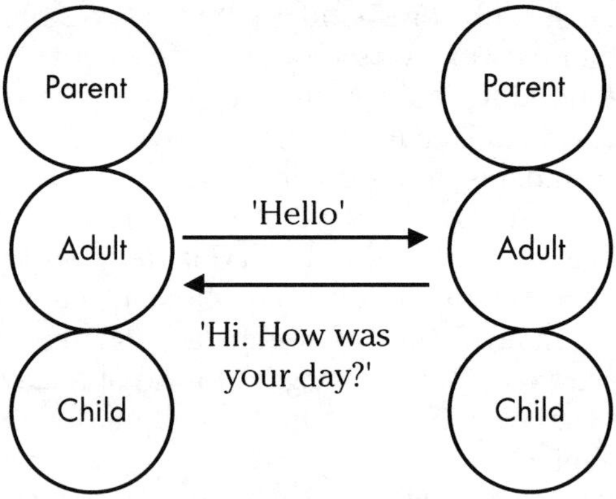

A simple two-way interaction like this is what Berne calls a transaction (hence the name of his theory: Transactional Analysis, or T.A. for short).

The interaction, shown below, uses a transactional diagram.

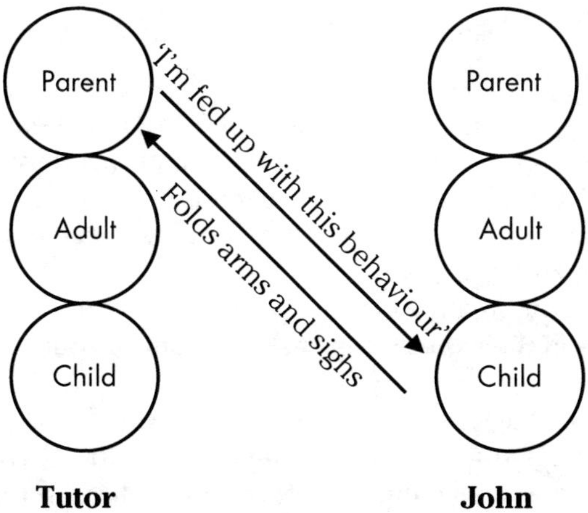

Crossed Transactions

Now, imagine that John had more flexibility about what state he was in (using some of the techniques discussed before). He might recognise that the tutor is talking to him from the Parent ego-state, but decides to respond Adult to Adult. In Chapters 5–11, we'll learn various ways of sorting out such situations 'Adult to Adult' (in Berne's terms), but for now we'll just take an example. John may have replied, 'I can certainly understand how their coming late makes it difficult for you. I'd like to check, with those who were late, whether they have some particular difficulty getting here. Perhaps that could be sorted out.'

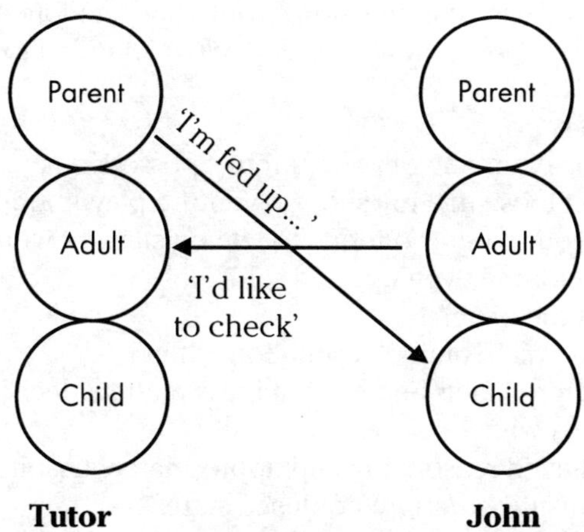

Now, instead of being a 'parallel transaction', as you can see the transaction is 'crossed'. A crossed transaction is an *invitation* to the other person to change their state. In this case it has some chance of getting the tutor to move into Adult state and sort out the problem instead of telling people off.

EXERCISE 2.8

Aim — to identify students' individual Parent, Adult and Child Ego-states.

1 Have people work in pairs, with a sheet of paper each. Each person's page should be divided into columns headed 'Parent', 'Adult', and 'Child'. The aim of the exercise is to write a list of ways you could tell which ego state you're in. These ways could include:

a postures and gestures.
b the way you breathe and the speed of breathing.
c changes in the expressions or skin colour of your face.
d the way you use your eyes.
e changes in the tone of your voice and the kind of words you say.

The job of the people in pairs is to take turns remembering a series of situations and explaining/demonstrating to their partner how they would respond. The partner will then assist them to identify the specific postures, gestures, tones of voice, and so on, which are related to each ego state *for them*.

2 *Parent Ego-state*: When thinking of these situations you may ask 'How would I respond to this?' *and* 'How would my parents respond to this?'

— a child breaking one of your possessions
— a child who fell off a bicycle
— a new neighbour from a different culture
— a 14 year old having a sexual relationship.

3 *Child Ego-state*: When thinking of these situations you may ask, 'How would I respond to this now?', but may get more accurate information by asking 'How would I have responded to this as a child?'

— a test at school
— having broken one of your parent's possessions
— being let loose in a toy shop/adventure playground
— one of your parents offering to let you stay up, when the other (who is out for the evening) had said 'No'
— a day at the beach.

4 *Adult Ego-state*: Think of a situation when . . .

— you gathered facts and on that basis made a decision you were pleased with
— you behaved reasonably and appropriately despite others being in a disturbed/angry/confused state.

5 Gather together as a group and share some of the things people discovered. Are there similarities? Did anyone discover that they had difficulty thinking of themselves in one of the states? Did anyone discover times when their Adult was 'contaminated' by another state?

EXERCISE 2.9

Aim — to explore group members' childhood 'life expectation patterns'.

1 Have each person think what their favourite childhood fairy tale, story, or even TV programme was.
2 In pairs discuss:
— who did you identify with in that story?
— what kind of person were they? What cultural values did they hold?
— what was their life like?
— what are the disadvantages of being that person?
— how would you like to change the story's ending?
— who introduced you to this story? What did the story mean to them?
3 Share in a group: What did you learn?

SUMMARY

This chapter has considered the state of mind you're in from three different angles. First, you learned four powerful techniques to create the state you'd like, whether it is relaxation, motivation, confidence, caring, or whatever. The four ways are (1)*visualisation*; using your ability to imagine and picture things, (2) *affirmation*; the way you talk to yourself, (3) *body position* and breathing style, and (4) *anchoring yourself into the desired state* using a stimulus associated with it.

Secondly, we discussed the effects of cultural and gender differences on your state of mind. Equalising power in society can make it easier for all of us to be in a state of mind where we feel good about who we are — a state of esteem. For Maori, this process involves making links to *the wider context of Maoritanga*. For women, it requires an increasing *respect for women's rights and contributions*.

Thirdly, the last part looked at the Transactional Analysis model of ego states. Eric Berne suggested that states of mind can be grouped as *Adult* (a response to the here and now situation), *Child* (a response first learned as a child), and *Parent* (a response copied from parents or parent figures).

References & Further Reading

Andreas, S. and Andreas, C. (1987) *Change Your Mind and Keep The Change*, Real People Press, Moab, Utah.

Awatere, D.(1984) *Maori Sovereignty*, in *Broadsheet*, Auckland.

Baird, J.E. (1976) 'Sex Differences in Group Communication: A Review of Relevant Research', in *Quarterly Journal of Speech* 62, no.1, (April), pp. 179–192.

Hoekelman, R.A. (1975) 'Nurse-Physician Relationships', in *American Journal of Nursing* (July), p. 1151.

Hutchinson, M.G. (1985) *Transforming Body Image*, The Crossing Press, Trumansburg, New York.

James, M. and Jongeward, D. (1971) *Born To Win*, Addison-Wesley Publishing, Reading.

McKay, M. and Fanning, P. (1987) *Self Esteem*, New Harbinger Publications, Oakland, California.

McMaster, K. and Swain, P. (1989) *A Private Affair? Stopping Men's Violence to Women*, G.P. Books, Wellington.

Menikheim, M. (1979) 'Communication Patterns of Women and Nurses', in Jervik, D.K. and Martinson, I.M. (eds) *Women in Stress: A Nursing Perspective*, Appleton-Century-Crofts, New York.

Metge, J. (1986) *In and Out of Touch*, Victoria University Press, Wellington.

Nairn, M. and Nairn, R. (1981) 'The Racism of Economics and the Economics of Racism', in Davis, P. (ed.), *New Zealand Labour Perspectives: The Challenge of the Third Depression*, Ross, Wellington.

Robbins, A. (1988) *Unlimited Power*, Simon & Schuster, London.

Rossi, E.L. (1986) *The Psychobiology of Mind-Body Healing*, W.W. Norton & Co, New York.

Sanford, L. and Donovan, M.E. (1984) *Women and Self Esteem*, Anchor Press/Doubleday, Garden City, New York.

Schaeff, A.W. (1985) *Women's Reality*, Harper & Row, San Fransisco.

Siegel, B. (1988) *Love, Medicine and Miracles*, Arrow Books, London.

Snitow, A., Stansell, C. and Thompson, S. (1984) (eds) *Desire: The Politics of Sexuality*, Virago, London.

Stewart, I. and Joines, V. (1987) *T.A. Today*, Lifespan Publishing, Nottingham, England.

Stirling, P. (1990) 'The Dangers of Dieting', in the *Listener*, October 1–7, pp. 10–18.

Waldegrave, C. and Coventry, R. (1987) *Poor New Zealand*, Platform Publishing, Wellington. (Unless otherwise stated, New Zealand statistics given in the section 'The Social Roots of Self-Esteem' of this chapter originate in *Poor New Zealand*).

Walker, R. (1989) 'Maori Identity', in Novitz, D. and Willmott, B. (eds). *Culture and Identity in New Zealand*, Government Printing Office, Wellington, pp. 35–52.

The Primal Institute Newsletter, (1988) Primal Institute, New York, 'The Birth of Suicidal Tendencies', vol XI, no. 1, (Jan/Feb), p. 3, 'Birth and Death' (1983), vol V, no. 10, (June), p. 3.

CHAPTER 3

The Context of Communication

KEY CONCEPTS:

'Proxemics' (closeness)

Body language and culture

Gestures and body language

Sensory system use (visual /auditory/kinesthetic)

Rapport

Approaching Others

Objective: to be able to recognise someone's intimate and personal zones according to Edward Hall's model.

CONTEXT

As you know, reading a book is very different from talking to someone. For instance, if I say 'Hello' to you here on the page, all you'll get is the word 'Hello'. In real life you might have received hundreds of other messages as I said that one word. Check it out and you'll see what I mean. Pause now and remember a time when someone you *really* liked, someone you were strongly attracted to, said 'Hello' to you ... Most likely, as you remember that, you're aware of the tone of voice they used, and how fast or slow they said it. Probably you can see that slight smile on their face as their lips form the word, and even feel the rush of interest inside you as you move physically a little closer to them.

What's different? The answers are about the *context* of the word they said; the things happening around and at the same time as the word Hello. Talking to someone is *high context communication*. By comparison, using an automatic teller machine to get money from your bank is *low context communication*. The machine does the same thing whether you smile or not, and no matter how sensitively you touch its keyboard, it's not interested in the context. Human beings usually are. In this chapter we'll explore the context of human communication; often called 'body language'.

Value of Body Language

You'll understand the reason for learning about body language when you think back to meeting that person you were strongly attracted to. As you spoke with them, you were probably very interested in understanding how *they* felt about you. It may have been important to you to know how they reacted to whatever you said and did. That's one good reason to learn body language: so you can tell what effect you're having. Another good reason is so you can create that sense of 'rapport' which I mentioned in Chapter 1: the ability to have that other person feel really understood by you, and for you to understand them. That sense of understanding doesn't just come from saying the right words to each other. It comes from using the right tone of voice, the right body gestures, even the right movements of your eyes (and by 'right' I mean right for you and the person you are with). That's what you'll learn in this chapter.

Although we are dealing with body language particularly in this *one* chapter, it's useful to remember that body language is the most important part of all person-to-person communication. Albert Mehrabian (author of *Silent Messages*) suggests that only about 7 per cent of the impact of a message comes from the words you say. The other 93 per cent is context. This is particularly amazing when you remember that most people are not even aware what messages they are sending non-verbally. Think about it. Most of your communication is happening at an unconscious level!

Pupil Size

Some of the messages you're sending aren't even under your control if you *try* to control them (ever tried to stop yourself blushing once you've started?). A good example is the size of the pupils in your eyes. Eckhard Hess has found in his research about pupil size that even 3-month-old babies will smile *more* when their caregiver's pupils are dilated (large) than when they are constricted (small). Adults tend to describe people with dilated pupils as 'open', 'warm', and 'gentle', and people with constricted pupils as 'harsh', 'cold', and 'sneaky'. So people are sending messages every time they look at someone; messages that even a 3-month-old baby is smart enough to pick up. And, of course, you may have realised this already. Sometimes people talk about 'bedroom eyes' to describe a person whose pupils are dilated in a way that reminds them of sexual attraction; or about 'beady little eyes' describing someone whose constricted pupils make them seem 'sneaky' or 'reserved'. In parts of southern Europe such as Spain, women used to put diluted juice from the poisonous plant Belladonna (the name means 'beautiful woman') in their eyes to attract men. Why? Because Belladonna dilates the pupils. In the same way, poker players sometimes wear dark glasses so that the excitement of a winning hand *can't* be detected from their dilated pupils.

Intuitively, people realise that they are sending and receiving messages just by the size of their pupils. If you've ever noticed this, you can congratulate yourself on your skill at reading body language. And you'll find it easier to understand that *communication is continuous*: it's always going on. The moment you look at someone, each of your eyes are sending messages — like it or not! Most of the time, you haven't even been aware that it's happening, let alone been planning what message to send.

'Proxemics'

So let's think again about how you're communicating as soon as you've met someone. Even the distance you stand or sit away from them is communicating things. It was Edward Hall who first called the study of how far apart people stand 'proxemics'. Hall observed that for every person you meet, there will be a distance between the two of you with which you feel comfortable. If they come closer than that, you will feel as if 'your space' has been invaded; you may feel cramped, anxious, even suffocated. Obviously, the distance at which *you can relax* will be closer for a friend than for a person you've just met.

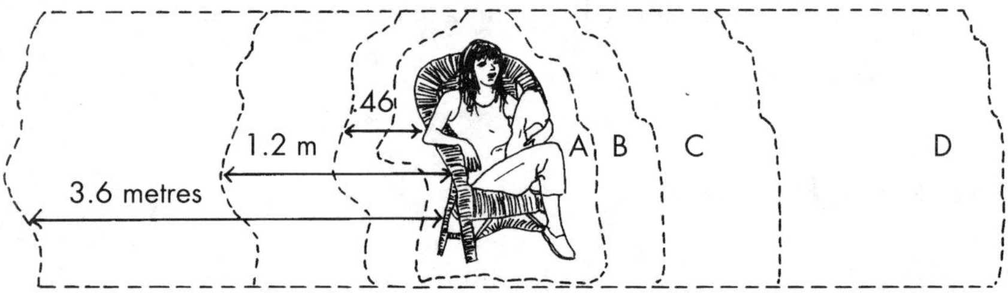

The close intimate zone (area A in above diagram) and the intimate zone (area B) stretch out to about 46 cm from the body, for most people. Generally in Pakeha culture, people only expect very close friends and family members to stand or sit this close to them. Of course what you expect and what actually happens are two different things. Other people are forced to move into your intimate space when you stand in a queue, in an elevator, in a crowded place, and so on. If you are a health professional, your job requires you to move into other people's intimate space quite soon after meeting them. Even in these situations, people usually feel anxious about their personal space being invaded. They may cope by avoiding eye contact more than usual, not talking, and so on. Watch next time you are in an elevator or a queue, and be aware of your own response as others move closer than 46 cm from you. You'll understand quickly why, in cultures with a British origin, this is not the best distance to stand from a person you're just meeting.

Personal and Social Zones

The personal zone (area C in the diagram) stretches from about half a metre to one metre out from the body. This is the distance people usually stand at friendly gatherings such as parties. Being this distance away demonstrates a deliberate interest in getting to know someone, whereas strangers and people not known so well tend to stand one to three-and-half metres away (area D, the social zone). Usually, when you meet people, standing somewhere between one and three metres away from them will tell them you are friendly, without making them feel invaded. Exactly how far away you stand will depend on both your cultural origins, and on whether you grew up in an urban or rural setting (people from the country stand further away than city people).

Area E is the public zone, used for speaking to an audience, for example. If you work in a group and sit more than three-and-a-half metres away, you will almost certainly create a sense of distance which makes it harder for others to share with you. Many group leaders prefer to seat people in a circle so that each person is actually in the personal zone or closer with the person beside them.

EXERCISE 3.1

Aim — to get used to the difference between intimate zone, personal zone, and social zone.

1 Get people into pairs and stand 3 m away from each other (this requires either a large space, or people standing in two lines facing their partners). With the other person in their pair, they then talk about:

- a in what situations they would stand this far away from the person they are talking to.
- b when was the last time they remember talking to someone from this distance away, and what relationship did they have with that person.
- c what it feels like *now* to talk to this person from this distance.

2 Have the pairs stand 1 m apart and again answer the three questions.

3 Have the pairs stand about 40 cm apart and answer the three questions, as well as, 'what things are you doing right now to manage being at this distance, if any?'

4 Return to the group and report back. You may also discuss what distance people usually sit or stand from each other in this group. Which zone are they in then?

Spot the Difference

Objective: to be able to specify one male-female difference and four cultural differences in body language.

CULTURE AND GESTURE

In their book *Talking Past Each Other*. Joan Metge and Patricia Kinloch recount the beginning of a fight in a hotel bar. A person from Niue accidentally bumped into a Pakeha man, spilling the other's glass of beer. The Niuean apologised, and the Pakeha replied, 'It doesn't matter', waving his hand away and down towards the floor to emphasise the point. Recognising the Niuean gesture for 'Come here', the first man moved into the other's intimate zone. Such a sudden move could only mean a fight, the Pakeha realised. He decided to get in the first swing, and hit the Niuean.

Just as surely as verbal language varies from culture to culture, so does body language. To a Pakeha New Zealander, the gesture 'come here' tends to be waving the hand up and towards the head. In most Pacific cultures, the hand is held palm *down* and waved in towards the body to say the same thing. Knowing such a simple thing can make the difference between a friend and an enemy.

Showing Respect

Mostly, when people meet each other, they are searching for ways to show each other friendship and respect. Both the people in that ill-fated hotel bar wanted exactly that. And yet, even aside from the different understanding of the downward wave, they probably misunderstood each other's most basic ways of *showing* respect. Eye contact is a very important way of demonstrating respect when listening to someone in Pakeha culture. Allan Pease describes (in what is an excellent study of Pakeha body language) the downturned eyebrows and sidewards glance, as well as the closed eyes gesture, as evidence of a negative or critical reaction. For Pakeha, someone who can 'look you in the eye' is honest and respectful of what you are saying; someone who does not is shifty and hostile. Maori and Tagata Pasifica (Pacific Island Polynesian) speakers, on the other hand, consider it impolite to look directly into another person's eyes while talking to them.

To do so is a gesture of conflict in these cultures, whereas looking down, looking to the side, and closing the eyes while speaking are often used to show respect and friendliness. Most Pakeha will understand how invaded a Maori or Samoan speaker feels by the Pakeha level of eye contact, if they think of the relentless (to a New Zealander) eye contact many North Americans expect. In some North American cultural settings, a speaker may keep their eyes fixed on the listener's throughout an entire speech, pursuing the New Zealander's eyes as they shift to look away while thinking. This can be compared with the Pakeha–Maori difference.

Standing or Sitting

Another important difference in showing respect involves standing or sitting down. In Pakeha culture, to stand up for someone shows respect. A student may be expected to stand in front of a teacher, and the court stands while the magistrate enters. In these cases, respectfulness means not sitting down until a seat is offered. Metge and Kinloch point out that in Samoan and Maori culture, the opposite is often true. People do not stand up in front of an important speaker (even if they must leave the room, they tend to do so in a crouching, bended over position). And the best way to show respect upon entering a room may well be to sit down and lower oneself. If you are working in a people centred job, it will be a relief to know that both the Pakeha who comes in and stands rather stiffly above you, and the Maori who comes in and slips down into their seat may be gesturing respect. In both cultures *brief* body lowering (a nod or a bow) tends to indicate respect.

Cross Cultural Gestures

Luckily, some gestures *do* work cross culturally. The smile is an example. Genetically coded as a response to pleasure, it occurs even in those who are deaf and blind, and is understood in every known culture. The handshake has *some* universality, despite its European origin. Pat and Hiwi Tauroa (in their book *Te Marae*) caution that the clasping of hand or forearm with the left hand, while shaking the right, may come across as a sign of insincerity to Maori. Allan Pease advises that clasping the arm or shoulder while shaking hands can seem insincere to Pakeha as well; so this may be a result of our general suspicion of people who seem *too* eager to reassure us.

None of this means, of course, that *every* Maori will prefer to look down more, while talking, than *every* Pakeha. I am merely describing what Metge and Kinloch found to be common patterns. One of the delightful things about human beings is their uniqueness. What we *can* learn from body language, is that each gesture is *unique* to that person and that moment. However, some gestures *are* common enough; therefore, it's worth us knowing their usual meaning. It could prevent a lot of pub fights, if nothing else!

The Use of Gestures

There are several situations, for example, where a Maori or Pacific Island Polynesian might choose to use body gestures to convey a message that a Pakeha would always say in words. A nod or an upward movement of the head and/or eyebrows conveys 'yes' to all these cultures. But for Pakeha, the word 'yes' needs to be spoken to be polite. To Maori, the gesture may be perfectly adequate, and the Pakeha's lack of understanding could easily seem a refusal to acknowledge. Similarly, in a Polynesian culture, shaking the head or staring unresponsively down may clearly indicate 'no'; and to catch someone's eyes and then move your head and eyes sideways can say quite clearly, 'Go over there please'. With such sensitivity to body language, it's possible in a Maori situation for Pakeha to get the impression that 'a lot is going on without anyone talking about it'. The raising of eyebrows which so obviously means 'yes' to a Samoan may be understood as puzzlement to a Pakeha; the fixed downward stare which says 'no' may be taken as agreement. Pakeha expect words to be added to clarify the intention. In the Maori or Samoan situation, the gesture is used more precisely.

Gestures Can Cause Confusion

There are a few gestures which have caused difficulty for Maori students in the Pakeha school system, and Metge and Kinloch particularly comment on the following three: first, hunching the shoulders up round the ears, which may well mean in a Maori context, 'I don't know', but in a Pakeha context also suggests '. . . and I don't care'. Another is a rapid, repeated frowning which *can* indicate 'I'm uncertain. Please assist me', but is often read by Pakeha as straight disagreement. Thirdly, the sniff can mean an acknowledgement of a mistake (sort of 'Okay, I goofed. Sorry'), and yet can be taken as 'Who cares?' by Pakeha. You can well imagine how these three gestures, used by a Maori student, could easily spoil their chances with a culturally unaware Pakeha teacher. It's another case where people's *best* intentions can be sadly misread.

In many such situations, the Pakeha expects a verbal explanation, where the Maori prefers a non-verbal gesture. This is so in the expression of feelings generally. And that means that a touch or a hug more often accompanies Maori communication of sympathy, gratitude or apology. The model of intimate and personal zones around someone, which we discussed before, needs to be modified when moving from Pakeha to Maori culture.

EXERCISE 3.2

Aim — to develop your skills in recognising the non-verbal expression of feelings.

1 Use two decks of playing cards, or enough so that each player can have six cards and there be at least six left in the deck. Shuffle the cards, give six to each player, and put the deck face down in the middle of the group. Keep your cards hidden from view.
2 Each card represents an emotion. Write this list down where everyone can see it:

Ace . . . love	2 . . . joy
3 . . . hope	4 . . . loneliness
5 . . . sadness	6 . . . fear
7 . . . anger	8 . . . shyness
9 . . . respect	10 . . . agreement
Jack . . . apology	Queen . . . disagreement
King . . . confusion	

3 The player on the dealer's left begins. This player selects a card from their hand and lays it face down in front of them. Their job is to express the emotion represented by that card, without speaking.
4 All other players then check their cards. If they think they have a card matching the emotion expressed, they place it face down in front of them. If not, they do nothing that round.
5 When all the cards are down, everyone who has placed a card down (including the person who expressed the emotion) turns their cards face up.
   a If one or more of the group have matched the emotion exactly, then they *and* the expressor put that card into the deck. Any player who put down a wrong card keeps it, and draws another from the top of the deck.
   b *However*, if no-one matched the card of the person expressing the emotion, then all other players simply keep their cards, and do not need to pick up another. The expressor must now keep his/her own card *and* take another one from the deck.
6 It is now the turn of the person on the left of the last expressor. *The aim of the game is to get rid of all your cards* by accurately expressing and recognising emotions.
7 As a variation, you may play assuming the context of a particular culture known to you.
8 Discuss:
— how easy was it to recognise/express emotions?
— were you aware of cultural differences in expression?

Men and Women

Even within a culture, people's body language varies depending on, for example, gender (male or female), and style of thinking (visual, auditory, or kinesthetic — to be discussed at the end of this chapter).

Research shows that from a very early age, men and women use different body language in most cultures. Allan Pease refers to the fact that when a man and a woman have to edge past each other in a narrow space, the man tends to turn *towards* the woman, while the woman turns *away* from the man. In her book *Invisible Women*, Dale Spender observes that men sit and stand so that they take up more space than women. This even happens at primary school, where little boys' wide-spread knees form an obstacle down the rows of desks, while little girls' generally do not.

Space Taking

Sometimes people rationalise this difference in space taking by saying that it's a result of women wearing dresses, or of men being naturally bigger. But if you check some tall women wearing jeans and some short men, you'll soon realise that this can't be the complete answer. The most convincing evidence that space taking is a result of our *attitudes* to 'manliness' and 'womanliness' is found in history. Only a few hundred years ago, in a Europe where women also wore dresses, women sat *very* wide legged. Take a look at a statue of 'Brittania' or some other older model of womanliness and you'll see that it's true. Similarly, now we tend to assume that for a man to put his arm round a woman's body and arms (actually pinning her arms to her sides) is a normal way for two people to walk together, while for a woman to do this to a man is odd. In statues from ancient Egypt, however, it is always the woman (as mother and protector of humanity) who holds her partner this way. Spender describes men's extra space taking as part of their general grabbing of more attention, resources, and control. This may not be their intention; however, it happens and is therefore important for us to be aware of. Men working in helping professions, for instance, will be able to increase their level of rapport with women clients and colleagues if they share the space and time available more fully.

A Hopeful Gesture

Increasing our rapport with others is important to all of us, male and female, from every culture. And an awareness of the meaning of body language can sometimes bridge the most extraordinary differences. Jane van Lawick-Goodall, an anthropologist working with wild chimpanzees, gives a graphic illustration of how the use of gesture can bridge such a gap in 'My Friends: The Wild Chimpanzees'). 'I was alone with David, a chimp, that day, deep in the forest. I held out a palm nut to him and, although he did not want it, he accepted my offering. For a full ten seconds, he held my hand gently and firmly in his. Finally, with a last glance at the nut, he let it fall gently to the ground. In that brief exalted moment, I felt a thrill of communication with a wild chimpanzee.... He had reached out to reassure me by the pressure of his fingers. Although he rejected my gift, he gave me one of his own.' Reading this story, it occurs to me that if a chimpanzee can reach across the gap between whole species, surely you and I will find ways to cross the much smaller space between human and human.

EXERCISE 3.3

Aim — to consider how 'masculine' and 'feminine' postures relate to 'male' and 'female' social roles.

1 Have group members close their eyes, and think of the *most* feminine body posture they can, using their own ideas about what 'feminine' means. The posture may be seated or standing. Still with their eyes closed, everyone gets into their posture.
2 Open your eyes and look around. Remaining in your posture, discuss:
— what are the similarities between postures?
— how comfortable is the posture?
— how confident do people look in their postures?
3 Repeat steps (1) and (2) using the most masculine posture people can think of.
4 Discuss: What does this tell us about men and women in this society?

The General Impression

Objective: to be able to recognise common gesture clusters for attraction, anxiety, dishonesty and confidence.

TWO FIRST IMPRESSIONS

There is a surprising similarity about the way people first meet and begin successful friendships. Marie Skodowska was a Polish woman living in France late last century. One day in 1894, at the home of a Polish friend, she was introduced to a 35-year-old French scientist named Pierre. She later wrote, 'When I came in, Pierre Curie was standing in the window recess near a door leading to the balcony. . . . I was struck by the expression of his clear gaze . . . . His rather slow reflective words, his simplicity, and his smile, at once grave and young, inspired confidence.' A year later their friendship and scientific partnership blossomed into marriage and Marie took the name under which she would, within six years, make the most important scientific discovery of the decade: the discovery of radium.

In 1942, George Adamson was working as a game warden in Kenya, when he was introduced to the young Austrian woman, Joy Bally. He describes his first impression of her in his book, 'Joy ... who turned out to be Austrian, was quite uninhibited. Fair-haired and slim, she wore a slinky, silver dress, and seemed entirely unaware that her growing animation accentuated the distortions of her curious English . . . . Within a few days I sensed a growing attraction between us, which Joy seemed to encourage.' Upon their next meeting six months later, Joy told him '. . . she had decided I was just the kind of man for her. Our few days on safari together had confirmed it. She fixed me with her blue eyes, and smiled an unspoken question.' Over the next forty years till their deaths at the hands of elephant poachers, George and Joy Adamson's friendship and work together protecting African wildlife (as immortalised in the film 'Born Free') were testimony to the power of that first meeting.

Attraction

The non-verbal signals of attraction (sexual or not) are usually quite strong. Both Marie Curie and George Adamson refer in their accounts to the other person's smile, their eyes, and their apparent openness. These, along with other, briefer gestures, would have come together in what body language expert Allan Pease calls a *cluster*. A cluster is a series of non-verbal signals which back each other up, enabling others to be more certain of their actual meaning. Someone smiling, for example, may or may not be pleased to meet you. They may be smiling to cover up nervousness, or smiling because they've just remembered a joke someone told them. However, if someone smiles *while* giving you slightly more eye contact than usual, with their pupils relatively wide, pointing their body towards you, gesturing with open arms and holding their palms outward . . . such a *cluster* is fairly convincing evidence of friendly interest.

Sexual Interest

When sexual interest is being expressed, two other types of gesture will probably be added. First, there are preening gestures (similar to a bird preening its feathers). These may include stroking, smoothing, or tossing back the hair, and straightening clothing such as a collar, tie, or belt. Even the muscle tone of the body is enhanced as the person 'presents' themself well for the other. The second type of gesture expressing sexual interest is that which draws attention (directly or by mimicry) to the sex organs. This includes widening the distance between the legs (or crossing and uncrossing them), stroking the thighs, putting a thumb in the pocket or under a belt so the hand points to the genitals, opening the mouth and moistening the lips, and fondling cylindrical objects such as wine glasses. At the same time, the person expressing interest may allow their gaze to wander down to the other person's chest or lower (whereas in most social encounters, it remains on the face).

There are of course two reasons for understanding these signals. One is so you can recognise them in someone else. The other is so you can choose to *send* them or *not*. There are, after all, some situations where you will choose *not* to express sexual interest, as well as some where you will want to.

Resistance/Anxiety

Resistance or anxiety about meeting someone is also expressed in clusters of gestures. These gestures will usually include facing the body away from someone and leaning back, constricting the pupils, and using the arms and legs to form a protective barrier in front of the body. Probably this last statement has caused more disbelief in body language than any other, so let's discuss it. Are people who cross their arms, or clasp one arm/hand with the other, or cross their legs really anxious? Well, the easiest answer is 'not necessarily'. They may be cold, or just used to the gesture as a habit. Again, the cluster of gestures is important. But another answer is that it doesn't matter: either way, other people will react *as if* they are anxious. Research (which you can easily repeat yourself) indicates that when shown photos of people crossing arms or legs, the general public identifies them as more anxious, more reserved, more resistant. If you want to appear open to others, it's to your advantage to have an *open* posture. And if you want to ensure others can relax and open up to you, it may be useful to encourage them to assume an open posture (e.g. by giving them a task such as holding a page of information, which is easier to do with unfolded arms).

Lying and Uncertainty

Related to the situation of anxiety is the situation of lying, or being uncertain about what one is saying. The most significant body signals displayed by people in such situations are hand to head movements; covering the mouth, rubbing the nose/eye/ear, scratching the neck, and pulling at the collar. Desmond Morris suggests that such movements both cover up the telltale signs of insincerity *and* deal with a physical discomfort felt by the person constructing a story. If you observe them in someone you're talking to, it will be useful to recheck the person's statement. Remember, these signals will not always mean that a deliberate lie is being told. They may simply indicate uncertainty.

Confidence

At the opposite extreme from signals of uncertainty are the gestures of extreme confidence and dominance. These include forming a steeple shape by pressing opposite finger tips together, clasping the hands together behind the back (not to be confused with actually clutching the arm behind the back, often a sign of frustration), displaying the thumbs while folding hands under a coat collar or into pockets, hands on hips, and leaning back with hands clasped behind the head. Most of these gestures expose the front of the body 'fearlessly'. Their meaning can vary from sexual confidence to dominance or simply general self-assurance. When you see these gestures in others, you will need to interpret the meaning based on the situation. For your own behaviour, be aware that these signals *can* come across as arrogant and overbearing. The gestures for openness and attraction will give you much safer ways of showing confident interest. Also, while hand gestures which move away from your body appear more confident than self-enclosing gestures, some of these so-called 'Baton' gestures will again create that impression of overbearing intention. Waving your finger at someone may seem to you to be simply a way of emphasising your point. To others, it may well carry associations with being told off. Open palm gestures will enable you to add similar emphasis, without being so threatening.

Subtle Changes

So far, we've listed various gestures which (in a *cluster*) would disclose attraction, anxiety, dishonesty, and confidence. You'll remember from the last chapter (on states of mind) that, as a person moves from one emotional state to another, they change in a great many subtle ways. Larger scale gestures are only one of the sources of information. Other minute changes occur, and these tend to be very individual. The changes which can be observed fit into five categories. Remember, as you read this list, that you already recognise and respond to all these subtle changes. We're just giving them names so you can be more consistently aware of them.

1 **Changes in posture and gesture:** Large scale movements.
2 **Changes in breathing**: The speed of breathing, the amount and type of pauses in breathing, the amount of air taken in, and the area of the chest/abdomen used, all vary.
3 **Skin changes**: These include colour, moisture on the skin, and apparent muscle tension, as shown by tightness of the skin. Some areas of skin (especially the lips) may expand or contract with different emotions.
4 **Eye changes**: These include pupil dilation (discussed before) and eye movements (discussed in the next section).
5 **Voice changes**: The speed of talking, the loudness, the tone of voice (high and low), and the type of words used all vary.

Practice

Generally the information comes in recognisable clusters (remember the 3-month-old baby who knew how to recognise pupil dilation), otherwise it would be too much to be aware of at one time. Imagine meeting someone for the first time at a Polytechnic or University cafetaria. You ask if the place beside her is taken, and she shakes her head. 'Help yourself', she says, smiling and gesturing with an open hand towards the seat, while sitting up and leaning forward a little. In the course of a brief chat while eating, she explains that she works as a chef at a local hotel. As she describes this job, she leans over the table, pressing her fingertips together so her hands form an inverted V shape. She raises her head and speaks more rapidly and fluently, still smiling.

'Are you doing a course here?' you ask. She frowns slightly while nodding, and closes her hands into a clasp. Looking down now, she explains, 'My boss asked me to do this course. They say it's really useful for the general hotel staff.' Her arms are now folded, and she is speaking slower. Some of the colour has gone out of her cheeks. 'I guess I'll learn a lot from it. Should be quite interesting', she adds, her hand covering her mouth slightly. 'Anyway, what are you doing here?' Her smile returns, as she waits for your reply.

What happened? That's right. Almost certainly, she's happy to meet you, feels good about her job, and isn't enjoying the course. Not so complicated in real life is it? And the only way to really develop this skill that you have is to practise observing people in various situations. The television is a wonderful tool for this. To observe the visual changes, try watching for a quarter of an hour with the sound turned *off*, and see how many of the things you've been reading about you can find.

EXERCISE 3.4

Aim — to remind you of your ability to identify correctly states of attraction and dislike from non-verbal cues.

1 In this exercise, even though we reduce the available information to a minimum, observers will still be able to recognise the subtle body cues as someone changes state. The exercise could be done first with the whole group observing, and then in pairs. In each case have one person (the subject) sit in a chair facing the observer/s. To reduce their anxiety, as well as the cues available to the observers, have the subject close their eyes. Ensure observers can see both sides of the person's face, and their whole body.

2 Ask the subject to think of someone they are strongly attracted to, someone they really like. Tell them (in these words) to:

a 'Get a picture of the person's face and see them in front of you.'

b Hear the kind of things they commonly say, in the tone of voice they'd use.'

c 'Get a sense of what it would be like if they were beside you right now.'

Have them keep repeating steps (a), (b), and (c) while observers mentally 'take a photograph' of them in that state.

3 Have the subject clear their mind and now think of someone who (at least at the time they think of) they strongly dislike. Examples are superiors they've had conflicts with, villains from TV series, or politicians they disagree with. Again, give the instruction to (a) see, (b) hear, and (c) feel that memory (use the exact same

words from step (2) above). Have the observers take a new photograph of *this* state.

4 Ask the subject to clear their mind, and now think of one of the two people at random, without saying which one they have in mind. Again, use the same instructions (a, b, and c) to encourage their full recall. Ask the observers to *guess* which person they are thinking of, then tell you how they know.

5 Repeat step (4) until most observers can detect the non-verbal changes, then do the exercise with another subject. Emphasise that the cues will differ from person to person.

Just Thinking

Objective: to be able to recognise sensory accessing from gesture, breathing, skin changes, eye movements, and voice changes.

SENSORY SYSTEM USE

Most people can tell *when* someone else is 'thinking'. For a start, they often don't look at you or the things around them while they do it: their eyes are 'somewhere else'. And often they touch their body with their hands, rubbing their forehead, stroking their chin, or clasping their hands on their tummy, for example.

In the early 1970s, John Grinder, Leslie Cameron and Richard Bandler found a way to be rather more specific about it. They discovered that they could tell *how* someone was thinking, from their body language. What we call 'thinking' involves seeing mental images (visual processing), talking to yourself and sounding things out (auditory processing), walking yourself through situations and getting the feel of things (kinesthetic processing), and even sniffing around and getting the flavour of a situation (olfactory/gustatory processing). In New Zealand, most people use one or more of the first three ways of processing information, but in some cultures, a lot of people's thinking is done by smell and taste. For example, the Yolngu people of Northern Australia can distinguish, by smell, minute amounts of the poison cycasin in cycad nuts. Anyone else needs a chromatograph machine to find which nuts are poisonous and which are safe to eat. The Yolngu way of understanding the world involves an acute sense of smell.

Other cultures encourage mental processing using the other senses. The Russian psychologist Alexander R. Luria spent decades studying a person he called 'S', whose extraordinary visual memory enabled him to almost instantly memorise a list of say 50 numbers and recall them 17 years later by 'seeing' the list again in his mind. While the European cultures have cultivated vision in this way, in Polynesia auditory memory has been enhanced. Hohua Tutengaehe, Kaumatua at Te Whare Runanga o Otautahi (Christchurch Polytechnic) is one example known to me of the several Maori Tohunga who can accurately recite tribal geneology (whakapapa) for several hours in a row.

Preferences

All of us who can see, hear, smell, taste, and feel will also think using these ways of accessing and representing information, but most of us will have a preference. Those who prefer the kinesthetic (body feelings) system will tend to move and talk more slowly. Their voices will have a deeper tone and they will talk about 'getting in touch' with 'something solid', 'feeling' that things are 'deep', 'shallow', 'close', 'distant', and so on.

People whose preference is for the auditory (sounds and words) system will move and talk in a measured rhythmic way. Their voices will be resonant and they will talk about whether things 'sound right', 'click', 'tune in' with each other 'harmoniously' or 'grate', and so on.

If your preference is for the visual (pictures and images) system, you will move and speak quickly. Your voice will be higher, and you'll talk about the way you 'see' things, whether you 'get the picture', and whether you 'take a dim view' of something, or have 'brightened up', and so on.

Conflict and Sensory Preference

In my work as a counsellor, I frequently counsel couples, and more often than not one of the issues is their different mode of thinking. A couple whom I'll call Carol and Ed came for counselling one day with just such a problem. Ed began speaking. He looked up to the right and said in a fast, relatively high pitched voice 'One of the things I see wrong is this: I can't imagine what Carol does all day. When I get home, all bright and looking forward to seeing her, the first thing I face when I open the door is the mess in the kitchen. If I've tidied up the hall cupboard that morning, by evening it'll be spread all over the show again. I mean, sometimes Carol doesn't even look like she's brushed her hair that day. It doesn't look to me like she cares about us at all.'

Carol, looking down to the right, replied in a low slow, quiet voice 'Well of course I care. I care about our family. I want it to be a warm, comfortable place for us all to live, and that's what I put my energy into during the day. Perhaps I'm just not so in contact with those things you describe. But when you come home you're so distant, I don't feel as if you really care at all. You just rush past us.'

One way to understand this conflict is to realise that these two people love each other, but they speak different languages. Ed, whose main sensory system is visual, looks to *see* if Carol loves him, but can't find the evidence (no matter how warmly and lovingly Carol holds him). Carol, whose preference is kinesthetic, reaches out to feel whether Ed is caring about her, but she doesn't 'pick up' very much (no matter how bright his manner or sparkling his smile). Each of them sends the messages they 'know' will tell the other person they love them, but the 'words' (to use an auditory expression) fall on deaf ears. Once I pointed this out to them, both of them had tears in their eyes. They just had never heard what the other was saying.

Other Differences

Visual and kinesthetic systems are very common in Pakeha society, where men are often encouraged to pay attention to visual images, while women nourish the feeling side. Even advertising plays along with this, providing flashy visual presentations to motivate men, and aiming at women sequences where someone strokes themselves with a towel or runs a hand over a tactile object. The education system, of course, is still mainly visual in its approach (books, diagrams, etc.), and creates needless difficulties for many women and for people from more auditory-kinesthetic cultures. If you find learning from a book (like this) hard work, relax. It's not because you're dumb; it's because your strengths lie elsewhere. *Talking over* the material and *doing* the exercises described will enable you to learn more easily. Does that click into place for you?

Cues to Observe Sensory Systems

In fact, you can tell in which system someone is thinking even before they talk about it. Remember that body language information comes in five main categories. As you read how each category changes depending on the sensory system, notice how much this fits in with what *you already know* intuitively.

1 **Posture and gestures**: When people think, they physically stimulate the sensory system they're using. To see pictures, they rub their eyes and forehead, and raise their eyebrows, using gestures which point upward. To talk to themselves, they rub their mouth, stroke their chin, fold arms over and press on their chest, and lean their head to one side to hear the messages. To contact feelings, they bend over and contact the body itself, gesturing downward, towards and away from the body midline.

2 **Breathing**: To think visually, people breathe fast and shallow into the upper chest, often holding their breath to get a picture. When thinking auditorally, people breathe into the chest, fully and rhythmically. Kinesthetic breathing is slower, and deep, using the tummy muscles.

3 **Skin changes**: In general, people's skin colour is paler or even greyer when they visualise, and when they are aware of feelings their skin is flushed and more coloured.

4 **Eye movements**: This is really the easiest way to recognise which sensory system someone is accessing. Each sense is stored in its own special area of the brain, and the eyes tend to move involuntarily to different places as different areas are used. Sometimes the eyes just flicker to the side; sometimes they stay there as the person thinks. Here's how it looks on most right-handed and some left-handed people (the rest usually have the same system, but with right and left sides reversed).

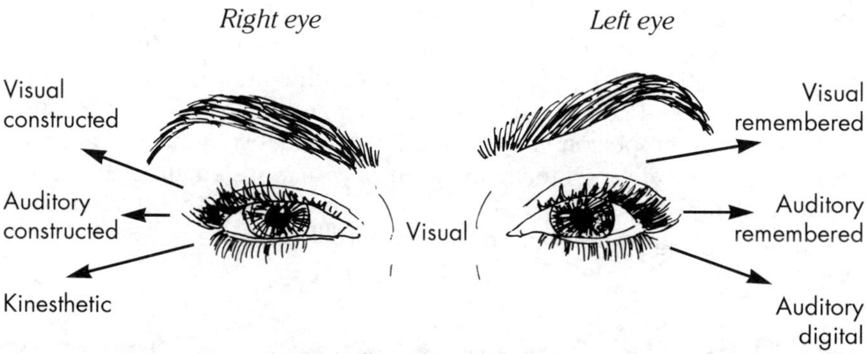

The specific areas are:
Visual constructed: Seeing pictures made up by the person, or seeing things differently to how they were in real life (e.g. get a picture of how you look reading this now).
Visual remembered: Seeing images of things seen before (e.g. remember which colour is at the top of a traffic light).
Visual: A general visual image is also able to be formed while staring straight ahead with defocused eyes.
Auditory constructed: Hearing words or sounds put together in new ways (e.g. imagine the sound of a parrot singing your favourite song).
Auditory remembered: Hearing sounds heard before (e.g. check which door in your house slams the loudest).
Auditory digital: Talking to oneself (e.g. say a favourite saying of yours to yourself, in your own voice).
Kinesthetic: Feeling emotions and sensations of touch (e.g. check which carpet in your house is the softest).

5 **Voice**: As already mentioned, when thinking visually, people use a high, fast voice, when thinking auditorally, a rhythmic, resonant voice (it may be melodious, *or* a monotone), and when thinking kinesthetically, a deep, slow, sighing voice.

Usually, the words people use to represent their thoughts (their 'representational system') will match the other cues you see and hear (their 'accessing system'). When they don't, you know that the person is getting information from one sensory system and explaining it to themselves in another. For example, a person may look up left and say in a high voice, 'I don't know why, but I just *feel* bad in this place'. In this case it is the picture of what happened before that causes the person to feel bad. The picture is 'unconscious' and only the feeling the person gets looking at it is 'conscious'. The words people use (their representational systems) will be discussed in greater depth in Chapter 6.

There are many ways you can use the above information about how people think. One is to enhance your own memory. For most people, looking up to the left is the best way to get their brain to remember visual images (how to spell words, where the right labels go on a diagram, etc.). Most importantly though, you'll be able to use the information to avoid the difficulty Carol and Ed encountered, by using gestures and language which *make sense* to the person you're with. Ever felt that someone could really see what you meant, was really tuned in to your wavelength, or had really made contact with you? That's the power of *rapport*. It isn't just 'chemistry'. It's a skill you can develop, and that's what I'll discuss after the following exercises.

EXERCISE 3.5

Aim — to recognise sensory accessing cues in others.

1 This exercise may be done in a group, with three people as subjects, or in pairs. Have the subjects seated so that everyone else can see their eyes clearly (if they have glasses, consider the lighting in the room). Check for left-handedness.

2 Ask them the following questions and observe for accessing cues (particularly eye movements) as they think of the answer and reply.

a Visual

— How many windows are there in your house?
— What colour was the last bicycle that you owned?
— How would you look with blue hair?
— Imagine the Prime Minister wearing a pink polka-dot dress. Does it suit him/her?

b Auditory

— What's the seventh word in the national anthem?
— Who in this group has the quietest voice?
— If you had to give a speech about body language, what would your first sentence be?
— What would it sound like if a window in the next room was smashed?

c Kinesthetic

— How cold was the sea last time you went to the beach?
— How warm do you like the water in a shower or bath?

— Where is the most uncomfortable place to be sunburnt?
— How did you feel when you first woke up this morning?
3 Ask them to tell you what they like and don't like about where they live (use *those* words). Check (a) what accessing cues they used, and (b) what sensory system they talked about.

EXERCISE 3.6

Aim — to discover which sensory system gives *you* the most important information about being loved.

1 In pairs, take turns to ask the other person: 'Think of a time when you really *knew* you were loved, when you felt inside that you were fully loved (or make up such a time, if you can't recall one). As you remember that time, seeing what you saw, hearing what you heard, feeling what you could feel, check: what is the *one thing* that is absolutely necessary that a person do, say, or show you so you will know you are loved. You don't need to tell me; just check what it is, and from which *sensory system* it is. Is it something you'd *see* (a look on their face, places you'd go and see, the beautiful things they'd give you, etc.), something you'd *hear* (the tone of their voice, the right music, certain special words, etc.), or something you'd touch and feel (the way they hold your hand, the kind of hug they'd give you, etc.). You'll know when you have the right one because you'll realise that even if the information from the other systems was not available, you'd know you were loved with that one key thing.'
2 Draw an imaginary triangle on the floor, with kinesthetic, visual, and auditory at its corners. Have everyone stand near the corner from which they get the most important information about being loved. Notice where everyone is, and discuss:
— Are people where you expected?
— Is there anyone who could benefit from knowing this information about you?
— Is there anyone you'd like to know this information about?
3 Discuss in pairs:
— What was it like to do this exercise?

Rapport

Objective: to be able to pace someone using visual, auditory, *or* kinesthetic behaviour.

WHAT IS RAPPORT?

When it comes down to it, *rapport* is so simple it can be summed up in a single sentence: to create rapport with someone, pace or mirror enough of their behaviours so they get the sense you understand them, elegantly enough so it doesn't distract them. The only complexity is knowing what to mirror or pace. The answers lie in: postures and gestures, breathing, skin changes (a little hard at first), eye movements and voice.

Observe two people who are getting on well with each other, and the chances are they'll be talking at a similar speed, at a similar volume, and in a similar tone. To do that, they probably breathe at a similar rate. Their posture and gestures will tend to be a *mirror* image of each other (when one waves to the side with their right hand, you'll see the other's left hand flick across a little), even to the extent that as one looks down, the other will gaze that way too. As we will learn in Chapter 6, they will also be likely to use similar language, and restate each other's main points before adding their own.

MIRRORING

If you're involved in any kind of group, watch people over the next sessions and notice who is in rapport with who. This isn't *mimicking* (which usually means exaggerating someone's body language to make a joke of it). It's something more subtle. If you are just learning to use rapport, you'll be safer to copy one or two things at a time, and to understate your own version slightly (so as to be sure not to overdo it). You'll know it has worked because, when you gently change your behaviour, the person you began to mirror will change with you. For example, parents often have excellent rapport with their young children. And when the parents are getting ready to go out — therefore, their pulse starts to speed up, they breathe faster, and so on — their child starts to speed up too (and is thus difficult to put to sleep). Mothers of young children often discover that the easiest way to get a child to sleep is to physically lie down beside them and to go to sleep too (once you realise how it works, you can choose just to gradually slow down your breathing to a sleeping rate, thus saving on wasted time).

In his book *Unlimited Power*, which covers much of the content of this chapter, Anthony Robbins gives several examples of his use of rapport. In one situation, he went to New York's Central Park to relax. Noticing a man sitting across from him, he began (without giving it much thought) to sit the way this man was, breathe the way he was, sway his head a little as he did, and so on. As the other man fed the birds breadcrumbs, so did Robbins. Soon the man came over to sit beside him. Robbins continued to mirror his voice tone and phraseology. Within a few minutes the man expressed a belief that Robbins was 'a very intelligent man' and that he felt he knew Robbins better than people he'd known for 25 years. Soon after this, he offered him a job!

Difficulties Mirroring

What would Robbins have done if the man told him to stop copying? This is something that often worries people learning pacing and mirroring skills (these words are used interchangeably to mean copying the other person's behaviour). My guess is that he would simply have apologised. He might have explained that he was trying to more fully understand the other person. Certainly, as he apologised, he would have continued to pace the man's use of sensory representational systems (talking about seeing, hearing, or feeling depending on which the other person used), just as he would have continued to use English, not German. Everyone expects to be mirrored to some extent; the only question is how much.

Empathy: The Feeling of Rapport

In rapport, the technical skill of mirroring blossoms into a *feeling* of having entered the other person's inner world, of being tuned into their wavelength, of seeing life as it appears in *their* maps.

This feeling, often called empathy, is an essential ingredient in all successful communication, but especially in helping. Hundreds of research studies, over the last fifty years, consistently show that empathy is the key emotional quality required to help another person. Carl Rogers, who developed the verbal mirroring skills discussed in Chapter 5, states 'Empathy is clearly related to positive outcome. From schizophrenic patients in psychiatric hospitals to pupils in ordinary classrooms, from clients of a counselling centre to teachers in training, from neurotics in Germany to neurotics in the United States, the evidence is the same.'

Empathy needs to be distinguished from sympathy. In empathy, it is *as if* you can experience the feelings of another, feeling these *with* them. In sympathy, one feels one's own feelings *for* another. Sympathy means feeling sorry for another, for example, and often has a sense of looking down at the person. Empathy comes with a sense of equality, of sharing this moment.

The feeling of empathy is an important clue that you have mastered the skill of mirroring.

How well do you think you'll be able to use this skill? Let me remind you. To be reading this page to yourself, you had to learn to talk English. This is a process so complex that we can't yet teach a computer to do it fully. And how did you learn to talk? By reading a book about it? By analysing the muscles of the mouth and throat? Not likely. You learned by mirroring other human beings, subtly, expertly, and consistently. You have always had the skills to create rapport. Now you can find new ways to use these skills to build the kind of relationships *you* want, and to create, for those you live and work with, the sense of being fully understood and valued that they need.

EXERCISE 3.7

Aim — to develop your skills in pacing someone auditorally, visually, and kinesthetically.

1 Get into groups of three. One person states a simple sentence such as 'Rapport is the key to good communication.' A second person restates this sentence trying to get the exact tone, speed, loudness, and emphasis as the original. The third person listens and gives the second person feedback on what they need to change to make their voice sound *exactly* like the original. The first person repeats the same sentence, and their partner again tries to create an identical statement. After three or four times, depending on the observer's comments, change positions, so that each person will eventually have a turn in each role.

2 Still in groups of three, one person talks for four minutes about how they think they could use these skills (or any other topic of their choice). The speaker should change position at least twice in the four minutes. The person who is listening may just listen, or add their own comments, but will mirror the posture and gestures of the speaker. Before changing roles, the observer can give feedback about how the mirrorer went. Again, rotate to give each person a practice.

3 The first person simply sits, breathing normally. The second person assumes a mirroring posture *and* breathes in time with them

till the observer is satisfied that their breathing matches for five breaths in a row. Breathing rate can be detected from subtle movements of the shoulders, chest, and tummy. Rotate roles, *remembering to return to your normal breathing rate* after each turn.

4 Discuss in your group how each type of rapport was: Which was most difficult for you to achieve? Were any uncomfortable to continue?

SUMMARY

In this chapter you've dived into the amazing world of non-verbal communication. You'll have realised that the context of what is said is even more important than the words we say. Like verbal language, body language differs from culture to culture. *Pakeha culture* for example, uses less physical contact, more eye contact, and less stand-alone gestures than *Maori and Tagata Pasifica cultures*. People from different cultures, and even different groups within a culture, may have a preference for *physical closeness or distance* (the study of which is called 'proxemics'). They may also have different preferred sensory systems. People can process information ('think') using the *visual, auditory, kinesthetic, or gustatory/olfactory sensory system*. And you can recognise which they are using from their body language.

In **verbal** language *words join together to make sentences*, and in **body** language *gestures join together to make clusters*. Understanding body language involves noting (1) these gesture changes, (2) breathing changes, (3) skin changes, (4) eye changes, and (5) voice changes. Once you can recognise these changes, not only will you have a good idea how the person feels, but you'll be able to *build rapport by mirroring them*.

References & Further Reading:

Adamson, G. (1986) *My Pride and Joy*, Collins Harvill, London.
Birch, B. (1988) *Marie Curie*, Exley, Watford, Herts.
Birdwhistell, R.L. (1952) *Introduction to Kinesics*, University of Louisville Press, Louisville, Kentucky.
Cameron-Bandler, L. (1985) *Solutions*, Futurepace, San Rafael, California.
Carney, C.G. (1977) *Exploring Contemporary Male/Female Roles*, University Associates, La Jolla, California.
Hall, E.T. (1959) *Silent Language*, Doubleday, New York.
Hess, E. (1975) *The Tell-Tale Eye*, Van Nostrand Reinhold, New York.
Kennedy, H. (1984) 'Food Secrets of The Aborigines', in *Omega Science Digest*, (July/August), pp. 86–89.
Luria, A.R. (1969) *The Mind of a Mneumonist*, Penguin, Harmondsworth, Middlesex, England.
Morris, D. (1977) *Manwatching*, Abrams, New York.
Metge, J. and Kinloch, P. (1978) *Talking Past Each Other*, Victoria University Press, Wellington.
Pease, A. (1990) *Body Language*, Camel Publishing, Avalon Beach, New South Wales, Australia.
Robbins, A. (1988) *Unlimited Power*, Simon & Shuster, London.
Rogers, C.R. (1980) *A Way of Being*, Houghton Mifflin, Boston, p. 150.
Van Lawick-Goodall, J. (1967) 'My Friends: The Wild Chimpanzees', in *National Geographic Society*, pp. 191–192.

CHAPTER 4
Problem Solving

KEY CONCEPTS:

Problem ownership

Problem solving/goal setting process

Learning stages

Problem Ownership

Objective: to be able to recognise who 'owns a problem' using Thomas Gordon's terminology.

PROBLEM OWNERSHIP MODEL

So far we've considered states of mind and how people can shift from one state to another; we've learned much about what people are saying before they use any words; and we've thought in a general way about how people introduce themselves and get in contact with each other. Once you have reached this chapter you already have a lot of skills for enriching your life and enjoying the good times that relationships bring.

At this point the bad news is: things don't always go well (you probably knew that though). The good news is: there's a *lot* you can do about it when something isn't right, either for you or for someone else. In fact, the rest of the book is mainly concerned with helping yourself and others find your way back to enjoyment when something is not going right.

This section is crucial to understanding the rest of the book! Basically, it'll help you work out when to use Part Two (caring for others) and when to use Part Three (caring for yourself). The answer isn't always what you expected. For example, sometimes people think that because they are a nurse (or a teacher or a parent) they mainly need skills to care for others. Actually a teacher, a nurse, or a parent who only knows how to help others is soon in serious trouble. Helpers need to be just as good at solving their own problems as they are at helping other people solve theirs. We'll see why in Part Three.

Knowing Which Is Which

Different communication skills work in different situations. Learning communication skills is no help unless you also learn when to use which ones.

The question you need to ask any time you are talking, or spending time with another human being is, 'Who here is feeling unhappy right now?' If the answer is 'no-one', that's great! In that situation *no-one owns a problem*, to use a new piece of jargon. If the answer is 'me', then *I own a problem*, in this sense. And if the answer is anyone else, then *the other person owns the problem*. This way of understanding situations was developed by Thomas Gordon, author of *P.E.T. Parent Effectiveness Training* and many other books.

Notice that this way of using the words 'own a problem' is different from the way many people use the phrase. For now, I'd like you to get used to this new way of thinking about it. When I talk about someone 'owning a problem', I don't mean that it's their fault, and that they should fix things up or anything like that. I mean that they are the ones who are not feeling happy about things. They are the ones who feel angry, hurt, sad, frightened, resentful, embarrassed, or otherwise unaccepting of the situation.

In Practice

Let's say your teacher enters your class and tells you, 'I'm very disappointed with you all. You're not getting through this work quickly enough. You may be enjoying yourselves, but you're really not treating this seriously enough'. Now, who 'owns' this problem? The question, restated, says *who here is feeling unhappy right now*? The teacher is, so the teacher owns the problem. That doesn't mean it's her fault, or that she's the one who has to fix it up: just that she is the one who is upset. Let's take another example. As you arrive at your work, you see a young man with a spray-can of paint writing slogans over your workplace walls. He's singing to himself as he writes. In ordinary language, we might well say, 'That guy has a problem', but in this new way of using the phrase, he probably doesn't. He's having a great time, painting the walls and singing. Who is feeling unhappy right then? Possibly you are! It's not your fault, and it doesn't mean you should clean it up. All we're saying is that it is very important to work out in any situation: 'Who is unhappy about this?' That's more important to understand than 'Who is to blame?' or 'Who will have to fix this up?'

Sometimes people say: 'Well, the guy painting the walls may not own a problem now, but he sure will once I finish with him.' That may be true. What we're doing here is checking who is feeling unhappy *right now*.

Difference from Usual Approach

So sometimes in everyday speech we'd say 'That person has a problem', when by this way of thinking, they don't. And sometimes we'd say 'There's no problem', when in our special sense there is! Here's an example of this: Your friend tells you he's lost one of the handouts from a course you're both doing. He say's he's really worried about asking the tutor for a replacement. You think he's getting worried about nothing. Does anyone own a problem? In the sense we're using it, yes. If your friend is worried, he's worried. It doesn't matter how trivial it seems to you. What counts is: 'Who is feeling unhappy right then?'

Reasons to Use the Model

There's a good reason for working out who 'owns the problem'. The ways of talking which will help when another person owns the problem (helping skills) are very different to the ways which help when you yourself own the problem (assertiveness skills, problem-solving skills). And as you may have realised, there will be times when you both own a problem (such as when you and your friend both want to use the same textbook at the same time). Those situations, called conflicts, require a third set of skills (conflict resolution skills).

I have another reason for wanting you to know about problem ownership though. That is to explain to you my role as the writer of this book. It's *not* my job to tell you when you should or should not own a problem. I don't intend to tell you which things you should feel accepting of or which things to be upset about. But once *you* have worked out what you want from your relationships, the skills in Part Two and Three will help you achieve it. This chapter discusses working out what you want.

What *you* want is special to you. Your dreams for your life may be different to anyone else's, and what 'gets on your nerves' may be totally different to what 'gets on someone else's nerves'. That's why my invitation to you is to use this book like a supermarket of new choices. Only you can know what choices will work well for you in which situations. If what you're doing already works perfectly, I'd say go for it! If it leaves you or others around you feeling less than delighted, this book contains some new possibilities.

Variations

Because you are human, you will even want different things at different times. Have you ever had one of those days when you wake up and realise you're half an hour late. As you rush your clothes on, it occurs to you that you've double booked yourself later in the day. Your bike or car has a flat tyre when you get to it. And as you head out the gate towards the bus stop, you grab the mail from the mailbox . . . and find the electricity suppliers are going to cut off your power if you don't pay that bill you thought you'd paid last month. On this particular day, when your friend at work says, 'I can't pay you back that $20 I owe you this week, sorry', you may own a problem!

Let's take another day though. You wake up fully rested. As you're getting ready, you receive a phone call from an old friend. They're coming over to visit tonight and you're really looking forward to that. As you're leaving you check the mail and find your tax return — the Inland Revenue Department are giving you back almost double the amount you expected. So, now, you go to work and your friend tells you about the $20. Probably it's not a problem.

People are not machines. At different times they feel differently. A behaviour that is no problem when one person does it may have you 'own a problem' when someone else does it. A behaviour that is no problem at home may be a problem at work. What counts is how you feel *right now*.

MY VALUES ABOUT PROBLEM OWNERSHIP

My belief, on which this book is based, is that when people own a problem, they have a right to get that problem sorted out. This is a very basic value underlying all the things you're reading. When other people (your family, your friends, your clients at work, and so on) are upset there *are* some things which research shows work better than others. You'll learn those skills in Part Two. Other people have a right to feel good about their life: that's why there's a Part Two in this book. When you are upset *you* have a right to get those problems sorted out. You'll learn the skills which have been shown to work there, in Part Three. You don't loose that right just because you are a parent, a child, a friend, a teacher, a nurse, a woman, a man, or anything else you might be.

The skills for solving problems you'll learn in this book are remarkable. I didn't make them up; they are the result of the collected wisdom of hundreds of thousands of skilled communicators. To use them, the first step is delightfully simple. It is to work out who owns the problem, by checking *who here is feeling unhappy right now*.

EXERCISE 4.1

Aim — to check understanding of the Problem Ownership Model.

1 Have group members individually read the following situations and check for each one whether:

- a there is no problem
- b they own a problem
- c the other owns a problem
- d both they and the other person own a problem.

Note that there is not always one 'right' answer, because different people will find different things a problem (e.g. some people are *always* upset to discover that someone close to them is unhappy, whereas others might want to help, but not feel upset about it).

2 Set out four areas of the room, one each of the above possibilities (no problem, I own a problem, other owns problem, both own problem). Read out each situation in turn and have group members stand in the area of the room they think they

would stand in for the situation. Discuss the result each time and check that people are using 'own a problem' to mean *who here is feeling unhappy right now*.

Situations:

1 A person working with you plays the radio so loud you're starting to get a headache.

2 Your friend tells you she's trying to cut down the amount of alcohol she drinks, but is finding it hard work.

3 Your child begins to cry when you tell him he has an appointment with the dentist tomorrow.

4 You need your bike to get to work each day. The repair shop told you they'd have it fixed in a day, but have so far taken three days and don't have it ready.

5 One of the people you look after in your job tells you he feels angry with some of the other staff.

6 A friend says he is really anxious about a meeting with his boss.

7 A fellow student hasn't returned the lecture notes which you need to study for next week's exam.

8 Your child forgot to do the dishes last night and you have to wash things before you can cook tea tonight.

9 Your mother tells you you should phone her more often.

10 You and your best friend often spend an enjoyable evening debating which sports team is doing best this season.

Setting Goals and Solving Problems

Objective: to be able to describe a problem or a goal in sensory specific ways; and list five steps in the problem solving process.

THE USES OF GOALS

In 1953, in a rather famous study at Yale University in the United States, graduates were asked if they had clear specific goals written down for what they wanted to achieve in their life, along with a plan of how to achieve these goals. Only 3 per cent of them had done so.

In 1973, twenty years later, the same researchers carried out a follow-up study. They established that the 3 per cent who had written down their goals now reported significantly higher enjoyment in their life. When they checked how much money the graduates had, they discovered that the 3 per cent with written goals were worth more money than the other 97 per cent put together.

Whether your goal is financial success, or a deeper sense of wellbeing, individual pleasure, or social change, this section makes the process that 3 per cent used available to you. When you own a problem, you'll be able to use this process to find the very best solutions for you. When you have a conflict, the same process (as adapted in Chapter 9) will help you find solutions which suit both you *and* the person you are disagreeing with. When your job is to help someone else solve their problems, understanding this process will enable you to know what stage of the process they are stuck at, and where they need to go next.

THE PROCESS: 5 STEPS

The problem-solving process is listed in various books and given a wide variety of stages. In other parts of this book I'll refer to particular models as appropriate.

Always, the process involves:
1 Defining the problem
2 Setting a goal

3 Planning how to get that
4 Acting
5 Evaluating how well you got what you wanted.

In this chapter you'll learn by using the problem-solving process to achieve a goal which is important to you personally. This is the very best way to learn this model. You'll understand how to help someone else much better once you feel able to help yourself. You deserve to do this well, so make sure you set aside an hour to work your way through this part of the book. You deserve more than a theory, do you not? As I said in the last section, one of my basic assumptions is that you have a right to feel good about your life, to *actually* achieve happiness. So before you read another word here, make sure you have a pen and paper ready.

1 **Defining the problem**

a *List all the changes you'd like to make in your life.*

Ever watched a child try and do a complex jigsaw puzzle for the first time? The trick is to turn all the pieces over and spread them out on the table before you start. It's the same here. We start by getting you to make a list of everything you'd like to change in your life, to improve or do better, to do more or do less. You could call this an 'inventory', or an 'assessment'. For now, you don't need to work out *how* you'd achieve this. Just allow yourself to dream. Take at least ten minutes. Think especially of what you would like to change about the way you communicate.

b *Choose one change you'd like to make. Describe in writing the problem this change would solve.*

Check through the list and choose one change you'd like to work on in the next couple of months. What we are going to do now is get specific about this one change.

Start by reminding yourself why you want to change. You could call this step 'diagnosis' if you wanted to be medical about it. If you know *why* you'd like to change, you will be more enthusiastic about reaching your goal. What difficulty, what problem, what limitation in your life would be solved by this change? Write down the answer to this question.

2 **Goal setting**

Write your goal, describing it:

— positively
— sensory specifically
— with you in control of it
— in a way acceptable to all of you.

In the last step you said what you don't want. Now say what you *do* want (e.g. say 'I want to arrive on time for my classes', not 'I don't want to be late'). Describe exactly what you plan to see, hear, feel, do, or say, instead of using general words (e.g. say 'I want to be able to say *no* when my friend asks me out and I'm intending to study', instead of 'I want to be more assertive'). The other thing about this is to describe how *you* will act, not how others will act. Working out what *you can actually do* about a problem is a lot more enjoyable than developing theories about what someone else should do (e.g. say 'I want to find new ways to reply when my father criticises me', rather than 'I want my father to stop criticising me'). Finally, ensure that all the parts of you can agree that this goal is appropriate. ('I want to find ways to relax in the week before my exams' may work better than 'I want to forget about the exams', for example.) Bearing in mind these four principles (positivity, specificity, control, and internal agreement) write your goal now.

Half Way There

Once you've done this, congratulate yourself. Knowing where you are going is more than half the job. One thing's for sure: if you don't know where you're going you'll probably end up somewhere else. Sometimes all that's stopping people living the life they'd love is not having done this simple exercise of working out specifically what they want. My own first professional training was as a nurse. I'd worked in a lot of factories, farms, and warehouses, and never really felt like I was doing anything worthwhile. Then a friend told me how much he enjoyed nursing. From that moment, I had a goal. The first time I applied I was turned down, and it was only the goal that kept me going. As the interviewers noted, at least I knew what I wanted, and why. After my second application, I got in.

I can't be sure what got me into that course. But I can be sure what got me to that next interview, because that part *was* within my control. What got me there was a clear, solid goal.

3 **Planning how to get that**

Just setting a goal, then, is part of achieving success, whatever success means to you. The next part of the problem-solving process is planning.

a *Write down what prevents you having the things you want*

One step in planning is to work out what stops you achieving your goal. There may be external difficulties, but there are quite likely internal obstacles as well, such as having too many goals at one time, not putting aside the time you need to get started, or spending your time thinking about what could go wrong, when you need to act. As you write these down, again, be as specific as possible.

b *List the resources you can use to achieve this goal*

Of course, there are also plenty of 'resources' that will help you reach your goal. If you were planning to bake a cake, useful resources might include flour, sugar, eggs, and so on. A recipe book or a friend who knows the recipe would also be a resource. For your goal, resources to list will include:

— friends who can support you to change
— role models (people who have achieved this goal themselves, who you know of and can learn from)
— time, money, energy
— information sources, including this book
— character traits of yours like determination or an enthusiasm for this goal.

c *Brainstorm possible actions*
Now that you have a better idea what you can draw on, it's time to think up possible actions which use these resources. Start by 'brainstorming' — listing ideas without criticising or discussing them. Think creatively and find new approaches wherever you can. There'll be plenty of time to be realistic in the next step. For now you can help your mind think up new ideas by *accepting* whatever occurs to you and writing it down. Give yourself ten minutes to do this. Actions for *your* goal may include talking to a resource person, studying a book, practising new behaviour, keeping a diary of your progress, setting aside time or money to use, and so on.

d *Choose the actions you will take*
The final stage in your planning involves narrowing down the list of possible actions. Check for each one:
— have I got the resources to do this?
— does it get me closer to the goal I wrote down?

When you know which actions you are going to take, you can list them in the order you will act. It's most effective to find a small part of one action which you can do *today*. People generally feel even better about goal setting once they have started doing something. Write down *now* which action you can begin first.

4 **Acting**
Each time you do one of the things on your list you'll remember to congratulate yourself. Each small step will add to your confidence. And every time something doesn't happen quite the way you had hoped, that gives you valuable feedback about what else you need to do or how you can change your goal.

5 **Evaluating how well you got what you wanted**
At the start, set yourself a time when you can check how you've gone. This involves asking:
— have I achieved my goal yet?
— which actions are working? Which should I change?
— is my goal still appropriate? If not, what is my new goal?

Goal setting and problem solving are 'course correction' models. It's like flying an aeroplane or paddling a canoe. If you find you haven't got where you want, that tells you to adjust the rudder to get back on course. It doesn't mean you've failed; in fact it's part of how you will succeed.

Conclusions

If you have any final doubts about whether goal setting can work for you, here's the answer. Check through your life for changes which have happened in the last ten years. Have you passed any exams, shifted house, started a new friendship, completed any projects, learned something new, even bought new clothes? Almost every positive change in your life began as a goal. Before you did it, you *thought* about doing it. This process works because it takes what you are already doing, and helps you to do it better. Doing it better means breaking it down into five simple steps:

1 Define the problem
2 Set a goal
3 Plan how to reach the goal
4 Act
5 Evaluate.

EXERCISE 4.2

Aim — to give group members a supervised experience of the goal-setting and problem-solving process.

1 Set each member an individual assignment to define a personal goal as described in the section above. After discussing the plan with them, give 4–12 weeks to act.
2 Group members write up individual evaluations of their progress, as a final report.

EXERCISE 4.3

Aim — to experience the value of goalsetting.
(Adapted from A. Robbins 1988)

1 Have the group spread out across the room and stand with feet slightly apart. Each person brings their left arm straight up in front so it's parallel with the floor. Now, keeping your feet still, turn your body to the left, pointing with the finger as far as you can comfortably turn. Notice, by the point on the wall, how far round you are pointing.
2 Turn back to the front, have everyone close their eyes and make a picture of themself turning again, but this time going much further. Sense what it would feel like to be that much more supple.
3 Now open eyes, and physically turn again to the left.
4 Check how many people have turned further. Explain the difference as due to programming the brain to achieve — the same

process we have called 'goal setting'. When people don't achieve in life, it's not 'laziness'. It's just a lack of adequate, compelling goals.

EXERCISE 4.4

Aim — to experience the value of creative brainstorming. (Adapted from Edward de Bono)

1 Tell the group the following story: 'You have agreed to bake a small, square cake for a children's birthday party. (Have the group decide what kind of cake, but ensure it has even icing over the top only.) There are four children coming, and you've said you will cut the cake into four pieces; each *the same shape and the same size.* All the cake must be used in these four pieces. How many different ways are there of cutting the cake to get this result?' Have group members think for a minute or so, and let them put their ideas on paper. Collect.

2 When you've collected all their ideas refer to the answer on p. 264. Discuss how our perceptions of problems often limit the answers we think up.

Learning

Objective: to be able to explain the four steps in Abraham Maslow's learning model.

LEARNING IN COMMUNICATION

Learning communication skills is an amazing business. In a way, most of it doesn't involve learning anything 'new' at all. It involves understanding what you already do well, so you can do it *whenever you need to*. It's like falling asleep. Everyone can do it. You've fallen asleep hundreds of times. And yet I'm sure that there have been times — perhaps times when you really needed to sleep, say because you had an exam the next morning — when you couldn't do it. Learning the skills of falling asleep means you can do it *every* time. It means that if you find it doesn't happen automatically one night, you can do it step by step anyway. Mostly, people's communication works okay. But when they *own a problem* their normal ability may not be available. For example, the person who can't get to sleep. That is the time they need to know the step by step how to do it.

Unfortunately, when people first hear about the idea of learning communication skills, they often suspect there's nothing to learn. After all, you can either talk to people or you can't. Aren't some people just naturally good at it and some not? And isn't it all just theories anyway?

This kind of question always occurs at the first stage of learning something. Remember learning to ride a pushbike? Quite often very young children are eager to get a bike. Perhaps they've had a tricycle before; that's much the same thing, right? Wrong. Going from three wheels to two turns out to be a major problem. The kid who was just waiting to ride off into the sunset suddenly comes to suspect that she or he may never ride a bike. Perhaps it's just not their scene. They have now reached the second stage of learning.

Stage One: Unconsciously unskilled. You can't do it but you don't know you can't do it.
Stage Two: Consciously unskilled. You can't do it and you know you can't.

A lot of people give up at stage two, but for those of us who stuck at it, riding a bike gradually became more possible. At first, someone pushed you, letting go for a brief time. You could ride at those moments, but you knew you had to hold on for your life. The slightest move to the side and you came off. Some people give up at this stage too. They say, 'Sure, I can do it. But it's a lot easier to get around the natural way — the way I always have before. Maybe it only works for certain people. I know when I'm doing it I feel really phony.' This is stage three.

Stage Three: Consciously skilled: You can do it, but it's something you have to keep remembering to do. It's just practice that enables you to get past this to stage four. Did you make it with bike riding? Can you ride a bike while thinking about where you're going, while carrying a parcel or waving to someone? If you can, the actual work of keeping your balance on a bike is now something you know so well, it's unconscious.

Stage Four: Unconsciously skilled: You can do it and it just happens without thinking about it. Learning communication skills is exactly like that. Ever known someone who got married and was unconsciously unskilled about building a relationship: someone who thought there wasn't anything to learn? Then watch them as they learn new ways of behaving. Probably they feel phony when they try and act or speak in new ways: they're consciously skilled. It takes a lot of practice to change fully. You may even 'fall off the bike' a few times in the early stages. But in the end, it works. The skills you learn in the next few chapters may seem trivial at first, or they may sound phony when you use them for the first time ... but once you have integrated them into your natural way of talking they *will* work. They will enrich your life beyong anything you could have imagined before.

Oops!

Does this mean that once you've learned a skill, you'll always use it perfectly? Unfortunately not. In most situations I find myself able to use the skills described here with ease. However, every so often I surprise myself. Some months ago I found myself shouting at a family member to 'shut up' — an approach which differs somewhat from that I recommend in the next chapters. It's always rather a humbling experience. In such a situation, something has 'pushed all my buttons'. To use a way of explaining it from Chapter 2, I've been *anchored* back into a state where I don't have the skills I need. I have two ways of coping with this experience. One is to excuse myself from the room and take the 'time out' to meet my needs and return to a resourceful state. The other is to apologise. In my first months as a single parent, when I was learning many of these skills, I did a lot of apologising! One of the really important things for me to remember at such times is this: making a mistake today doesn't prove that I'm doomed to live a life of mistakes. The fact that I've *recognised* the mistake does mean that I'm learning to respond differently.

Conclusions

Learning happens in four stages:

Unconsciously unskilled: I don't realise that I can't do it.

Consciously unskilled: I know that I can't do it.

Consciously skilled: I need to think about it to do it.

Unconsciously Skilled: I do it without having to think about it.

SUMMARY

In this chapter I've introduced you to a process which is the basis for most of the skills you'll learn in Part Two and Part Three of the book. Problem solving in communication begins by *identifying who owns the problem* (meaning who is feeling unhappy at that moment). It then works through the 5 steps of *the problem-solving process*:

1 Defining the problem
2 Setting a goal
3 Planning action
4 Acting
5 Evaluating.

Another model presented in this chapter was *Maslows 4 steps of learning*, through which you will move as you learn any new communication skills. These steps or stages are:

1 Unconsciously unskilled
2 Consciously unskilled
3 Consciously skilled
4 Unconsciously skilled.

Bibliography & Further Reading

Gordon, Dr T. *T.E.T. Teacher Effectiveness Training*, Peter H. Wyden, New York.

Kaufman, R. (1976) *Identifying and Solving Problems: A Systems Approach*, University Associates, La Jolla, California.

Robbins, A. (1988) *Unlimited Power*, Simon & Schuster, London.

PART TWO

Caring for Others

CHAPTER 5
Hearing someone else fully

KEY CONCEPTS:

Rescuer/victim/persecutor roles

Roadblocks to listening

Non-verbal attending skills

Open and closed questions

Reflective listening skills

Rescue, Persecution, or Help?

Objective: to be able to recognise common 'roadblocks' to helping according to Thomas Gordon's model, and identify the assumptions of Rescue which underlie these.

A LIFE OF WAITING

The very first person I ever visited in my work as a Public Health Nurse was an elderly lady. Most of my nursing training had been done in hospitals. It was odd to walk up to her, sitting alone on a tree stump round the back of her little house, and think of this as 'nursing'. My visit was essentially routine, but I had the time to listen as well as the intention to get to know her. Her mind wandered over nearly a century of memories, as she attempted to introduce herself to me. The youngest child in her family, she had continued to live with and care for her mother until her mother's death a few years before.

When she was about twenty she had fallen in love. The young man involved went off to World War I and then moved to England. He wrote to her assuring her that he would return to marry her soon. She waited faithfully for him . . . for over forty years. Gradually she had realised that he was *never* coming back, and that she was going to be single all her life. Her mother's last words to her, on her deathbed, were to the effect that she had always been a selfish, lazy daughter, and never looked after her well enough. At that moment, as her mother's life ended, she understood that she had wasted her own entire life. An elderly woman herself now, she had never ever lived. 'And now', she concluded, 'it's too late.' I held her hand as she wept for the tragedy of a life given up to the demands of others.

Over an hour had passed as I listened to this woman's tale. I had said only a few sentences, but, as I left, she pleaded with me to accept some gift for what I had done and asked eagerly when I would be able to return.

What had I done to earn this gratitude? I had been the only person who happened to have the time to listen for an hour to her sorrow. I was twenty two. This woman had lived four times that long, and she certainly was not asking for my advice. What she did crave, above all, was to be heard.

'HOW DO I HELP?'

All of us will come across people who are hurting, who are unhappy, angry, afraid, or otherwise 'own a problem'. They will range from those who experience their whole life as 'a waste' to people who are momentarily annoyed. In the next two chapters we will discuss how to respond to this situation. Ever met someone who has been through some distressing event, or who has suddenly off-loaded their anger, their hurt or their confusion in front of you? Perhaps your job involves you working with people at times when they are anxious or in pain? In all these situations, people often wonder 'What can I say?', 'What do I do to help?', or 'How do I show the other that I care about them?'

One of the temptations of such situations is to forget who really owns the problem: to start thinking that it's *my* problem and I need to find the right solution to it. It's hard to accept, when someone else is hurting, that *only They can find the very best solution for them.* They have to live with the solution. So it doesn't matter how well my ideas would work for *me*, if the other person doesn't think they will work for *them*.

Rescuer Role

Once I forget that *the other person owns their problem* I start to believe that I can take away their pain for them: that I can 'make them feel happy'. I may even think that I *have to* rescue them from their problem because they are not smart enough or strong enough to do anything about it themselves. Once I believe these things, I'm in what Stephen Karpman calls the *Rescuer* role. He uses the word Rescuer with a capital 'R' to distinguish it from genuine rescue, which does happen (e.g. when a firefighter rescues someone from a housefire). The Rescuer believes that helping someone means doing things *for* them (whether they asked for it or not), even when it creates difficulties for the Rescuer.

Victim Role

The elderly woman I described above had spent much of her life being a Rescuer for her lonely mother. The result of Rescue, Karpman says, is to encourage the other person to act like a helpless Victim (again he uses the capital 'V' to distinguish someone in the Victim role from someone who is a genuine victim asking for a specific kind of assistance). The woman's mother began to do less and less for herself; she too began to believe that she was not smart enough or not strong enough to solve her own problems. She became a 'Victim'.

Persecutor Role

Instead of thanking their Rescuer (as an *actual* victim of a real misfortune might thank their helper), the Victim often comes to resent and complain to their Rescuer. They then move into a third role, the role of the 'Persecutor'. And that's exactly what the woman's mother was doing on her death-bed. The mother had come to *demand* that she be looked after in every way by her daughter, and was resentful when asked to do something for herself. Her calling her daughter selfish and lazy was like a slap in the face: it was action from the Persecutor role.

Rescuers also slip into the Persecutor role. At times, the daughter in our example would begin to suspect that her mother was 'not as sick as she made out'. She would then become angry at being manipulated and decide not to respond to the mother's requests at all. From being her mother's Rescuer, she would shift to being her Persecutor, angrily blaming her for ruining her life. It's a bit like a game of musical chairs; everyone keeps changing places around this triangle:

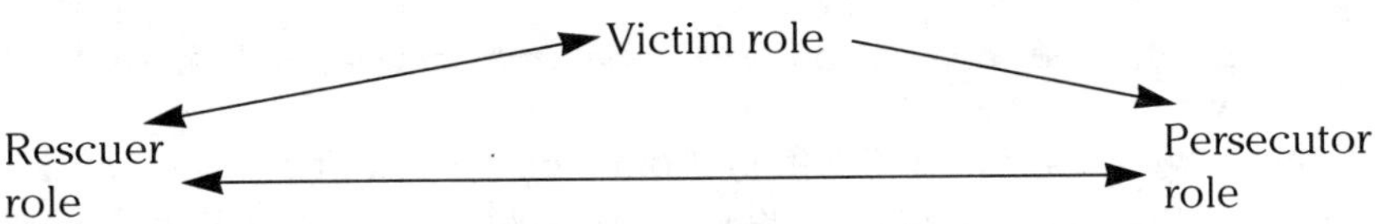

The daughter herself also felt like a Victim much of the time. She dreamed that the young man who had promised to marry her would Rescue her from life with her mother, because she herself didn't feel strong enough or smart enough to get out.

ROLE THEORY

The term 'role' is similar to the terms 'state of mind' and 'ego state' which we discussed in Chapter 2. The word 'role' was borrowed by psychotherapist Jacob Moreno (1892–1974) from the world of the theatre, where actors play various roles. Moreno described a role as 'the functioning form the individual assumes in the specific moment he reacts to a specific situation in which other persons or objects are involved.' This definition emphasises the way a state of mind is a response to a specific situation, to other people or things.

The role of Rescuer is a *response* to the Victim, and vice versa. They are 'interdependent' — one can't exist without the other. Moreno called this a *role set*. Victims need Rescuers, and Rescuers also look for Victims to save. Each role has a *context* or surrounding situation, *feelings*, *beliefs* about what is happening, *behaviour*, and *consequences* of what the person does. The Rescuer role has a *context* where someone else owns a problem, *feelings* of guilt, and responsibility, related to a *belief* that the other person is not able to contribute to solving their own problem, *behaviours* such as advice giving and reassuring, and the *consequence* that the Victim does even less to help themselves.

The Rescue Triangle In Action

The Rescue triangle is so common that you can easily think of times when you've been caught in it. In my work training nurses and counsellors, I often find that the people who choose such 'helping' professions are people who have a strong Rescuer role. They're the one who always helps out in their families, who helps sort it out when others are fighting, who's there whenever a friend is in a tangle. The problem is they feel like they *have* to do these things, and forget who actually owns the problem. If you want to be able to help others when they are upset (and that includes helping your friends, family or clients) the first thing to understand is how to avoid Rescuing or Persecuting them.

ROADBLOCKS

In his book *T.E.T. Teacher Effectiveness Training*, Thomas Gordon points out four basic ways that people can do damage when someone else owns a problem. Each of these ways of talking involves a confusion about problem ownership. Each of them is either Rescue or Persecution. Gordon calls them 'Roadblocks' because they tend to block the other person from sorting out solutions to their problem.

1 **Solution giving**
This includes straight out advice giving ('Why don't you try . . .'), lecturing ('Well, the fact is that research shows . . .'), commanding ('Stop behaving like that right now!'), warning ('If you carry on that way you'll . . .), and moralising ('You're old enough now to be more considerate'). When you give solutions as a response to someone feeling upset, there is a high risk that the person will feel put down, told they are too dumb to work it out, and pushed into something. If someone tells me 'I'm having trouble with my marriage. I'm beginning to wonder if it's all

worthwhile', for me to say, 'Get a divorce or you'll be stuck for life', is of very little use. It's as if someone came to see a doctor and said, 'I'm not well' and the doctor said, 'Take these pills. I was sick last year and they worked for me'. The doctor hasn't listened well enough to really understand what it's like for the patient. In most cases giving solutions just leaves people feeling misunderstood. Even when they agree with the suggestion, they rarely act on it unless *they* have chosen it. Real helping means enabling people to choose solutions *they* will act on.

2 **Judgements**

Included here are blaming ('It's your own fault: serves you right'), name-calling ('You numbskull. You're incompetent'), and analysing ('I think deep down what you're really doing is ...'). These kind of messages simply tell people you theory about how bad they are. They often leave the other person feeling ashamed, insulted, hurt, and angry. Take the person who says to me, 'I'm having trouble with my marriage. I'm beginning to wonder if it's all worthwhile'. For me to reply 'It's your own stubbornness that's really causing your problem' may make me feel better, but is of very little use to anyone else. People are generally better at finding good solutions when they feel respected and understood then when they are told off.

3 **Denying**

Denying that there is a problem can be done by praising ('You don't need to worry. You'll do fine as always'), reassuring ('Never mind. It'll all work out in the end'), and distracting ('Come on, let's think about happier things right now'). The most likely result of such attempts is to leave the other person feeling misunderstood, or sensing that they have been told off for the way they feel. To respond to 'I'm having trouble with my marriage. I'm beginning to wonder if it's all worthwhile' by saying 'I'm sure it's worthwhile. A nice person like you will work it out', may stop the other person talking about their worry. But it won't stop them worrying. They'll just need to find someone else who really listens to them.

4 **Interrogating**

Asking a lot of questions, like 'Why did you do that?', or 'Can't you talk about it with him?', or 'Did you tell her?' is the fourth main type of roadblock. Oddly, such a question produces the opposite effect to what was intended. The person often says less and less, waiting for the next question to tell them what to reply to. They may feel defensive, exposed, and distracted from the things they meant to talk about. By asking repeated questions you take charge of the conversation and stop the person's own natural way of working it all out. In our example where someone tells me, 'I'm having trouble with my marriage', to ask, for example,

'Why haven't you gone to see Marriage Guidance?' is more likely to lead to a lot of defensive explanations than to any useful sorting out.

Mostly, people who use a lot of advice giving, judging, denying, or interrogating aren't *trying* to hurt someone. They're more often trying to help in the only way they know how. It's sad because all of us enjoy helping. Some of your most precious memories of being with others are probably of times when you were able to help in some way.

An Example of Roadblocking

See if you can recognise the particular roadblocks being used in the following conversation between Tony, aged ten, and his father, John. Notice how very much John wants to help, and yet how far from helpful his comments actually are.

Tony: I'm really worried about this maths test tomorrow.
John: You should be learning for it right now then.
Tony: But I don't understand parts of it.
John: Didn't you talk about it in class? Why didn't you ask the teacher?
Tony: I don't know. Just didn't want to.
John: Well read it again. You can do it if you want to. You're good at maths.
Tony: No I'm not. Not this maths anyway.
John: Honestly, Tony, how do you expect to get anywhere in life with such a negative attitude? You're hopeless. I don't want to talk about it any more.
Tony: (Begins to cry)

Remember, we're not saying it's never a good idea to ask a question, to praise someone, or to give advice. But sometimes it's not the right time (e.g. when someone is upset). As a rule, the stronger the person's feelings, the more risky these four types of roadblock will be.

Often when I point out the risk of using roadblocks, people say to me, 'But that covers 95 per cent of what I can say when someone is upset!' In the next section we'll discuss the other 5 per cent.

EXERCISE 5.1

Aim — to provide practice identifying roadblocks and their effects.

1 Group members each write down five *imaginary* situations where they could be upset, worried, angry, hurt, etc. — where they would 'own a problem'. (e.g. 'I've lost all my money', 'I can't wake up in the mornings', 'None of my friends came to my party.') Don't use real situations — we are not going to be getting very helpful responses.

2 In pairs, each person takes a turn telling one of their imaginary problems to the other, who then responds using one of the four main roadblocks (Solutions, Judgements, Denial, or Interrogation). The first person checks how they would feel if this were a real situation and tells the other. Reverse roles so that the other now states one of their own imaginary concerns. Continue till all the situations have been tried.

The Listening Attitude

Objective: to be able to attend and to ask open questions as an invitation to talk.

PEOPLE'S NEEDS

When people are upset and try to get help from others around them, what do they want more than anything else? John Mayer and Noel Timms studied a large number of people who visited 'helping' professionals, to find out *what* helped. A few comments they heard were as follows:

> *The first time I went, I was there for two hours and I didn't stop talking once. It was marvellous and I felt very much better when I left. I was a completely different person.*
> *I just felt like I was talking to an old friend and just pouring out my troubles. She heard all I've got to say and out it goes.*

It's very much the same thing people want from non-professional helpers like friends, parents, or spouses. Here's what author and University Professor Judy Katz said about her friend Richard's help, after her experience of being raped:

> *He was very understanding and compassionate about the rape. What was particularly helpful was just his being there. He took all the cues from me and responded to my needs, not forcing his own.*

Benefits of Listening

Not only do people *want* helpers who can 'just be there' and listen to them, they actually are physically better off if they have someone to do this. James Pennebaker, psychologist at Southern Methodist University in the USA, studied men and women whose spouses had died suddenly (reported in Siegel 1988). He found that those who had no one to talk it over with had a much higher than average rate of illness over the next months. Those who had *someone to listen* stayed well. Listening is a powerful message to the suffering person. It conveys respect, acceptance, and understanding of their difficulty. Learning how to listen will increase your success in people-oriented jobs, and will help you to be a valued friend, lover, parent, or relative. Your very presence around people will help them to heal and protect them from stress-related illness.

Commitment to Listening

Listening requires a commitment though. After all, if you really learn to listen, you may sometimes hear things you don't like or don't agree with. And listening only works fully when you have a willingness to find out what it's really like for the other person (when *you* don't 'own a problem' with what they're saying). Listening requires love. The word 'love' comes from an old English word related to the word 'leave', meaning permission to be free (e.g. to give someone leave, or to take annual leave from work). So to love is to give permission to someone to be who they are, and to find solutions which suit them. In this sense 'love' is a *state* (see Chapter 2) which you need to be in to listen well.

If you are interested in listening fully, and you have someone who wants to share a concern, what next? What do good listeners actually do? First, they use all the body language skills we studied in Chapter 3, to show the other person that they are listening. This non-verbal skill is called *attending*.

Attending includes:

1 Being close to the person and at their height. (How close varies from person to person as discussed in Chapter 3) and people from some cultures will find it easier if they are a little lower than you, as a gesture of respect.)

2 Facing the person and/or leaning towards them. (People who get a lot of information visually — through their eyes — will want to face you, while people who get more information from your voice or from how they feel may prefer to sit next to you.)

3 Using open body gestures (legs and arms uncrossed) and to some extent mirroring the speaker's body posture. (This way of creating rapport, discussed in Chapter 3, needs to be done carefully so the other person doesn't feel made fun of.)

4 Nodding your head occasionally as they speak.
5 Having your eyes facing somewhere near them, so they are *available* for the other person to make eye contact as they need to. (This will be more for Pakeha than for Polynesian people, for example, and more for people who get information visually.)
6 Not doing other things such as gazing out the window, playing with a pen, or reading a book, while the person is talking. (If you need to do something else, perhaps right now is not a good time for you to listen, and you will have to tell the person that.)

This may sound like a lot to remember when it's written down in a list here, but in real life good and bad listening are both pretty obvious. You can probably remember a time when someone *didn't* listen to you (perhaps a parent, a child of yours, a teacher, a health professional, or someone serving in a shop or office). Check through the list and find out which of the six principles of attending they forgot. Once you remember how it feels not to be attended to, you'll realise how very important it is to actually *show* someone you're listening. It's not enough to know that you can sometimes listen while you do other tasks. People need to *feel* listened to, and they need to *see* that you are attending. Nowhere is this more obvious than in a group or classroom. Try it out. When you and your fellow students lean a little forward and *attend*, the teacher's energy will improve. And as you know, if you all started packing your books away, the teacher would falter and might even experience 'strong negative feelings'.

EXERCISE 5.2

Aim — to experience the effect of attending.

1 Get into groups of three (triads). Have each person think of a topic that interests them, or a book/film/TV programme they've enjoyed recently.

2 One person will talk about their interest while a second person listens to them, talking only minimally. The third person will be the observer and time keeper. For the first two minutes the second person (the listener) should break three of the principles of attending. In the next two minutes they will use all the principles of good attending.

3 After the four minutes are up, the talker describes what each section felt like, and the observer gives feedback about the listener's ability to attend. In this case 'feedback' simply means to tell them what you saw.

4 Change roles and start again. Repeat a third time so that each person tries out each of the roles.

VERBAL LISTENING SKILLS

There are times when attending is just about all you need to do with someone who is upset. Someone who is crying may appreciate your silent presence or simply a hand on their shoulder. Remember that at such times you can increase their sense of being understood by the use of pacing (e.g. breathing in time with them).

However, there are also things you can *say* which actually increase the other's sense of being listened to and understood. These skills were first identified by people such as Carl Rogers, Robert Carkhuff, Allan Ivey, and Gerard Egan, American researchers who developed modern counselling. Anne Munro, Bob Manthei, and John Small have written an excellent New Zealand exposition of them. Others, including Thomas Gordon, Linda Adams, and Robert Bolton, have shown (with courses such as Parent Effectiveness Training) that not only counsellors but anyone who wants to be able to help others can learn these skills. In this chapter we consider the three most basic verbal listening skills: minimal encouragers, open questions, and reflective listening. Reflective listening is discussed separately in the next section.

Minimal Encouragers

These are the 'sound effects' for attending — what Thomas Gordon's Youth Effectiveness Training Course calls '*helpful grunts*'. They are brief grunts or words of acknowledgement ('Mmm', 'Uh-huh', 'Right', 'Sure', 'Yeah') which tell the speaker that you are still awake and listening. They don't imply agreement or disagreement, just interest. On the phone, they may in fact be the only way you have to assure the speaker that you are still there, without interrupting.

Questions

Questioning can either help or hinder your ability to listen. Overuse of questions (interrogating) is one of the four roadblocks to listening, discussed before in this chapter. Often the challenge to beginning listeners is to use *less* questions, not more.

Helpful questioning is best understood as an *invitation* to the other person to talk. Sometimes people will prefer not to talk when they are upset, and just to be nearby may be the very best thing you can do. But at other times, a simple question such as 'What's on your mind?', 'Tell me about today.' or 'How do you feel about that?' may help them to start talking. Such questions can be used well in the middle of a conversation too, to help the person say more or direct them to start again if they got lost. There are two kinds of questions; open and closed.

Closed questions: Closed questions can be answered with the words 'yes' or 'no', or with a specific piece of information such as a number. Examples are 'Do you like it here?', 'Don't you think you could ask him?', and 'What time is it?' In ordinary conversation when nobody owns a problem, closed questions usually get perfectly good answers. However, when people are upset, they often reply with a straight 'yes' or 'no', forcing you to ask another question to get the extra information you expected. This easily degenerates into an interrogation, with the speaker saying less and less, as the listener asks more and more. Closed questions are best used to check a very specific issue and are a skill to use sparingly.

Open questions: When you are in a listening situation and want to invite someone to talk more, open questions (which cannot be answered 'yes', 'no', or with a specific number) will work better. Open questions usually begin with words like 'what', 'how', or the phrase 'Tell me about', e.g. 'What was that like for you?', 'How is your new job going?', 'Tell me what happened before that.'

The word 'why' also begins open questions (such as 'Why did you do that?') but most people find why questions difficult to answer. This is because 'why' asks the person to explain what was happening underneath. It suggests that the simple facts are not good enough, and deserve explaining or justifying. Often people hear 'Why did you do that?' as a judgement about what they did. 'How' questions get a better response (e.g. 'How did you come to do that?'), because they ask for a simple description of what went on, more than a justification.

Okay. Before we read on to learn the most important verbal listening skill, let's summarise these basics. Good listening includes both non-verbal and verbal skills. The non-verbal part is called attending, and includes (a) nearness, (b) directing your body towards the speaker, (c) open and mirrored gestures, (d) nodding, (e) appropriate eye contact, and (f) avoiding distractions. Verbal skills include minimal encouragers and the use of questions (particularly open questions such as those beginning 'how' or 'what').

EXERCISE 5.3

Aim — to practise forming open questions.

Directions: In each of the following six situations, the listener asked a closed question. Write an open question which would give you a fuller response. Compare answers in pairs, and discuss.

1 A 26-year-old woman has been discussing her mother's overuse of alcohol. Closed question: 'Do your mother and you get on okay usually?'

2 An 8-year-old boy has been telling you about how he doesn't enjoy maths. Closed question: 'Don't you like anything at school?'

3 A 17-year-old woman is talking over her feelings of resentment about her boyfriend. Closed question: 'Have you told him about this?'

4 A 35-year-old man has just explained that as a child he hated social events. Closed question: 'Do you hate social events now?'

5 Having explained his difficulty finding a job, a 19-year-old man says he will have to do a training course on carpentry as it's all that's available. Closed question: 'Do you want to be a carpenter?'

6 Your friend stops talking in mid sentence and begins to cry. Closed question: 'Are you Okay?'

EXERCISE 5.4

Aim — to increase awareness of the different effect produced by open and closed questions.

1 Get into pairs. One person is to interview the other with the aim of discovering (a) more about them in general, (b) what kind of books they enjoy reading, or (c) some other such information. The first time, they are to ask six closed questions. Write these down before. (It helps to be in a pair with someone you know *less* well.)

2 Now begin again, but this time change each of the closed questions into an open question.

3 Reverse roles and repeat step one and two.

4 Discuss, in pairs, the difference between the effect of open and closed questions. Report back to the group.

Reflective listening

Objective: to be able to verbally reflect (a) feelings expressed in words or behaviour, and (b) information described in words.

THE CRUCIAL SKILL — the third verbal listening skill

The skill described here is the single most important verbal skill I know. It is the skill which helpers and counsellors use more often than any other. Group leaders use it to help discussions flow, and in conflict situations it has the power to bring the temperature down and get people sorting things out again. As you'd expect with such a widely used skill, it appears in hundreds of best-selling books, under a wide variety of names (names like 'active listening', 'reflecting', 'accurate empathy', 'responding', 'feedback', 'the helping response', understanding response', 'paraphrasing', and 'verbal pacing'). As you'd also expect with such a widely used process, it is something which can be misused or even overused, and in those cases it can feel annoying or condescending. If you'd like to have the ability to get in rapport with others, to fully understand others and have them value your listening, then learning to use this skill well is a *must*.

VERBAL RAPPORT

In Chapter 3 we discussed how to build rapport by 'pacing' or 'mirroring' enough of the other person's behaviours so they feel understood, but not distracted. Reflective listening is the verbal part of this process. To reflect you simply restate the basic idea or feeling in what another person has said. This helps each of you to know whether you've understood them. It also tells them that your *intention* is to understand and accept what they said. If done well it helps the person clarify their own thoughts and feelings. Naturally, you've done this many times when listening. It's no newer to you than asking open questions, and like questioning, you can greatly improve your ability to do it.

The Beach Problem

Consider the following example, in which John, aged 23, is listening to his 25-year-old friend Andrew. John has recently attended a listening skills course where reflective listening was taught. Recognising the situation as one where Andrew 'owns a problem', he uses this reflective process to help him clarify the feelings involved.

John: How did you and Beth get on at the beach yesterday? (open question)
Andrew: Oh ... not so good I guess. I don't think I'll bother again.
John: Not so interested in her? (reflective listening)
Andrew: Well, I was when we were just going to parties, that sort of thing.
John: So it's the way things were at the beach. (reflective listening)
Andrew: Yeah. Turns out she owns a windsurfer, and .... (shrugs)
John: You're not into windsurfing. (reflective listening)
Andrew: No. Where as she's really a pro.
John: Uh-huh. (minimal encourager)
Andrew: Hell, I couldn't even stand on the thing. I was a wipeout!
John: Embarrassing, eh! (reflective listening)
Andrew: Yeah, I'll say ... But it's more than that. I suppose I always back away from situations where I'll have to learn something.
John: You tend to stay with what you know. (reflective listening)
Andrew: Yeah. Which is stupid really. I mean, I get so worried about what other people will think of me ... that I give up the whole relationship anyway.
John: And avoiding that embarrassment leads to even worse losses. (reflective listening)
Andrew: Mm-hm ... I mean, heck, everyone has to learn sometime. Obviously Beth didn't just climb on a windsurfer and zip across the harbour.
John: Right. (minimal encourager)
Andrew: And, anyway, if I wasn't being so down on myself I'd probably enjoy having her show me.
John: Starting to feel interested in another try. (reflective listening)
Andrew: I guess. She's going out again on Thursday. I think I'll ring up and see if I can invite myself along.
John: Sounds great!

What happened here? Well, Andrew solved his problem ... by himself. All John did was listen.

Possible Responses

What would you have been tempted to do? Mostly, when I ask people about this, they say they'd either avoid the issue or give some advice,

'Why not get some windsurfing lessons', or 'Let me show you how it's done'. The saddest thing about this advice is that it may actually work .... Because if it does, and Andrew learns how to windsurf, he may well carry the *basic* problem (of embarrassment learning in front of friends) into several more relationships. If the advice doesn't work, Andrew's going to spend a lot of energy convincing John that windsurfing's not for him. He's then worse off than before. Neither advice nor denial will create that sense of safety for Andrew to explore how he actually feels about the problem.

That sense of acceptance and understanding (or empathy, to use a word which means to feel *with* someone) is uncommon in life. Empathic, reflective listening is like a precious jewel. In a society full of loneliness, anxiety, and frustrations, it is rare indeed that you find someone who really wants to listen, someone who trusts that *you* can find solutions which will work for you. This skill is too important to leave only to the counsellors and other professionals.

How to Reflect

Obviously, what Andrew does needs to be different from parotting, just as non-verbal pacing needs to be different from mimicking. Take the sentence where John said 'I was a wipeout'. For Andrew to reply 'So you're a wipeout' is not very good reflective listening, even though it uses John's own word! Andrew's actual reply is 'Embarrassing, eh!', a shortened version of 'So you felt embarrassed'. He's interested in checking the basic meaning of what the speaker has said.

Content and Feeling

This basic meaning includes the information (or 'content') about what happened when John tried windsurfing, in this case) *and* the feelings the person is experiencing. When the person hasn't *named* the feelings themself, the listener needs to ask themself 'In this situation, how would I be feeling?', and 'From this person's body language, what do they seem to be feeling?' Being in a similar body position to the speaker can help you identify feelings (see Chapter 3, on rapport). When you reflect feelings, you are often less certain of having understood then when you reflect information. Sometimes it helps to explain this in the way you reply, for example, 'It almost sounds like you felt ...', 'You feel ... is that it?', 'From the way you say that, I get the impression you feel ...'. Having reflected the meaning as you've understood it, your next step needs to be listening for confirmation. If your reflection was accurate, the person will usually nod, say 'yes', or continue talking almost unaware of your presence. If your reflection sounds different to what they meant, they may frown, shake their head, or attempt to re-explain. Either way, your reflection has worked! You now have a better idea what the person meant (or didn't mean) and they know your intention is to understand.

If your reflection wasn't accurate, you can listen again and offer a new statement. To summarise, reflective listening has three steps:

1 Ask yourself what the basic meaning of the person's message was.
2 Put this into a brief statement and say this back, in words that can be understood by the person.
3 Check the person's response to find out whether you understood.

LEARNING TO REFLECT

Reflective listening really makes sure that you listen. New students sometimes say 'I always thought I was listening, but when I have to say it back I realise it's actually hard work'. It is, at first. As we mentioned in Chapter 4, when people are first learning a new skill, it can feel like work, and it may also sound less natural. With practice, you'll integrate reflective listening into your natural way of talking. Once that happens, you won't have to think out every response, and — most of the time — no one will even notice you're using a new process. You can then simply enjoy being fascinated by what the person is saying to you. Reflective listening itself doesn't require a lot of effort. You don't have to think up the solutions. You don't have to find smart questions to lead the conversation the right way. Actually, the main mistake learners make when counselling or helping is to work too hard. Christchurch counsellor George Sweet explains, 'It is becoming clear to me that when I am working effectively with a client, I have ceased working altogether, ceased striving to be helpful. My questioning and searching for answers is over. I no longer "leave the room" to go into my head. I am with What Is. Part of the way What Is is flowing. The more I am simply with, the more healing occurs.' This is a very simple and a very old idea. George Sweet finds it origins in the gentle Chinese philosophy of Taoism. Christians will recognise it in the words of Paul, 'Rejoice with those who rejoice, and weep with those who weep' (Romans 12.15).

Deeper Messages

When you are listening to someone, you will certainly discover that what people say to you (especially early on in a conversation) is not always a complete description of what is happening inside them.

In our example before, Andrew's initial comment about his day at the beach is simply that he didn't get on so well and doesn't think he'll bother again. He doesn't say, 'I felt embarrassed by my difficulty windsurfing, and — as usual — am backing away from that situation'. Later on, that's how he describes it, but first he himself may just have a general uncomfortable feeling about the day. Each time John reflects back to him, it acts as a kind of feedback, helping Andrew understand and explain his experience more deeply and more clearly. Often you will find in listening to someone, that the basic problem the two of you end up discussing is very different from the first thing they presented to you.

Listening is a voyage of discovery for both speaker and helper. I urge you to use it with respect and with affection.

Types of Reflecting

Sometimes, in order to teach reflective listening, counselling trainers will divide it up into several smaller 'microskills'. These include:

1 *Reflecting content (paraphrasing)*: This part of reflecting is less intense, and helps concentrate on solving the specific *out there* problem. For example, 'You had difficulty standing on the windsurfer.'

2 *Identifying and reflecting feelings*: A deeper response which focuses the conversation on how the person talking *is*. Feelings can be described:

a *single words* (e.g. 'You feel embarrassed')

b by comparison to other situations–i.e. *metaphor* (e.g. 'You feel as if your pants just fell down')

c using the *body response* the feeling causes (e.g. 'You went red all over')

d by the *action* it makes you want to take (e.g. 'You felt like running away and hiding').

Feelings are *not* the same as beliefs or opinions though. To say 'You feel she's putting pressure on you' is *not* actually reflecting a feeling. It's reflecting a *belief* about what 'she' is doing. As a simple test, if the word 'that' is or can be put after the word 'feel' in your sentence and it still makes sense, you have an opinion or belief. For instance:

— 'I feel you're being rude' is a belief, because 'I feel *that* you're being rude' still makes sense.

— 'I feel lonely' is a real feeling, because 'I feel *that* lonely' loses the sense of it.

— 'I feel I'm a good loser' is a belief, because 'I feel *that* I'm a good loser' still makes sense.

— 'I feel like jumping for joy' is a feeling, because 'I feel *that* like jumping for joy' is not correct English.

3 *Perception check*: This refers to checking your understanding, not just of what the person said, but of all the 'messages' you get from their body language as well. For example, 'You've become very quiet.' I have the impression you're feeling sad. Is that right? As in this example, it helps to

specify the non-verbal behaviours from which you made your guess about how the person felt.

4 *Summarising and sorting issues*: Restating things expressed over a longer period of conversation or reflecting several pieces of content/ feelings at once. The listener may invite the talker to do this (e.g. 'Well, where have we got so far?') or may do it for them (e.g. 'So although you found it difficult to be in that situation yesterday, you'd like to stop telling yourself off and try just enjoying being with Beth there.').

Summarising helps the person 'put the pieces together' and clarify their thoughts. A good example occurs in psychotherapist Carl Jung's account of his first interview with Sigmund Freud, in 1907. For three hours Jung talked with great enthusiasm about his own ideas. At the end of this time, Freud interrupted him and, to Jung's astonishment, grouped the content of this talk into several categories. These formed the basis for the rest of their discussion.

Simpler Than It Sounds

Because the descriptions of microskills come from the field of *professional* helping (discussed in Chapter 6), they may make reflective listening sound more complex than it is. Reflective listening is a very simple skill which I use many times every day. Whenever I'm in a discussion with someone, I use it to check my understanding of what they're saying. Usually this involves my saying one sentence. Some time ago, I passed the scene of a fairly serious car accident. After I'd checked each of the people injured (including a child with a skull fracture) I saw the driver of the car, and father of two of the injured, standing by himself staring blankly ahead. Bystanders were busy assisting each of the injured, but no one was looking after him. He seemed to be in a state of shock. I stood beside him and said, 'It's a hell of a shock isn't it. Hard to believe it's happening to you'. 'It's a hell of a shock!', he replied emphatically and launched into an explanation. Mostly, I just listened, but my first comment was reflective listening. Had I said nothing, he could have been left to assume I considered him a bad driver or a poor first aider or he might have just withdrawn into himself. Had I 'reassured' him he could well have felt I didn't realise how serious it was. Reflective listening gave me a simple third choice. It involves:

a listening for the basic meaning of the speaker's message
b restating this to the person
c checking to see whether you have understood. Once you have some practice with it you can use it to:
  i convey understanding and acceptance, and
  ii help the person clarify and resolve their concern — a concern

which may well differ from their original comment. Reflective responses include:

a reflecting content (paraphrasing)
b identifying and reflecting feelings
c perception check, and
d summarising and sorting several comments.

Reflecting feelings involves being able to distinguish beliefs from feelings, and having a wide variety of ways to describe a feeling.

EXERCISE 5.5

Aim — to practise developing reflective responses.

Directions:

1 Read each of the following ten statements. For each one, write a response which reflects the information (content) the person is talking about. Check the responses in pairs.
2 Next, go through the examples again. For each one, identify the feeling involved using (a) a single word, (b) a metaphor, (c) the body responses you'd expect, and (d) the actions a person with this feeling feels like taking. Discuss in the group and collect ideas on whiteboard or newsprint.
3 Write a response for each statement, reflecting the feeling. Check your responses in pairs, and report back to the group.

a A student in your class asks, 'Do you think it's fair the way half the class is late like this? I mean, you and I get here on time, Why can't they?'
b A 39-year-old friend of yours, with a teenage son, confides, 'I thought it was bad enough when he was a kid. But now! . . . I never know what he's doing in the evenings. He won't talk to me. He could be on heroin for all I know!'
c A client who is seeing you for counselling explains, 'I've talked about this *so* often — including with my last counsellor. Nothing seems to help, and I guess I've just given up on ever feeling better.'
d A 25-year-old woman whose son died in a car crash explains tearfully, 'I play those minutes over and over in my mind. Could I have swerved away? I don't know. But I don't think I'll ever really forgive myself.'
e A friend announces, 'Amazing! I passed my biology exam! Honestly, I'm just over the moon. Wait till I tell my mother. She'll do a flip.' (Note that this is *not* a situation where the other person owns a problem. Use it for practice anyway).

f A 64-year-old woman explains haltingly, 'Since Mathew — that's my husband — died, I've been aware of how big the house is. Some days I just wander around from room to room, listening to the sound of my own footsteps and wondering where everybody is.' She begins to cry.
g A friend explains, 'I thought I'd decide what I was doing this year — that I'd just be doing the university course. But this new information has thrown all that into confusion. I can't decide which thing to pick up: worse, I don't even know how to choose!'
h 'I'm no good at parties', a friend tells you. 'Just go without me. I always feel so awkward, and I'm sure everyone else is staring at me.'
i A 27-year-old-man, discussing his wife, complains, 'I've had it. Every time we make an arrangement to share the housework, it ends up being me who does the extra! This is the last time. Either something changes or this relationship is over!'
j A 56-year-old man who has recently lost his job confides, 'Most mornings I just stay in bed and sleep. I wish the day would go away. There's nothing to look forward to, and I just don't have the energy to keep on trying.'

EXERCISE 5.6

Aim — to practise reflective listening in a group setting.

1 Go around the group checking in (saying how each person is, how their week has been). Before each group member describes their own week, they restate the essence of what the last person said (begin with the group leader), and check that they've understood it.
2 As a group, choose a topic for discussion (something people are likely to have different opinions about, such as euthanasia or a current issue). Set aside 30 minutes for discussion, using the following rule: Anyone may state an opinion, but before they do so they must reflect the comments of the last speaker, to that person's satisfaction. (If the previous speaker doesn't feel understood, they can help the new speaker to rephrase their reflection.)
3 Discuss the effect of reflecting on (a) the previous speakers (did they feel more understood), and (b) the next speakers (did they find they had to listen more carefully than usual).

EXERCISE 5.7

Aim — to practise reflective listening in a one-to-one situation (this exercise takes at least an hour).

1 Have the group divide into threes (triads). In each triad, one person will be the speaker, one the listener, and one the observer.

a *The speaker* will talk for six minutes about any actual concern of theirs (if your group repeats this exercise, extend the time to ten minutes on the second round). If you are speaking it may help to choose one of the feelings identified in exercise 5.6 above, and talk about a recent time when you felt that way. Unless you are an excellent actor, roleplaying an imaginary situation will not give a useful practice. The issue you discuss does not need to be a major problem or life crises: we're only doing a six-minute practice. Also, when you talk, pause after each couple of sentences and give the listener a chance to reflect: remember, they are learning. If you take up the full six minutes talking, they won't have a chance to practise their skill. As you listen to their reflection, think about whether it sounds as if they have understood, and check what else comes into your mind to continue talking about.

b *The listener* will listen and use reflective responses. If you are listening, check first of all that you are in an attending posture — ask the person who will be speaking what feels right for them. Remember, you don't have to 'solve' the concern the person raises. Your job is simply to understand. Use *only* reflective listening, so you get the chance to really learn this new skill. At the end of the six minutes, give a summarising response.

c *The observer* will keep time, and observe the listener. At the end of the six minutes, the observer will encourage the speaker and listener to say how they found it went. The observer can then tell the listener what they seemed to do well. If you are the observer, remember that it helps the listener to hear specifically what was said or done that was useful. It also helps them to know if they lost track of what they were doing or used any of the roadblocks (denial, judgements, solution sending, or interrogating).

2 Swap roles and repeat the exercise twice more, so each person has a practice.

SUMMARY

This chapter has discussed listening fully when someone else is upset. The four most common *Roadblocks* to listening were considered; namely: Solutions, Judgements, Denial, and Interrogating. These approaches treat the person with the problem as a helpless Victim and put the would-be helper in a Rescuer or Persecutor role.

Instead, real listening begins with *non–verbal attending*, such as directing your body towards the speaker. *Minimal encouragers* like 'ah-huh' emphasise this attending, and *open questions* invite the person to begin talking. When listening it is most important to make a comment which restates the basic meaning of what the speaker said. This comment tells the other person that you are interested in understanding and 'feeling with' them and is called *reflective listening*.

Bibliography & Further Reading

Adams, L. (1979) *Effectiveness Training for Women*, G.P. Putnams Sons, New York.

Bolton, R. (1979) *People Skills*, Prentice–Hall, Eaglewood Cliffs, New Jersey.

Carkhuff, R.R. (1972) *The Art of Helping*, Human Resource Development Press, Amherst, Massachusetts.

Egan, G. (1975) *The Skilled Helper*, Brooks/Cole Publishing, Monterey, California.

Gordon, Dr T. (1974) *T.E.T. Teacher Effectiveness Training*, Peter H. Wyden, New York.

Ivey, A. (1972) *Microcounselling: Interviewing Skills Manual*, Thomas, Springfield, Illinois.

Jones, E. (1961) *The Life and Work of Sigmund Freud*, Basic Books, New York, p. 253 (Quoted in Bolton, R. 1979).

Katz, J.H. (1984) *No Fairy Godmothers, No Magic Wands: The Healing Process After Rape*, R & E Publishers, Saratoga, California, p. 22.

Mayer, J.E. and Timms, N. (1970) *The Client Speaks — Working Class Impressions of Casework*, Routledge and Kegan Paul, London, p. 82.

Munro, A. Manthei, B. and Small, J. (1988) *Counselling: The Skills of Problem Solving*, Longman Paul, Auckland.

Siegal, B.S. (1988) *Love, Medicine and Miracles*, Arrow Books, London.

Steiner, C.M. (1974) *Scripts People Live*, Bantam, New York.

Sweet, G. (1989) *The Advantage of Being Useless: The Tao and the Counsellor*, Dunmore Press, Palmerston North.

CHAPTER 6
Helping Someone Change

KEY CONCEPTS:

Models of helping: problem solving, catharsis, holism

Ethical issues in helping

Other perspectives: Maori and Women's models

Refining the listening skills

Advanced helping skills: confrontation, reframing, self-disclosure, immediacy

The Helping Process

Objective: to be able to explain the ways in which helping skills can be used to promote (a) problem solving, (b) catharsis, (c) an ethical 'contract' between helper and client, and (d) a reintegration of personal, social, and spiritual life.

LISTENING AND HELPING

The situation 'where someone else owns a problem' covers a wide field. Everything from a 30-second chat where your kid tells you they grazed their knee at school today, and you say 'ouch, that much have hurt!' to a three-hour evening spent with a friend whose marriage is ending and who feels like committing suicide.

For most of those situations, attending, minimal encouragers, questions, and reflective listening are all you need to use. These are the simple listening skills presented in Chapter 5.

Mostly, people don't *want* you to use fancy counselling techniques to help them find new solutions and resolve lifetime problems. They just want you to listen. This chapter discusses the times when someone wants more. People like teachers, nurses, doctors, lawyers, social workers, clergy, physiotherapists, naturopaths, and counsellors are helpers. They're around at some important times in people's lives. They deal with people who have major issues to resolve. In my opinion their clients have a right to expect high quality listening from them. Someone who has recently learned they might die of cancer deserves a doctor who won't deny they're upset. A person who has just managed to get out of an abusive marriage has a right to a social worker who doesn't dump a load of judgements on them.

This chapter is for people who want to refine their listening ability and become excellent helpers. Helping is a serious business. Robert Cakhuff has shown through research that — left alone — people with a major problem tend to 'struggle on'. But when they receive 'help', they tend to either get much better *or* much worse.

Letter to A Helper

Judy Freespirit's 'Open Letter to My Former Shrinks' gives a very specific example of this. In it she explains how she felt used and betrayed by her first two counsellors. Then she goes on to talk about Marshall, her third therapist. Of him she says that it was as if he 'taught her how to feel'. Tragically, Marshall died in an accident, leaving their journey of exploration unfinished. In the part of the letter addressed to him, Freespirit expresses the mingled love and grief she bears for him, concluding:

> *When I die I hope I'll have a memorial service like that. But I'm not going yet, and while I'm here I'll have a special place in me reserved for your memories. I wish that you, Marshall, more than anyone else could be here now that I'm so close to really becoming a whole person. I wanted to be able to show you — Look, Marshall! Look at me! I feel anguish, and joy, and the tears flow freely from my eyes and my nose. I'm angry and sad and ugly and very weak and needy and terribly, terribly beautiful and strong and warm and potent and loving. I want to share that with you because you're the one person who knew all that about me before I did — and I want to share my knowing, too, but you went and died before I could show you. Hey, look, Marshall, now I'm awakening and becoming and being! — and, best of all, I'm a therapist now, too, and what I learned from you and others is spreading out into the world from you through me to others, and from them to others still. That's really what it's all about isn't it.*

What Helps?

How does a psychotherapist or a counsellor have this powerful impact on a person's growth? What can those of us who may never formally train as a 'counsellor' learn from their skills? The answers won't make you a therapist, but they will build enormously on your basic listening skills. If someone is prepared to accept you as a helper, these skills will sometimes enable them to work their way through difficult issues to successful life-solutions.

That is an *if*. Judy Freespirit *chose* Marshall as her helper. He didn't just walk up to her in the street and offered her advanced new ways of understanding herself. The skills listed here will work *once* someone has 'hired' you to seriously explore an issue. Otherwise, this is merely a recipe for being a 'busy body'. If in doubt, stay with listening skills.

Three Scouts

You may have heard the story of the three little boy scouts. At the end of the day they reported to their troop leader. It is, of course, a boy scout tradition to try and do one good deed every day. 'Well,' the leader asked, 'and what was your good deed for today, Johnny?'

'Please sir,' smiled Johnny, 'I helped an old lady across the road.'

'Very good,' the scout leader encouraged. 'How about you, Timmy?'

'Please sir,' said Timmy, just a little less certainly, 'I helped the same old lady across the road.'

'Well,' said the leader thoughtfully, 'that was very good too.'

After all, he considered, some old ladies require a bit more assistance than others. 'How about you Andy?', he asked of the third little boy scout.

'Please sir,' added Andy, 'I helped the same old lady across the road.'

'Now hold on', said the scout leader, suspecting some mistake here.

'This can't be right. How come it takes three little boy scouts to help *one* old lady across the road?'

'Please sir,' explained Andy, 'You see sir, she didn't want to go.' This does not count, in our terms, as 'helping'. But if that's *not* helping, what *is*? So far, we've said that helping is something you can choose to do when someone else 'owns a problem'.

We've also said that helping is based on *listening*. We'll now discuss four other ways of thinking about helping. Then, we'll learn the specific skills to achieve what is described here.

1 HELPING AS PROBLEM SOLVING

If helping skills are skills to use 'when someone else owns a problem', then helping must be a process of enabling others to solve problems. When we studied problem solving in Chapter 4, we listed its five stages as:

— *Defining* the problem
— *Setting* a goal
— *Planning* action to reach the goal
— *Acting*
— *Evaluating* the action, to check whether the goal has been reached.

A helper who understands this simple process can identify what stage their client is at, assist them to find their way forward through the steps, and even know which helping skills to use when. Most of the real work in helping occurs in stage one: Defining the problem. Often all a person wants the helper to do is enable them to identify what's going wrong. They can then work out what to do by themselves. The skills which are of most use in helping a client define the problem are the ones we studied in Chapter 5:

Skills for stage one: defining the problem

— attending
— minimal encourages
— questions, especially open questions

— reflective listening (reflecting content, reflecting feelings, perception check, and summarising).

In the second stage, as the client begins to work out where they are going, a skilled helper can offer the 'stronger medicines' of confrontation, reframing, self-disclosure, and immediacy, which we'll discuss in the next section of this chapter. That doesn't mean that the helper stops attending or using the simpler skills now. They continue to use the basic listening process, adding more challenging comments as appropriate. What it does mean is that it's not a very safe idea to use a stage two skill, such as a confrontation, as your first comment on meeting someone who wants your help. That would be like trying to start a car in top gear.

Skills to add in stage two: setting a goal

— confrontation
— reframing
— self-disclosure
— immediacy.

Other new skills come into their own in the planning action stage. One of these — asking the person to speak in here and now — will be explained in the next section. It's at the planning action stage, when the person knows where they want to go, that you as a helper may have useful information about how to get there. The skills you've learned earlier in this book — to help change state of mind — are an example. If you work professionally as a helper you may know what agencies, courses, and so on would be of use to the person. But, this information is useless *until* the client has set their own goal. Given *before* this point, good information is mere advice, a *roadblock* to the person working out what they actually want.

Skills to add in stage three: planning action

— speaking in the here and now
— giving information.

Once the client has taken action, you may well want to meet again to check how things went — *stage five: evaluation*. This may lead you back to the defining of a new problem, or on to the end of your helping relationship. Ending a relationship is as much a skilled process as beginning one. We'll explore this more fully later in the book.

2 HELPING AS CATHARSIS

When a helper reflects *feelings*, he or she is giving their client permission to become aware of, recognise, and express those feelings. By naming a feeling, you make it obvious that acknowledging feelings can be safe to do. By sharing your own feelings (as in self-disclosure and immediacy) you further demonstrate that having feelings is not only normal but is an important part of healthy living.

The release of strong feelings is known as emotional catharsis. The word 'catharsis' comes from the Greek word *katharsis* meaning to purge or to clean out. A cathartic drug is a laxative — it cleans out the bowels. In 1971, Fred and Brenda Forster (reported in Frey, 1985, p. 132) studied the responses of nursing students to crying patients. They found that the students generally behaved in the following ways:

1 Offered a ready made solution such as turning on the TV.
2 Belittled the patient's reaction, e.g. by saying that other people have just as big a problem as they have.
3 Ignored the crying, changed the subject, or told them not to worry.

These are, as you'll realise, the first three main types of roadblock we studied in Chapter 5 (Solutions, Judgements, and Denial). This response is particularly sad because we know for certain that crying helps the body heal. An old Jewish saying advises, 'What soap is for the body, tears are for the soul'. William Frey's research for his book *Crying: The Mystery of Tears* showed that 85 per cent of women and 73 per cent of men feel *better* after shedding tears. Frey points out that tears of sadness (*not* tears caused by irritants like onions) contain stress hormones such as the adrenocortico-trophic hormone (ACTH). A good cry may *literally* wash away your worries. Other studies suggest that those who cry more have a lower incidence of such stress-related disorders as colds, and duodenal ulcers.

Frey urges helpers to directly give permission to a crying person ('It's alright to cry', 'Thats it, let it out'), and assist by silently staying nearby while the person weeps. In terms of the helping skills we are studying, this makes attending the most important skill to assist catharsis.

Skills to assist catharsis

— attending
— reflecting feelings
— self-disclosure and immediacy
— asking the person to speak in the here and now.

Creating space where a client can allow themselves powerful feelings such as grief, anger, and fear is one of the most precious gifts of helping. In many models of psychotherapy (such as psychodrama, co-counselling, bio energetics, and primal therapy) the release of previously suppressed feelings is thought of as *the* central healing act. Judy Freespirit, in her letter to Marshall quoted before, also expresses this belief.

3 HELPING AS AN ETHICAL PROCESS

When helping is part of your job, the person you help can be considered your *client*. Just as you may expect them to arrive on time for appointments, for example, they have a right to expect certain standards from you. 'Ethics' is the study of the standards of behaviour which you keep to. Important examples are *touch* and *confidentiality*.

Touch: In the professional helping situation, an issue often comes up about the non-verbal part of listening. It's the question of physical touch. Ashley

Montague, in his book *Touching*, points out how powerfully healing human touch is. He quotes evidence that a 'course' of regular human touch will cure such illnesses as asthma and eczema, as well as enhancing children's physical growth.

In some professional situations (such as hospitals) helping routinely involves physical touch, and so to hold someone's hand or put an arm around their shoulder may be an accepted way to offer comfort. Similarly, some cultural settings allow more touch than others (e.g. physical touch is an important part of any Maori greeting, according to psychiatrist Mason Durie). There is also a difference between the way people in our society feel about being touched by men, on the one hand, and women, on the other. Munro, Manthei, and Small suggest that female counsellors 'may still be seen more naturally and effectively to initiate such contacts with both males and females'.

But there are two concerns that helpers need to think about when using touch. The first is that your client needs help and, therefore, may find it difficult to ask you to *stop* touching them if they don't feel right about it. Secondly, in our society there is often some confusion about whether touch has a sexual meaning. How do you balance the value of touch and the risk of a client feeling uncomfortable with it? A good general principle is only to use touch when (a) you sense that the client will appreciate and benefit from it, and (b) you feel comfortable with it yourself. Once you have a sense of rapport, or empathy, with a client, the very best way to find out what *they* feel right about is simply to ask.

Confidentiality: When you listen to a friend talking over their worries, you will often have a sort of understanding that you won't tell anyone else what they said. As a professional helper, of course, this becomes even more important.

At times it will help clients to know exactly how much confidentiality they can expect. Do you need to report back about your discussion to your colleagues or teachers. Do you understand which situations (such as child abuse) you are legally required to report? And what if you find out your client is planning to drive off a cliff tonight? For me, these are the three main limits to my confidentiality:

— professional requirements such as reports or supervision
— legal restrictions
— someone's life being endangered.

If I thought I was in one of these situations, where I needed to discuss a client with someone else, I'd like to tell the client as soon as possible about my intention.

Other than these three situations, I think clients have a right to know that their helpers won't discuss their affairs with others. This commitment is often acknowledged by a helper at the start of their time with a client, as part of their making a 'contract'. In what helpers do say to others (e.g. in case discussions), the sense of respect is important. A client's information is precious, it is a treasure, and not an amusing story for the curious. When I go to a doctor, a lawyer, or a counsellor, my hope is that they have this sense of respect and affection for what I share with them. In some cases, *who* they tell is not so important to me as *how* they tell my story.

Discussing Ethics

The skill which enables you to discuss ethical issues like touch and confidentiality is called 'Immediacy'. When you explain your limits and check your client's limits about what is happening between you, that's immediacy. It's also part of the process of maintaining a *contract* (see Chapter 1).

Whenever you begin a helping relationship, the questions 'what will we do here?', 'What are the rules?', and 'What will I get out of it?' need to be answered. As was pointed out in Chapter 1, it helps to set aside a little time at the beginning to ensure these questions are answered for both of you. In some cases the agency you work for will do this routinely. When both you and your client know what to expect from each other, this sense of contract adds to the feeling of safety which you are building.

4 **HELPING AS A HOLISTIC PROCESS**

'Helping', as we have been discussing it here, developed out of western (particularly American) male culture. Initially, it has taken for granted the western, male tendency to approach life by dividing things into even smaller pieces. For example, we have accepted so far that helping is something one individual does for another individual. Actually, people always exist in families and other groups. It doesn't make any sense to try and fix up one person in a system without thinking about how they relate to the others (as the theory of ego states in Chapter 2, and roles in Chapter 5 both emphasise).

What Is Health?

Often, in western cultures, there is an assumption that to be totally independent is to be mentally healthy. Fritz Perls, who founded Gestalt Therapy, summed up his definition of mental health as: '*You do your thing, and I do mine. I am not in this world to live up to your expectations and you are not in this world to live up to mine. You are you and I am I. And if by chance we find each other, it's beautiful. If not, it can't be helped.*'

Most helpers nowadays would question the absoluteness of this. Robert Bolton, for example, says quite simply 'You can't be human alone'. If Bolton is right, and 'by chance' we don't find each other, we'd better damn well discover why not!

Another part of our tendency to divide things into small pieces is the separation between mind and body. In Chapter 2 we discovered that mind and body are completely interrelated, so that a person's 'state of mind' is also their physical state. We must ask ourselves how much sense it makes, then, to help someone 'emotionally' without nurturing their body, or at least considering their posture. In this sense, touch (although culturally sensitive) is an important helping skill. To communicate 'acceptance' while staying physically aloof from someone is almost self-contradictory.

Connection with the Universe

The other major example of the western dividing process is the separation of humans from the universe which surrounds them, from nature, from what we might call 'the spiritual side of life'. Consider psychiatrist Viktor Frankl's initial response in the following story of his visit to a young woman in a Nazi concentration camp. Her own comments are a moving reminder of the healing power of a sense of unity with the universal life-force. Pointing through the window of the hut, she said 'This tree here is the only friend I have in my loneliness.' Through that window she could see just one branch of a chestnut tree, and on the branch were two blossoms. 'I often talk to this tree', she said to me. I was startled, and didn't quite know how to take her words. Was she delirious? Did she have occasional hallucinations? Anxiously, I asked her if the tree replied. 'Yes.' What did it say to her? She answered, 'It said to me, "I'm here — I am here — I am life, eternal life"' (Frankl 1969, p. 109).

All this dividing is quite odd because the very concept of 'healing' comes from the old English word *haelen*, meaning 'whole' (the same word from which our words holy and whole come). In old English to heal was to reunite with the universe, to join together all your parts, to reconnect body and mind, to re-establish your relationship with others. The word 'holistic' is being used today by many health professionals to describe care which has this aim of reuniting. What would it mean in practice?

A Maori Model

Psychiatrist Mason Durie discusses this from a Maori perspective in a video available from the New Zealand Mental Health Foundation. Holism, he suggests, has always been central to Maori culture (although it is the Americans who are marketing it most enthusiastically). Helping, for Maori, needs to incorporate (using Durie's key words):

- Whanaungatanga: family involvement
- Whakamanawa: encouragement, including the sharing of food and other supports (manakitanga) as well as the physical embrace (awhi). This could mean welcoming clients with a hug and an offer of a cup of tea, for example

— Mauri: vital or life force, including the spiritual element (wairua) and the geneological background (whakapapa) of the tribe and subtribe. These elements are treated as being significant in any 'personal' concern.

Durie also points out that in a holistic culture, talking 'about' feelings is less valued. Actually experiencing the feelings (see 'helping as catharsis') is more appropriate, and being asked to name feelings may even pull a person away from this. In terms of the skills we will study, Durie's suggestions seem to me to emphasise the following:

Skills for holistic links

— attending (including physical support)
— reframing
— asking the person to speak in the here and now.

Professional Helping: a Pakeha Model

Even the division between professional helper and client is culturally specific. The very words 'helper' and 'client' come from American counselling models. Maori counsellor Hinekahukura Barrett-Aranui states in *Counselling: The Skills of Problem Solving* that:

> *Counselling as a one-to-one relationship between a professional and a client is a concept foreign to Maori culture. In Maoridom, helping involves the whole whanau (family) and beyond in an intense sharing which takes physical, emotional, spiritual, and practical forms. The essential elements are the family network (whanaungatanga), the help given by the people (manaakitanga), and the spiritual dimension (wairuatanga).*

While it may be appropriate for people to receive help from those who share their own culture (e.g. for Maori to assist Maori, and Pakeha to assist Pakeha), *all* helping is obviously enriched by the recognition of the unifying trend of holism. As the word 'haelen' reminds us, Pakeha culture too had it's roots in the holistic world view.

The Human Electrical Field

One way of directly experiencing the interconnectedness of human beings is by training yourself to feel and control the electrical field around yourself and others. N.L.P. (Neurolinguistic Programming) is a communication skills model partially described in Chapters 2 and 3. N.L.P. researcher Robert Dilts has developed a way of teaching people how to feel and control their own electrical energy. Once taught, people can feel this field several feet from a person's body.

To help people get used to feeling this subtle electrical field, Dilts uses a 'biofeedback' machine which measures changes in skin electricity (or G.S.R.), like a lie detector. As he points out, though, certain people in almost every culture around the world have discovered by themselves how to feel, and even see, changes in the electrical field around the body. Like the people he teaches, these 'naturals' have learned to increase the power and stability of their own field, often using breathing techniques (people who are breathing less, such as depressed people have a lower amplitude G.S.R. People in a state of anxiety have a high amplitude, erratic G.S.R. (see Lader, 1975, pp. 98 and 130).

Wide Use of Bio-Electrical Field

In Maori culture, for example, the ability to see and feel a person's energy field is well recognised. There are numerous descriptions in religious sources such as the Bible which may be related to this natural phenomenon. Once people realise they can feel this field, and even direct their own energy so as to 'recharge' someone else, it often produces a deeper respect for the interconnectedness of all life. Dr Dolores Krieger, Janet Macrae, and others teach this process (under the name 'Therapeutic Touch') as part of basic nursing training in a number of hospitals in the US. Their research (see Macrae 1988) supports it's healing benefits. No particular beliefs about the 'meaning' of the electrical field (e.g. a belief that this is a 'spiritual aura') are necessary to learn to use this process.

Empowering: A Feminist Model

Miriam Greenspan's description of feminist helping is also about holism. She says the helper needs to go beyond 'the old divisions between feeling and thinking, emotional release and theory, love and work, male and female. The therapist must know how to combine the feminine skills of empathy, intuition and relatedness with the masculine skills of discipline, distance and theory'. (Greenspan 1983, p. 251)

Greenspan too, is critical of Fritz Perls' individualistic definition of health. 'A female-style model of therapy must acknowledge that not only children but adults have legitimate needs for caring, reassurance, nurturance and support.' The fact that women ask for and give support has often been used to suggest that they are less independent and, therefore, less healthy than men. Both extremes (being a 'rugged individual' and being always dependent on others for feeling good) may be equally unhealthy. Helping women understand how the male definition of mental health (as being alone and unemotional) has left women feeling inadequate is part of 'listening for the connections between personal and political in women's stories'. A helper, she suggests, needs to understand the way social pressures affect self-esteem (see Chapter 2). In the same way that reflecting *feelings* helps a person recognise their own feeling states, reflecting people's experience of what it is like to be a woman, a man, poor, Pakeha, Maori, Samoan, and so on, helps them recognise their own identity. Understanding the social causes of their situation, they are less likely to blame themselves, and more able (empowered) to change things. Again, in terms of helping *skills*, Greenspan's approach emphasises the importance of what we will call 'reframing'.

Skills for empowering
— reframing
— immediacy

So far in this chapter we have discussed the following four processes:

1 *Problem solving*. Basic listening skills especially work in the first (Defining The Problem) step of problem solving. More advanced skills, including several to be discussed after Exercises 6.1 and 6.2, are better introduced in the later stages of problem solving.
2 *Emotional catharsis*. Attending, and skills which focus on feelings will help this important process of releasing blocked feelings.
3 *Maintaining an ethical 'contract'*. Immediacy is the skill which helps you clarify what the 'rules' in your relationship are and how these rules are working.
4 *Reintegrating body and mind, personal and political, individual and family, or human and universal.* To help make a holistic process may mean changing the physical setting (involving family, offering food, using touch). It also means using helping skills such as reframing.

EXERCISE 6.1

Aim — to feel human electrical energy 1–10 cm out from the body.

1 Use the relaxation process described in Exercise 2.3. Then give the following instructions:

a With each *in* breath, imagine that energy of some kind is flowing from the area above your head, down the centre of your body to your heart. You can imagine this as you like as an electrical energy, or as a spiritual energy which you know and trust. Actually feel the flow down to the area of your heart.

b Continuing to 'breathe in' energy, imagine that as you breathe out, the same energy flows from your heart out down your arms and out your fingertips. Think of this energy as being as abundant as the air you breathe. You may be aware of tingling in your fingers.

c Get into pairs, continuing to imagine the energy flow. Place your hands palms facing each other, and about 5–10 cm apart. You may feel your own energy as you move the hands a little. Have your partner move one of their hands down through the space between yours, back and forth several times. Check for the feeling. Once you are aware what it's like, you may be able to feel the field a similar distance away from your partner's body in general.

2 This part of the exercise does not require any particular imagining:

a Stand with one leg straight, and the other in front of it with only the toes touching the ground. Hold both arms up in front of the chest forming a horizontal circle, with the fingertips almost touching (as if you were holding up a large beach ball). Place your tongue lightly against the top of your mouth and breathe relaxedly. Keep this posture for three minutes. This is hard work, but it builds a powerful electrical response.

b After three minutes, keep your arms up but reverse the position of your legs. Stand another three minutes.

c Place both feet on the floor and slowly lower your arms. For the next minute or so, your hands and arms will have a high energy level. Run the fingers of one hand along beside your arm or over your cheek, keeping them just under a centimetre apart. You may feel as if you are touching (a similar effect is often produced by touching someone who is lying on an electrical blanket, but in this case the electricity was generated in your own body).

d Discussion: Gather together as a group and share your response to the exercise.

EXERCISE 6.2

Aim — to practise the use of touch as a helping process. (*shoulder massage*)

This exercise can be done in pairs, taking turns to do the massage, or in a whole group, simultaneously. The group stand in a circle, facing the back of the next in line.

Relaxing the shoulders, upper back, and neck has a calming effect on the body in general. Massage strokes can include tapping using the finger tips, *gentle* pounding with knuckles or fists, kneading (grasping areas of the shoulder and squeezing), and pressing firmly in a circular rubbing motion with the hands/thumbs/fingertips. When pressing, with one hand, you may find it helps to steady the shoulder with the other.

The following areas are particularly good to massage in this way:

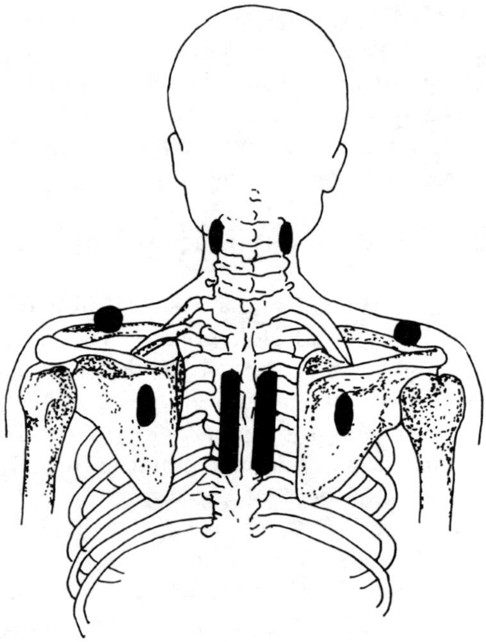

Skills of Helping

Objective: to be able to use metamodel questioning, matching sensory systems, confrontation, reframing, self-disclosure, immediacy, and directions to speak in the here and now.

ATTITUDES AND SKILLS

I'd have to be crazy to believe that helping was nothing more than a set of skills: 'Do this, do that, and someone will feel better'. No amount of fancy communication skills can replace the attitude of affection which is the basic principle in helping someone.

But, on the other hand, without skills a whole lot of nice ideas about love, holism, or anything else can end up as 'just nice ideas'. Once you feel confident with the listening skills described in Chapter 5, you will have many of the skills to *express* that love. We will, however, discuss several more skills. These are:

1 Refining your questioning skills
2 Refining your reflecting skills
3 Confrontation
4 Reframing
5 Self-disclosure
6 Immediacy
7 Directing the person to speak in the here and now.

1 **Refining Your Questioning Skills**

In Chapter 1, I indicated that people's map of what the world is like is *only* a map. Mostly, what causes pain in people's lives is not so much the actual events around them: it's their internal beliefs, or maps, about what happens. Leslie Cameron–Bandler, Richard Bandler, and John Grinder have developed a method of recognising which parts of a person's map create difficulty for them, and of asking questions to help the person change that map. They call this method the *metamodel*. Here are some examples of using the metamodel.

a If a client says 'I can't . . .' the metamodel response could be either 'what stops you?' or 'What would happen if you did?' e.g. 'I *can't* tell my husband what I really think of his jokes.'

'What would happen if you did?'

b If a client says 'I must ...' the metamodel response would be 'What would happen if you didn't?' (similar to (a))
In both cases the person's map of the world assumes things have to be the way they are. Your question challenges that limit to the map.

c When a client says something is 'wrong' or 'right', you could ask 'According to whom?'
e.g. 'It's *wrong* to accept charity.'
'According to whom? Who believes it's wrong?'
This question helps the person identify whose map of the world they are using. Is it their own? their parents? Whatever the answer, the question reminds them that it's only a map.

d Sometimes a client simply misses out important parts of a sentence, leaving you to guess what they were. The metamodel suggests you actually ask what they are.
e.g. 'I can't cope with this.'
'What, specifically, can't you cope with?'
Such questions help the person explain what is wrong in a sensory-specific way (see Chapter 4 on problem solving for an explanation of 'sensory specific').

e A client may also describe what happens so generally that you don't know who did what to whom. You could then ask for this information.
e.g. 'My brother annoys me all the time.'
'What, specifically, does he do that annoys you?'
e.g. 'You've hurt me very much.'
'How, specifically, have I hurt you?'
e.g. 'People are always picking on me.'
'Which people are picking on you; and what, specifically, do they do?'

f As a final example, often people's maps contain beliefs that are totally magical, such as mindreading.
e.g. 'I *know* what he thinks of me.'
The metamodel suggests you ask how this magical process is happening. 'How, specifically, do you *know*. What do you see or hear?' Another magical belief is that one person can make an emotional response happen inside another person's body.
e.g. 'You make me feel very sad.' (This magical belief is challenged by Exercise 1.1.)
A metamodel response might be 'How, specifically, does what I do force you to be sad.'

Practise with the Metamodel
Try using the metamodel to respond to these statements:

— 'I *can't* face my teacher ever again.'
— 'I *must* spend more time with my family.'
— 'It's not *right* for a woman to argue with a man.'
— '*This* is hopeless.'
— 'My children *push me around* a lot.'
— 'I can *tell* you don't like me.'
— 'My mother *makes* me so angry!'

2 **Refining Your Reflecting Skills**

The aim of reflective listening is to create verbally that sense of shared understanding, called either empathy or rapport. This will work better if you use similar language to the client. For example, if an 8-year-old child said to you, 'I'm sick of my brother. He always gets his way', to reply 'You have a sense of resentment about your sibling's interpersonal persuasiveness' is not as useful as 'You don't think it's fair'.

One way in which you can make your language more understandable with clients of all ages is to use the knowledge about sensory systems, explained in Chapter 3. When someone speaks mainly about what they see (visual system) your reflective reply can do the same. Similarly, this applies equally to auditory and kinesthetic responses. For example:

Client: 'I can't see any way forward. It looks really gloomy to me.'
Reply: 'There's no light at the end of the tunnel.'
Client: 'I tell myself we can just tune into each other again, but all the conflicts keep echoing round my head.'
Reply: 'Sounds like you keep hearing the past arguments replaying, and that stops you listening to what she's saying now.'
Client: 'It's too much. I've been carrying this relationship for years, and I just have to have a bit more distance from it.'
Reply: 'You want to stand back from it more and share the load with your husband.'

Practise Matching Sensory Systems

Try writing reflective replies *using the client's sensory system*, for the following examples:

— 'The first time I spoke with her, we just clicked. She's really on my wavelength.'
— 'It's been a long hard struggle, ploughing through all these decisions, but I feel like I'm almost there now.'
— 'The way I see it, it's black and white. Either he wants to be part of this scene or not.'
— 'Wherever I look, I see problems obscuring the way forward.'
— 'It was so quiet while the kids were away. Now I can hardly hear myself think!'
— 'I don't really feel like I make contact with her anymore. She's always so distant.'

These word lists may help:

Visual	***Auditory***	***Kinesthetic***
see	listen	fall
view	hear	move
spot	sound	hold
glimpse	ask	run
eye	tell	struggle
gaze	ring	walk
show	click	push
read	scream	feel
look	groan	grip
picture	buzz	contact
bright	call	touch
clear	tone	soft
focus	tune	rough
flash	loud	hard
perspective	harmonise	smooth
colourful	clash	tight
dark	crunch	close
vision	quiet	distant

3 **Confrontation**

One of the most common human experiences is for someone talking to you to *say* something that doesn't fit with what you see of their body language; or to say one thing one day and the opposite the next; or to tell you they plan to do something, but then never quite get round to it.

In all these cases, the person is sending you *two* messages. The jargon term for this is 'incongruity'. I once had a counselling client who came to see me each week and began by starting to cry. As she sobbed, she would say to me 'Well, Richard, I'm feeling a lot better this week,' (pause to wipe her eyes) 'and I think I've really got over the separation now.' Of course, a reflective listening response might be 'You feel on top of it all now', but this would miss a lot of what she was telling me.

When someone is incongruent, to ignore the incongruity is not the most useful helping response. Another approach that's not so helpful is to believe that one of the messages is 'real' and the other is 'phony'. Using that approach I might have said to my client 'You say you're fine but obviously that's not true. You're pretending to be okay, but I can tell that really you're still upset'. As you can guess, this approach ends me up in an argument. It's actually a judgemental roadblock (interpreting).

Acknowledging Both Messages

The most powerful response to incongruity is to acknowledge (and reflect) *both* messages, that is, literally to 'believe all things'. My opinion is that *both* things are, in some sense, true. The woman who tells me that she feels better may well be aware of more positive feelings. There is *certainly* a part of her which *wants* to feel better. I don't want to deny that part, just because there is another part which is still needing to feel her grief. My comment will be something like, 'On the one hand, you say you feel a lot better. On the other hand, you still cry as you talk about it', or 'There's a part of you that has got over it, and a part of you that still cries as you say that.'

What will the person make of this reflecting both messages? I can't be sure. She may come to understand the way in which both things are true, or she may decide she isn't fully over her separation. My job was simply to *confront* her with the difference between the messages. By confront, I mean to put it in front of her clearly enough so she cannot pretend that one message doesn't exist. The name of this skill, 'confrontation', sounds a little aggressive. Actually, this is simply an extension of the basic skill of reflective listening.

Confronting Addiction

Another example might be my response to a client who begins drinking gin and tonics at 11 am each day, and is routinely drunk by tea time, but who tells me 'I'm not alcoholic. I could stop any time. I just need to relax lately'. I might respond 'You say you're able to stop if you want and at the same time, you've been drinking every day for several weeks because of a "need to relax".' To emphasise the confrontation I might explain my awareness of the difference by adding 'Those two things don't seem to fit together'. The first example (crying and saying 'I'm fine') was an incongruity between words and body language. The second (alcoholism) could be described as an incongruity between words and actions or between one statement and another. Any of these incongruities is a signal to the helper to use confrontation, *if* there is enough sense of rapport built up. To use this skill *before* the person feels listened to in a more gentle way will create resistance.

Practise Using Confrontation

Try writing your own confrontation responses to the following statements:

— A 15-year-old boy, laughing enthusiastically, tells you 'I guess I do push my brother around a lot. Poor kid. I feel sorry for him. He never gets a break.'
— A 31-year-old man tells you 'My wife and I have a good relationship really. It's surprising because, as I say, she can be a real bitch at times.'
— A 21-year-old woman, who told you last week that she intended to give up smoking before her next visit, comes in. Lighted cigarette in hand, she explains, 'Well, I've decided for sure now. I'm stopping smoking . . . sometime soon, mark my words.'
— Smiling, and speaking in a quiet, musical voice, a 25-year-old man tells you 'I'm absolutely furious about what my father said, and I mean to tell him too.'

4 **Reframing**

Some pictures look cold and dark in one frame, but warm and bright in another. The colours may clash when you put a picture up on one wall, but harmonise with the wall next to it. People's life experience is like that too. Put it in one frame and they feel powerless or meaningless; put it in another and they discover all sorts of new ways forward. Think back to a time when *you* made a major decision in your life; perhaps a decision about what job you'd do or a decision to begin or to leave a relationship. Once you'd made that decision, it *reframed* the rest of your life. Maybe it gave you a whole new perspective on what was possible, maybe it restored the balance you needed to move ahead.

In helping, to reframe means to reflect what the person has said, but putting it in a different context or giving it a different meaning. This new meaning should offer more choices, or create a more positive state of mind. All the reflective listening skills are really a kind of reframing. When someone says 'My mother is really stubborn' and I respond 'You're annoyed with her', I've given quite a different meaning to the statement. The person says something about their mother. I reframe it as something about *them.* This reframe is useful — they may not be able to do much about their mother's stubbornness, but they do have choices about dealing with their feeling of annoyance.

From Problem to Goal

Another example of reframing is used to help move someone to the goal-setting stage of problem solving. If someone says 'I'm hungry', I may reply 'You'd like something to eat'. They've defined their *problem*, but I've said back something about their *goal.* If someone says 'I can't stick up for myself', I may say 'You'd like to learn how to be more assertive'. This problem → goal reframe will only work once the person understands their problem enough to start thinking about what their goal might be. Most reframing will work best later in the helping process. Used at the beginning, it may come across as a denial of the person's real problem.

Finding Usefulness instead of Blaming

To reframe, I ask myself 'In what context would what the person tells me about be useful?' or 'In what way could this experience have a useful meaning?' If I offer a reframing and the person seems to resist, then I need to go back to listening and more simple reflection.

Many people who come for help have a judgemental or 'blame' frame. When they talk about their problem they talk as if they or someone else is bad, at fault and to blame. The 'blame frame' is not much use for working out what to do next, so I usually offer them a reframe. An example is the man I described in Chapter 1, 'Culture and Meeting' who came to me and explained that he was 'no good' at communication because (for instance) he couldn't make eye contact as much as his wife wanted. I encouraged him to reframe this situation by comments which, in essence, said 'Sounds to me like you're a *good* communicator with a Maori cultural experience'. Did this mean his wife was the 'bad' person? No. She was just a communicator with a Pakeha cultural experience. Our reframe put the personal situation in a social or even 'political' context, instead of one in which individuals are at fault.

Symptoms and Society

Symptoms, such as 'depression', 'anxiety', or a stress-related illness can also be reframed as social events rather than as an individual's fault. Such symptoms have usually been very sensible choices which the person first made early in their life. At that time, to be depressed may have been the only safe way to shut down feelings of hurt and anger which were not allowed in the person's family. To develop an illness may have been the only way to get quality time with pre-occupied parents. *Now*, the person may be able to find other even better ways of dealing with hurt, anger or loneliness. But we don't need to blame them for a wisdom which has just outlived its time of usefulness.

Let's say someone tells me 'I feel really worried about it. Ever since my childhood I've had an explosive temper'. I may reframe 'Sounds like you learned then that the best way to cope with that situation was to be aggressive, and now you're really choosing to learn new ways that are suited to the kind of relationship you'd like to have'. There are two reframes here. I reframe the person's temper (which they saw as a problem) as something that 'worked' in one context. I reframe their worry about it (which they felt as a weakness) as 'choosing to learn new things' (a strength).

Practise Reframing

There are as many ways to reframe as there are stars in the sky. In this chapter I've reframed 'helping' as 'listening', as a set of skills, as 'problem solving', as 'catharsis', as 'healing', as 'love', and now as 'reframing'. Read the following comment and write reframes of it as:

— a feeling (reflecting feelings)
— a goal instead of a problem
— an example of a social situation
— a good choice which has outlined its usefulness
— evidence that the person is choosing to change.

A 26-year-old woman explains: 'My problem is that when my husband Karl gets annoyed about something, I just shut down. It's the same as it was with my father. When he got angry — boy, nobody had better say a word! I know Karl's not like that, but I suppose I'm still stuck in the same response. So I say less and less, and Karl gets even angrier. It's odd, because with some feelings I'm fine. I'm quite supportive when someone's sad. But I realise now that I can't seem to handle anger.'

5 **Self-disclosure**

This skill and the next skill both involve sharing my feelings and opinions with the person I am helping. In helping, these are probably the highest risk skills — in the sense that, unless they are used very carefully, the client can feel as if I'm giving them advice or sorting out my own personal problems instead of listening to their concern. And yet there are times when telling my own experiences can help the other person know that I understand, and can model the type of self-exploration I'm encouraging them to do. This is especially so later in a helping conversation, when the client already knows my main role is to hear *their* story. Self-disclosure involves me telling the other person briefly about my own experiences. The two most important things to remember when I do this are:

a When talking about myself, I always say 'I' and 'In my experience'. For example, 'I've found it hard to cope with that kind of conflict myself' rather than 'People find that hard to cope with', 'We find it hard to cope with', or even 'You always find that kind of conflict difficult'. I want to make sure that my client knows when I'm reflecting *their* comments, their feelings, and when I'm offering *my* ones. Self-disclosure uses 'I' language.

b After self-disclosing, I want to encourage the conversation to shift back to its focus on helping, not to become a two-way 'chat'. Often I will include a question which does this, at the end of my self-disclosure; for example, 'When that has happened to me, I know I've felt pretty embarrassed. *Is it like that for you*?' Or I may reflect and then self-disclose, 'You say you've been wondering who to talk to about this for a long time. I always find that half the problem is getting the courage to ask someone. Once I've made that step, I sort of relax'.

Practising being in the *client* role when learning helping skills is an excellent way to develop your ability to use self-disclosure.

6 **Immediacy**

Immediacy means talking about what's happening right here and now, in the 'immediate' situation. When I am 'upfront' in this way, I honestly but respectfully tell the other person how I feel, or what response I have to the things they've said and done. This can encourage them to be more open and 'honest' with me. It can also give them important real-life feedback about how others react to them.

Most people have certain ways of behaving that invite a similar reaction in each person they meet. Someone who is 'depressed', for example, may behave in ways that invite others first to feel sorry for them but later to get annoyed and frustrated (see Chapter 5, 'Rescue, Persecution, or Help?'). When I am helping this person, it's quite likely that I'll start to have these feelings too. Instead of telling myself that 'I shouldn't feel this way. I'm the helper and I need to be gentle and caring'; *immediacy* is another choice. I might say, at various times:

'As I listen to your story, I feel a real sadness inside me.'

'I'm starting to get frustrated here. You said you wanted to explore this, but you're saying less and less. I begin to feel as if I'm left to do all the work.'

'I find myself starting to get anxious when you're sad: almost as if I need to look after you. Actually, I know it's safe for you to feel your sadness. I want to make sure I don't block that in any way.'

'You've stopped talking, and I really don't know right now what you want from me.'

'I appreciate you telling me about this.'

All these comments are examples of immediacy. One important function of immediacy is to help us to clarify the 'contract'. I might say such things as:

'Mostly my intention is to listen to you and help you find your own solutions', or

'I intend to treat this conversation as confidential. Unless I thought your life was in some kind of danger, I won't discuss this outside this room', or

'I need to stop in ten minutes time.'

As with self-disclosure, my language in immediacy makes it very clear which are *my* thoughts and feelings, and which are the ones I've heard from my client.

Using Immediacy

Immediacy is powerful. It needs to be used gently, and with a good understanding of how this comment will *help* the other person. To develop your skill with immediacy, take time after practising the use of helping skills to talk with the person who was your 'client'. You could discuss what your feelings were as you listened to them, how you chose which things to say back to them, and so on. Then check — would any of what you've just discussed be useful for you to say *while* you were helping?

7 **Directing the Person to Speak in the Here and Now**

This skill was first developed by helpers such as Jacob Moreno and Fritz Perls. It gives the power of immediacy (see above) to situations from outside in the rest of the person's life. Notice, in the following example, how much more impact the 'here and now' statement has than the client's earlier 'there and then' statement.

Client: 'I wish I could tell Lisa how much I love her, but I never do. It's kind of sad. I suppose she wonders . . .'

Helper: 'Imagine she was sitting beside us here. Try saying that to her now.'

Client: 'Well . . . okay . . . Lisa, I never say it but . . .' (begins to cry). 'But I really do love you. I know this is a hard time for you and I want to be here for you.'

Helper: 'That sounds great. How do you think she'd respond?'

Two Uses

Here and now statements can be used in two ways. First, they can be used to 'practise' for real life. Once a client has gone through the problem-solving process and worked out what they'd like to do about their situation, they can rehearse a conversation while talking to you. Secondly, here and now statements can be used to help the client more fully experience what they feel and think about a situation. They may say things they'd never want to actually say to the other person, but which express where they stand and the way they really see things.

If you're the helper, you need to know which kind of *here and now* statement you are encouraging. You might begin by explaining: 'Let's practise, so you have an idea what you want to say' or 'It may help you to work out how you feel about this if you pretend you're saying these things *to* her. These aren't things you're choosing to tell her in real life, but they are your real feelings.'

Simple Form

Directing the person to speak in the here and now can be done in a simple form with an open question such as 'How do you feel about that *right now*'. For example:

Client: 'I felt confused at the time. I couldn't work out exactly what was wrong. He sort of convinced me to go with him, but I didn't want to.'

Helper: 'How do you feel about it right now?'

Client: 'I feel damned angry!' (Pounds the chair.) 'He tricked me. I'm furious about it. I want to say "Damn you!"'

Helper: 'Sure. Tell him now.'

Client: 'Damn you! I'm so sick of your manipulating me. I hope I never see you again!'

Re-experiencing a State

Encouraging the client to use the gestures and body positions that go with their words, and to imagine the scene in which they are speaking, will enhance the use of speaking in the here and now. If you, as a helper, are not comfortable with catharsis, then it's best to avoid this skill. As the examples suggest, this skill can assist a person to fully re-enter the 'state' they are describing, with the feelings anchored to it. Something interesting happens then, because the safety of your helping situation can tend to be anchored (see Chapter 2 for the meaning of this term) to the situation in which those strong feelings occur. The feelings need not be blocked as they were before. It becomes safe to feel them. The result is a kind of healing which N.L.P. counsellors call 'collapsing anchors'.

This sort of healing happens in everyday life. A person who is grieving for a dead relative will often speak 'to them', releasing the feelings they've held back. Judy Freespirit's letter to Marshall (at the start of this chapter) is a written example. Obviously, directing the person to speak in the here and now is a skill which can only be used later in helping, if at all. In the next chapter you'll practise assertion using 'speaking in the here and now'.

Finding out what that feels like is a useful first step, before inviting others to use it.

Now you have been introduced to seven 'advanced' level helping skills, appropriate to situations such as counselling. These skills are:

1 Using the metamodel to develop *questions* which challenge the limits in a client's map of the world. These *limits* include unquestioned beliefs about what can't be done, what must be done, what is wrong or right, and people's ability to read minds or cause feelings in each other, as well as missing information.
2 *Matching* the client's use of *sensory systems*, when you use reflective listening.
3 *Confronting* the incongruity between two messages a client has sent (by restating *both* messages).
4 *Reframing*, that is, offering new frames for understanding the meaning of what the client is exploring, for example:
   — changing a comment about events into a comment about feelings.
   — changing a description of the problem into a description of a goal.
   — changing a blaming statement into a description of social causes.
   — changing a description of a problem into a recognition of a solution which worked in an earlier situation.
   — changing a story of failure into an affirmation of the person's intention to change.
5 *Self-disclosure* of the helper's own experiences and past responses in ways helpful to the client.
6 Talking about what is happening right at the moment, between helper and client — *immediacy*
7 Directing the client to *speak in the here and now*. This can be used to practise for real life, and to assist the client to more fully enter a state and become aware of their thoughts or feelings.

EXERCISE 6.3

Aim — to practise the use of helping skills and receive specific feedback.

1 Follow the procedure described in Exercise 5.7, except that the time should be extended to 10–15 minutes, and the listener may use the full range of helping skills as appropriate.

2 After each practice, the observer can give the listener feedback using the following chart. Functioning at level 3 could be considered a successful or 'pass' level.

Skills	Level 1: Dangerous	Level 2: Unhelpful	Level 3: Helpful
1 Attending	Not in an attending posture. Distracted by other activities.	Mechanical use of attending posture. Gestures and smile absent. No pacing of client's gestures.	Posture and gestures are relaxed and appropriate for attending. Some indications of rapport (e.g. simultaneous gestures).
2 Reflective listening	Comments are often unrelated to client's feelings/ experience. Repeated use of roadblocks (denial, judgements, solution giving, interrogation).	Reflects some of the feelings expressed. Occasional use of roadblocks.	Accurately reflects all major feelings expressed. All comments come from a base of empathy.
3 Self-disclosure and immediacy	Either overwhelms the conversation with own stories and views, or denies and lies about own feelings.	Avoids personal material or 'shares' own 'feelings' incongruently.	Congruent verbal and non-verbal responses. Shares own feelings and view/ experiences in ways which are helpful to the client (if appropriate opportunity occurs).
4 Confrontation and reframing	Ignores important incongruities or use of blaming frame by the client, or reacts to these only with roadblocks. Repeatedly confronts or reframes too forcefully for client.	Reflects the feelings in incongruity or in client blaming statements, but does not fully use these statements by confronting and reframing.	Able to specifically and empathically challenge client incongruity or blaming statements. Finds useful new ways to reframe the problem situation.

Skills	Level 1: Dangerous	Level 2: Unhelpful	Level 3: Helpful
5 Problem-solving skills	Uses roadblocks (solution giving, interrogating) to direct the client's problem solving, or responds with abstract and vague statements.	Asks the client to be specific and to problem solve, but does not model this process.	Uses open questions, reflecting skills, etc., to model specific language and assist the person to problem solve.

EXERCISE 6.4

Aim — to practise the individual skills of metamodel questioning, matching sensory systems, confrontation, reframing, self-disclosure, and immediacy.

Suggestions for practice of these skills are included at the end of the description of each skill, above.

SUMMARY

There are times when simple listening is not enough to help another regain their sense of wellbeing. This chapter has explored four different ways of understanding this 'helping' situation, and suggested several verbal skills you can use to help someone change. We considered helping as (a) a step by step *use of the problem-solving process*, (b) a process of releasing blocked emotions (*catharsis*), (c) an *ethical commitment* to assist another in ways respectful of them, and (d) a *holistic process* which relinks body and mind, personal and political, and human and universal.

As was noted, each of these four models suggest particular advanced helping skills. Then, we explained the following seven skills:

1 *Questioning* the limits in the person's map of the world.
2 *Matching* the person's use of sensory systems.
3 *Confronting* the incongruity between two of the person's messages.
4 Offering new *reframes* of the person's situation.
5 *Self-disclosing* your own experiences and past responses.
6 Talking about what is happening at the moment (*immediacy*).
7 Directing the person to *speak in the here and now*.

Bibliography & Further Reading

Bolton, R. (1979) *People Skills*, Prentice Hall, Englewood Cliffs, New Jersey.

Cameron-Bandler, L. (1985) *Solutions,* Futurepace, San Rafael, California.

Carkhuff, R. and Berenson, B. (1977) *Beyond Counselling and Therapy* Holt, Rinehart and Winston, New York.

Durie, M. 'Maori Mental Health', Video, Mental Health Foundation, Auckland.

Frankl, V. (1969) *Man's Search For Meaning: An Introduction to Logotherapy*, Simon & Schuster, New York.

Freespirit, J. (1976) 'Open Letter to My Former Shrinks', in Wyckoff, H. (ed.) *Love, Therapy and Politics*, Grove Press, New York.

Frey, W.H. (1985) *Crying: The Mystery of Tears*, Winston Press, Minneapolis, Minnesota.

Greenspan, M. (1983) *A New Approach to Women and Therapy*, McGraw-Hill, New York.

Lader, M. (1975) *The Psychophysiology of Mental Illness*, Routledge and Kegan Paul, London.

Macrae, J. (1988) *Therapeutic Touch: A Practical Guide*, Alfred A. Knopf, New York.

Munro, A., Manthei, B. and Small, J. (1988) *Counselling: The Skills of Problem Solving*, Longman Paul, Auckland.

Montagu, A. (1971) *Touching*, Harper & Row, New York.

Perls, F.S. (1969) *Gestalt Therapy Verbatim*, Real People Press, Moab, Utah

The Holy Bible: Revised Standard Version (1973) Collins, New York.

PART THREE

Meeting Your Own Needs Along With Others'

CHAPTER 7
Assertive Communication

KEY CONCEPTS:

The assertiveness model

Addiction and codependence

Assertive I messages

Sources of anger

Using listening skills in assertive situations

Assertiveness

Objective: to be able to discriminate assertive, aggressive, and unassertive behaviours.

THE NEED FOR ASSERTIVE SKILLS

As a counsellor I have sometimes been called out to visit a family where communication has 'broken down'. Like an ambulance driver, perhaps, I often don't know till I get there what sort of help is needed.

In one family I visited, the woman (whom I'll call 'Kerry') had phoned out of concern about the way her husband ('Sam') dealt with their kids. 'He looses his temper', Kerry explained as the three of us sat down to talk. 'Social Welfare have warned us that if he hits our oldest girl again like he did last month, she'll be taken off us.'

Sam nodded. 'The thing is, I know what I have to stop, but I don't know what I'm supposed to do instead. It's easy for the Social Welfare people to say "Don't hit her". They don't hear how she goads me, how she hassles me.'

'You really want to change, and the question is what do you do to cope with her at those times. Tell me about what happens when she "hassles" you.'

He shrugged his shoulders. 'I guess I mainly just try and ignore her. I'll be sitting here, just like now, watching TV say, and she'll come up to me and thump me or something. I might say "Be a good girl and sit down. You don't want to get daddy mad." But honestly; it's as if she does. I take it for as long as I can, just pretending I don't notice it. And then I can't take any more. I explode. I let her have it — in words as well as hitting.'

Kerry leaned forward. 'That's right. It's not just the hitting. He calls her all the names under the sun. And I think, that can't be very good for her either. Most of what he says to her is telling her she's no good.'

A Key Skill

Already I knew a lot of ways in which this family could change, to create relationships which boosted each other's self–esteem instead of wrecking it.

But in that first hour I needed to leave Sam with something he could use. Rather than impose my own solution, I listened until he was certain *he* knew what he most wanted. It turned out that that was the ability to send what I call an assertive 'I message'. When I explained how to use this skill, Sam was elated. It was exactly what he'd been trying to find. Having never been to a counsellor or read anything about 'communication skills' before, he'd had to get to a crisis before he risked talking to me. At that stage, even I wasn't sure how much use assertive skill would be to him. He seemed a pretty down to earth, no-nonsense kind of guy, and I wondered if this new way of talking would be too 'middle class', too text-book sounding for him to really get into. Within a few minutes he'd convinced me that he was going to be an expert. As he said 'what I've been wanting is a way to get my message across, tell her what I want, but not put her down, eh! And this is it. It's fantastic!'

Most of us want exactly the same thing for our own lives. We're searching for ways to get our needs met, to express our opinions and concerns, and we don't want to hurt or humiliate those around us in the process. What's missing is often the *skill* to achieve this.

When I Own the Problem

Let's think about Sam's situation using the Problem Ownership model introduced in Chapter 4. When Sam's daughter comes up and hits him, he 'owns a problem', in the sense that it's him who is immediately annoyed. He's the one whose needs are not being met, the one who is unaccepting of the situation. In this situation, helping skills — such as we discussed in Chapters 5 and 6, won't work. Helping skill are the most effective response when someone else owns the problem, while assertive skills are the best choice when I myself own the problem. Far from just listening, which is useful when the other person owns the problem, when I own the problem I want *others* to listen to *me*. When the other person owns the problem I'll help them find solutions that suit *them*, but when I own the problem, the solution has to suit *me*.

You Messages

If it's me who owns the problem, you might expect that most of what I say will be about my concern. In fact though, many people respond to this situation by saying a whole lot of things about someone else. Look at what Sam tried. He says '(You) be a good girl and sit down', 'You don't want to get daddy mad', and 'You're just a little bitch!' All his messages are *you*

messages. They may tell his daughter she's good or she's bad, what she wants to do, or what she must do . . . but they don't say anything much about what *his* problem is. There are four main kinds of you message:
— denials: e.g. 'You don't want to get daddy mad.'
— solutions: e.g. 'Sit down!'
— judgements: e.g. 'You're just a little bitch!'
— interrogating: e.g. 'Why do you do these things?'
These are the same types of response which cause difficulty in the helping situation, when someone else owns a problem. Thomas Gordon calls them 'roadblocks'. Some roadblocks may work quite okay when no one owns a problem, but in the area where I am not happy about something, they are likely to:
— create resistance to change
— leave the other person feeling bad about themselves
— damage my relationship with the other person.
Because they are *you messages* they actually *encourage* the other person to think more about themself ('*Am* I a bad person?', Do I *have* to do this?', Why *did* I do that?') at a time when I'd like them to consider my own concerns.

Unassertive Behaviour

Denial statements and what Sam called 'pretending I don't notice it' are *unassertive* ways of behaving. They don't tell others that I'm upset, they expect others to guess what I'm upset about (an unassertive person will sometimes say 'You should *know* I was upset. I shouldn't have to tell you') or they suggest that my needs aren't as important as other people's. The likely results of unassertive behaviour are:
— the unassertive person builds up resentments until they explode
— the unassertive person becomes depressed (shutting down their feelings) or develops physical illnesses (from the stress)
— others avoid the unassertive person because they can't work out what they want
— others walk all over the unassertive person. They decide only to meet their own needs because they can't work out what the unassertive person wants.

Aggressive Behaviour

Judgements, interrogation, and solution sending (ordering), along with actions such as hitting, are *aggressive* ways of behaving. They violate others'

rights, use more force than is necessary, and suggest that others' needs are not as important as mine. The likely results of aggressive behaviour are:
— the aggressive person becomes anxious about others' resentment
— the aggressive person feels guilty about their 'overkill'
— others avoid the aggressive person because they feel abused by them.
Although unassertive and aggressive behaviour seem very different, they are really only the opposite sides of the same coin.

Both unassertive and aggressive people believe that things can't be sorted out so that *theirs and others'* needs are *both* met. Both of them think that 'someone has to lose'. Both are afraid to take the risk of discussing the matter openly. In fact many people (like Sam) swing between unassertive and aggressive and back. When they are unassertive they build up resentment which pushes them to explode aggressively. When they've been aggressive they feel guilty and resolve not to be so violent again, and so become unassertive.

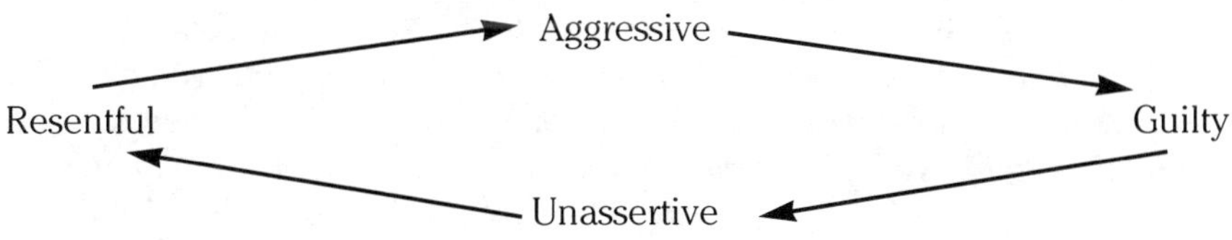

Assertive Behaviour

Being *assertive* means stepping right out of this system, expressing your own opinions and feelings in ways that don't put others *or* yourself down. Assertive messages suggest that my needs and others' needs are equally important and worth meeting. They invite others to act in ways that also respect both sets of needs. The likely results of assertive behaviour are:
— the assertive person becomes increasingly confident of their rights, and trusting of relationships
— most others are attracted to the assertive person because of the mutual respect and honesty they offer. Some others will avoid the assertive person because they are not willing to risk such relationships.
This last comment reminds us that there *is* a risk in being assertive. The risk of listening and helping skills is that you will hear what people are saying, and sometimes that may not be what you wanted to hear. The risk of assertive skills is that others will hear what you think and feel, and there are times when they may not want to. Relationships which have been unhappy but 'stable' can be destabilised when only one person learns communication skills. Of course if you learn assertive skills and then discover that one of your friends or family doesn't want to hear what you think and feel, you could just choose to stop using the skills. Mostly, though, people who learn to be assertive begin to realise that they *can* build the relationships they want, they can create the

kind of life they'd really enjoy. They then either work to change or to leave those relationships which deny this. We'll discuss that situation in Chapter 9.

Assertiveness and Whakaiti

Interestingly, the word 'assertiveness' may refer to an attitude similar to the Maori quality of 'whakaiti' (humility). Consider Tipene Yates description (quoted in Metge 1986, p. 86) of his kaumatua (elders):

> *I observed them and watched them, and they all had one thing in common, whakaiti. To me that is how these old people conducted their whole way of life. You didn't see them abusing people; you saw them talking fire, not abuse. Always they were polite and humble. But they made their points and they would not turn away from them. They would say, 'Well, I am sorry. You say this is white, I know it is black, and you are misguided.' Something nice like that in Maori.*

The Assertive Attitude

So far in this chapter, we've talked about assertive, aggressive, and unassertive ways of responding to the situation where 'I own a problem'. An assertive response in this case does what Tipene Yates suggests: it makes the point politely, neither backing down *nor* abusing the other person. We'll discuss this issue later in this chapter. The assertive attitude or state of mind (to use a term discussed in Chapter 2) can be thought of more generally. An assertive attitude is one which values my own feelings and opinions, my own needs, and also those of others. Such an attitude is 'confident' and includes a sense of 'self-esteem' (see Chapters 2 and 3). Like other states, the state of assertiveness is one you can develop using body language, visualisation, and self-affirmation. For example, assertiveness is helped if you:

1 Use postures, gestures, and voice qualities which express confidence (including (a) open hand gestures and open arm/leg positions, (b) culturally appropriate eye contact, (c) a voice with a relaxed tone and a steady delivery, loud enough to be heard, and (d) posture, gestures, and voice which are *congruent*, that is, which fit with the words you're saying).

2 Visualise situations, from your memory, in which you were relaxed and confident. Use all your senses to fully recall these times and anchor yourself

back into that sense of confidence: remember what you could see, hear, smell, feel, and even taste.

3 Tell yourself beliefs about your situation which are realistic and supportive of your assertion. This was discussed in Chapter 1 in relation to the skill of introducing yourself to someone else. People are more able to assert themselves when they believe that assertion is likely to *work*, for them and for others. This means reminding themselves of the differences between assertion, and aggression and non-assertion.

Assertive Rights

Another way of thinking about the beliefs that support assertiveness is the model of assertive rights. You will behave more assertively when you fully believe *you have the right to*:

— have and express feelings and opinions
— be different from others, and set your *own* priorities
— ask others for information or help
— say 'no' when others ask you for things, without feeling guilty
— change your mind or recognise you've made a mistake without feeling guilty
— choose not to express feelings and opinions.

Others around you also have these same rights. As you reread the above list, think about the very specific everyday rights which are a part of these six main rights. For instance, 'the right to have and express feelings and opinions' may mean in your actual daily life things such as:

— the right to tell your parents you disagree with them
— the right to say you felt insulted by a certain joke
— the right to a religious belief your friends don't share
— the right to really enjoy your favourite music.

Basic Right

Marjorie Manthei suggests that such assertive rights all spring from one basic or ultimate assertive right:

'You have the right to be the final judge of your own behaviour, thoughts and feelings. You must, however, take responsibility for them.'

Assertiveness, then, is about the right to be who you are. There's an old Jewish saying which suggests that 'You don't give glory to God by trying to be more like Moses. That was Moses job. You give glory to God by being true yourself.' Whatever the most important thing in the world is to you, this saying is likely to make sense: giving glory to that most important thing means being true to yourself.

ADDICTIVE, CODEPENDENT, AND INTEGRATED BEHAVIOUR

In the last few years, several writers have used the addiction model to explain how destructive communication happens. Charlotte Davis Kasl (1990, p. 374) points out that people who have an unmanageable desire or compulsion (whether for alcohol, for food, for sex, for power, or whatever) become increasingly concerned only for themselves and for winning. *The addict is, in that sense, aggressive.* Kasl describes addiction as often being an escape from the opposite pole of feeling empty, as if one has no self to be concerned for. This opposite pole is one she names 'codependency'. The codependent is concerned almost entirely with other people's happiness, unable to live their own life and ensure their needs get met. *The codependent, then, is unassertive.* Men's conditioning, Kasl points out, usually moves them towards the addict position, while women's conditioning usually moves them towards codependency. But both positions are based on the same sense of low self-esteem, and are interchangeable.

In her book *When Society Becomes An Addict*, Anne Wilson Schaef suggests that many of the institutions in our society are addictive systems. They require people to function as addicts (e.g. workaholics) or codependents; to be one up or one down in relation to others.

Recovery

If your aggressiveness or unassertiveness is a result of addiction/ codependency, how do you find your way to 'recovery' and what Charlotte Davis Kasl calls 'integrated behaviour'? Traditionally, organisations like Alcoholics Anonymous have recommended a series of twelve steps. Kasl says that she finds these steps themselves to be full of one up/one down assumptions. Her forthcoming book *Many Roads, One Journey: Moving Beyond The Twelve Steps* offers a reframing of these steps. Her new 'twelve steps' involve acknowledging that your addiction has been controlling you, being willing to tune in to your own inner wisdom and spirituality, examining your life and committing yourself to resolve issues in an assertive way, and sharing this understanding with others. Most of all, Kasl invites us to 'move from *re*covery to *dis*covery. Then we can break through the limitations imposed by hierarchy, work together for a just society, and free our capacity for courage, joy, power and love' (quoted in *MS* magazine, Nov/Dec 1990, p. 3).

Loving Yourself

Helping skills begin with the attitude of love for others: assertive skills are founded in the ability to love yourself (in self-esteem, to use the term we discussed in Chapter 2). To discover this ability in yourself, what I'd like you to do *right now* is to search through your memory for someone who you know loves you. This person need not be someone present in your life today; they need not even be someone who *you* love; but it is extremely important that, as you think of them, you know *they* love you. Continue checking until you've identified this person, and then read the next paragraph.

Get a picture in your mind of this person, with the kind of look that reminds you of who they are. Listen to the sound of their voice, saying the sort of thing they might say to you; remembering their particular tone of voice and way of saying things. Sense what it would be like if they were with you now, nearby. Feel the feelings which pass through you as you remember their particular personality, their idiosyncracies, all the little things that make them who they are.

And now, gently feel yourself change your position. In your imagination, float out of your body and over to the form of the person who loves you. See the altered perspective as you look back out of the eyes of that person. Hear from their ears as you now become aware of their thoughts, the thoughts that occur in the mind of someone who loves you. If you listen carefully, you will hear how *they* describe the you that is in front of them, with your particular personality, with all the little things that make you who you are. Seeing yourself, through the eyes of this person who loves you, you may notice qualities in yourself which you never saw, or which you thought of as unacceptable. And yet, seen through these eyes, understood in this person's words, you can recognise what it is that makes you loveable; what it is that enriches this other person's life just by being you. Take all the time you need, now, to look at yourself through the eyes of this person who loves you, and to hear how they would describe the unique person that is you.

Gathering this understanding, holding it deep inside you, and remembering what you have seen or heard, return to your own body, slowly, gently, respectfully. You may like to reread that first list of assertive rights and check how much more you can accept them, when you hold this new understanding (adapted from an exercise in Cameron-Bandler 1985, p. 185).

So far in this chapter we have considered the general concept of assertiveness. Assertive behaviour means expressing your own feelings and opinions in ways that don't put down either others or yourself. Assertiveness can be thought of as a *state*, with body language, feelings, and thoughts which back it up. Amongst the thoughts which back it up is a belief in your assertive rights, including the ultimate assertive right to be the final judge of your own behaviour, thoughts, and feelings. The feeling of self-love is an important basis of assertive behaviour.

Assertive behaviour can be contrasted with unassertive behaviour in which a person denies their own feelings and opinions, and aggressive behaviour in which a person overrides others' opinions and feelings. When I 'own a problem', assertive ways of talking explain my problem, while unassertive or aggressive responses tend to be 'you messages'.

EXERCISE 7.1

Aim — to assertively give and receive compliments.

1 Give the group time to prepare for this exercise by inviting each person to look around and remember what they genuinely like about each other person in the group. Whether you like someone a lot or even dislike them, there are *always* things you can genuinely appreciate. To be genuine is important in this exercise.

2 Point out that what people have done in (1) above reminds us that we cannot 'measure' how much people like us, based on how many things they say, or how long they take to find the words to compliment us. This is worth reminding yourself *as* we do this exercise.

3 Each person takes a turn being the focus of compliments. (The order may be simply the seating order, or could be decided at random.) When it is someone's turn, there should be no particular order in which other people speak, and no requirement that each person does. Note again the point made in (2) above. Until it seems like people have said what they want to say, group members give compliments to the person focused on. These could begin with statements like, 'One thing I value about you . . . ', 'I like . . . ', or 'I think it was really good the way you . . .'. Compliments are most effective when delivered *congruently* (not with a tone of voice or side comment which makes fun of or contradicts the compliment).

4 The person who is the focus can receive compliments most effectively by not denying them, and by maintaining an open, attentive body posture. Having heard the compliments, the person writes down all those comments which they can accept as being valid in some way. They may like to add their own self-compliments, describing qualities or actions not obvious to those in the group.

5 After each person has had a turn, discuss:
- — how was it to give compliments? to receive them?
- — was people's body language assertive? how could it improve?
- — what effect does this exercise have on the group?

EXERCISE 7.2

Aim — to experiment with different intensities of disagreement.

1 Have people in pairs, standing one metre away from their partner.
2 One person in each pair will say 'yes', the other will say 'no', taking turns. Begin by saying this as quietly as possible. Gradually increase the volume until both people are shouting as loud as possible.
3 Reverse roles ('yes' and 'no' swap) and repeat.
4 Discuss (in medium voices) what this was like, still in pairs:
  — was it difficult to say either word?
  — how was it to say the word quietly? loudly?
  — how was it to hear the other person's disagreement?
  — how do you usually respond to disagreement (please notice, *this* method is not being recommended).

I Messages

Objective: to be able to write and say assertive 'I messages', using reflective listening to deal with the other person's response.

Before discussing I messages, we will look at three examples.

Example 7.1
Sam has an important exam coming up in two days' time, so tonight he's set aside five hours to revise his work. He's a little uneasy when, at 6.30 pm, Eliot rings him up to tell him about the party they're having. 'Come on', Eliot urges, 'You're always wound up in that study. The exam will come and go, but your friends are here for keeps. It's about time you remembered us.'

Consider his choices, using the model of *assertive-aggressive-unassertive* from the last section. Which of the following responses fits in which of the three categories?

a 'Ah, um, well, I don't know Eliot. I may come over in an hour or so then. Don't wait up for me though: I've been feeling ill today so I might not make it.' (After an hour of study, feeling guilty, Sam leaves for the party.)

b 'Oh yeah? Well, how about you guys spare a thought for *me* once in a while. How do you think I feel stuck here with my study? You've got a lot of nerve. Get off my case Eliot.' (Slams phone down.)

c 'Well I certainly don't want to lose your friendship. I *am* studying for this exam in two days though, and if I leave the study now, I'm worried that I'm going to end up with even more pressure next year.'

Example 7.2
Marge has an arrangement that her kids will take turns doing the dishes, seeing as she cooks the meal each night. But it's now the third night in a row that they have forgotten the arrangement and gone in to watch TV for the evening instead. Seeing the dirty dishes there, she considers what to do about it. In terms of assertive, aggressive, and unassertive options, her actions might include the following (check again that you recognise which is which):

a Walking quickly into the TV room, turning off the TV and announcing 'There'll be no TV until the three of you have got into the habit of doing your jobs. You're the most ungrateful, selfish slobs a mother could ever be cursed with.'

b Walking into the TV room during an ad break, turning the TV down and explaining 'We have an agreement that you'll organise the dishes, and I feel really resentful when I end up having to remind you each night. This is the third night they haven't been done.'

c Doing the dishes and resolving not to cook anything the kids enjoy for tea the next night.

Example 7.3

Andrea and her husband John are going out to tea this Friday with some of the people from John's work. She's fairly tense about this. Last time they went out with John's workmates, John got pretty drunk, and told some rather embarrassing stories about their sex life. Andrea doesn't want to end up in another situation like that. Which is the most effective way for her to express her concern?

a Not mention the subject and encourage John gently to slow down with his drinking, hoping it won't happen again.

b Find a time when he seems able to listen and tell him 'I'd like to talk about Friday. I think I'll enjoy the dinner, but it's really important to me that I don't end up feeling embarrassed there. Last time I found some of the things you said about me hard to handle.'

c Catch John as soon as he gets back from work that day and tell him 'Your one track mind has got me all tense about this Friday dinner. So help me, if you carry on like last time, I'll walk out then and there.'

Usually, people find it easy enough to *recognise* an assertive response (such as the third of Sam's choices, the second of Marge's options, and the second of Andrea's possible actions). What people have more difficulty with is actually working out the right words to use in their own real-life situations. In this section we'll learn a simple three-step process for making up your own assertive messages, and think about how to carry on talking when the other person disagrees with your message.

I MESSAGES

Remember that assertion is about expressing your own opinions and feelings; for example telling someone when you 'own a problem' as discussed in Chapter 4. This means that assertive messages are mostly 'I messages' (to use a term coined by Thomas Gordon). Instead of focusing on what you think of the *other person*, they describe the situation you yourself are in. This includes:

— the actual *behaviours* which are a problem to you
— the concrete effects (if any) that these behaviours have on you
— *the feelings* you have about those effects, and about the behaviours.

(You don't have to 'cover up' your feelings when you use an I message. In fact, using an I message is a more *direct* way to express your feelings than a you message.)

The Behaviour

In the assertive I messages from the examples above, here are the descriptions of the *behaviours* which were a concern:
1 'I *am* studying for this exam in two days though, and if I leave the study now . . .'
2 'We have an agreement that you'll organise the dishes . . . This is the third night they haven't been done.'
3 '. . . some of the things you said about me. . .'
The important thing about describing the behaviour is to describe things that you could see, hear, or physically touch — not opinions or guesses. In the terms we discussed in Chapter 4, this means being 'sensory specific'. The dishes haven't been done is a description of a behaviour, whereas 'You kids are being ungrateful, selfish slobs' is an opinion or a guess about what goes on inside them. When you describe the behaviour you're unhappy about, check that the other person is likely to agree that those things did happen. (Probably the kids won't agree that they were 'being selfish slobs', but they can agree that 'the dishes haven't been done'.)

It's just good 'tactics' to describe behaviour this way. Otherwise you'll end up arguing about what actually happened, instead of telling the other person your problem, and getting their help.

For the same reason, avoid saying 'you never . . .' or 'you always . . . e.g. 'You never do what you've arranged', 'You always say things that embarrass me.' Those words just end you up in an argument about whether there are any times when this wasn't true.

A second set of words to avoid includes 'deliberately' and 'on purpose'. These are guesses about the other person's intention. The aim of assertiveness isn't to argue about whether your friend 'deliberately' said things that embarrassed you, or did it by accident. The aim is to get them to stop! If you're uncertain how to describe the behaviour, a simple beginning suggested by Thomas Gordon is the word 'When . . .' e.g. 'When I give up my study two days before an exam . . .', 'When the dishes don't get done . . .', 'When you tell your friends details about our sex life . . .'.

Concrete Effects

Once you've explained exactly what behaviours concern you, in this non-blameful way, the next step is to check whether the behaviour has any concrete effects on you. Does it cause you more work, cost you money, physically hurt you, and so on. Or do you believe it will cause these effects in future? Not all problems cause actual effects. Sometimes you just have feelings about it.

Probably Andrea, in the example above, doesn't have to do more work or pay more money as a result of her husband's comments about her personal life. She just *feels* embarrassed. People have just as much right to get problems solved when there isn't any concrete effect on them as when there is (these 'no-effects problems are *values conflicts* and will be discussed further in Chapter 9).

Sam, whose friend Eliot rang about the party, *is* worried about the possible concrete effects of leaving his study ('I'm going to end up with even more pressure next year'). And Marge is already experiencing concrete effects when her kids leave the dishes ('I end up having to remind you each night'). I messages which include a clear description of the concrete effect are much more likely to produce results. They help people understand exactly how their behaviour causes you a problem.

Feelings

The really *powerful* part of an I message though (and the part most easily forgotten by people learning this skill) is the feeling. Sam feels 'worried', Marge feels 'resentful', and Andrea feels 'embarrassed'. Remember from Chapter 5 that feelings are not opinions or beliefs. 'I feel that you are very mean' is *not* a description of a feeling. It's a description of a belief. Feelings can usually be described in one word (e.g. 'sad', frustrated', 'afraid', 'left-out', 'insulted'). If you can put the word 'that' in front of the word 'feel' in your sentence, you have a belief or an opinion. To discover a word for your feeling, you might ask yourself 'How does someone who gets *those* effects feel?', How does someone who experiences *that* behaviour feel?'

Using I Messages

A clear I message has three parts:

a The *behaviour* — described in a way the other person could recognise, without blaming words like 'always', 'never', or 'deliberately'.

b The concrete effects which are happening or will in future happen to you.

c The feeling you have.

Some people ask 'Shouldn't I suggest the actions I'd like the other person to take; the solution?' Our experience is that solution suggesting is only helpful when the other person resists acting because they have a problem of their own. This situation is a conflict, and we'll explore it further in the next two chapters. Suggesting solutions in your first I message runs a high risk of leaving the other person feeling cornered, insulted, and ordered about. It's as if you said 'I'm going to spell out step by step what you must do to solve my problem, because you're too dumb or too selfish to understand'.

You're quite right that often an I message won't solve your problem instantly. It's not the complete answer — that's why there are more chapters in this book. But an I message is a lot more effective way of *starting* to assert yourself than a you message. The I message:

— explains exactly what your problem is instead of leaving the other person to guess
— does not put the other person down, so protects their self-esteem
— opens discussion rather than closing it, so protects the relationship.

When to Use I Messages

I messages can be used:

a When you own a problem. When you are unhappy about some behaviour that's already happening (e.g. in Marge's case with the dishes).
b When you think you may own a problem in the future (e.g. at Andrea's dinner).
c When you want to say 'no' to a request which could cause you a problem (e.g. in Sam's study situation).

As with any skill, you will need to practise to be able to use I messages well. At first it may help you to write out your I messages and even roleplay sending them (as in Exercise 7.3) before using them. In a short time, I messages will feel more natural than you messages. You won't always need to say all three parts of the I message. Let's say you were standing in a queue and someone stood on your foot. A full I message might be:
'When you stand on my foot (behaviour) the bones get pushed into the floor (effect) and it hurts (feeling)'. In this case, you'll probably get a good response just by describing the behaviour:
'Excuse me, you're standing on my foot!' If the person looked puzzled and nodded though, I'd recommend sending the *full* message *and* moving!

Why I Messages Are Not Enough

More often than not, an assertive I message *in itself* is not enough to ensure things change. There are four basic reasons for this:

a The I message wasn't a complete I message as described above.

b The other person felt upset when they heard the I message and *their* upset didn't get listened to.
c The other person has a problem of their own: a conflict of needs.
d The other person doesn't believe their behaviour affects you: a conflict of values.

We'll discuss (c) and (d) in the next two chapters. Here we'll think about (b) how a person feels when you send them an I message. If you've ever been 'told off' or had it pointed out to you that another person is finding your behaviour a problem, you'll know that it can feel pretty uncomfortable. Remember some of the times when someone has complained to you, criticised you, or asked you to change. What did you do? You might have defended yourself, argued back, or got angry. You may have been embarrassed, gone silent, looked down more, shrugged your shoulders, cried, blushed, or even laughed nervously. Whatever you did, all these responses are clues that you 'owned a problem'. The person who complained to you started off owning a problem about some issue. When they told you; *you* owned a problem.

Listening to the Other

I messages minimise this effect, but they don't eliminate it. Send an I message to someone and they'll experience feelings such as embarrassment, anger, hurt, confusion, or even guilt. If you read Chapter 5, you already know the skills which will be useful in this situation where someone else owns a problem. They work just as well when the problem is about *your* behaviour as when it's about some outside situation:

— Attending: physically paying attention
— Minimal Encouragers: 'Ah-huh', 'Yeah', 'Mm', 'Right', and so on.
— Questions, especially open questions which begin 'how', 'what . . .', or 'tell me about . . .'
— Reflective listening: which restates the person's meaning, acknowledging the feelings, and summarising or sorting the various issues they've raised.

Using Reflective Listening After I Messages

The easiest way to respond to someone's distress, after being sent your I message, is to acknowledge it using reflective listening. Carry on using reflective listening till the other person nods, says 'yes', or otherwise tells you that they feel understood. You can then repeat your I message if need be. Here are a couple of examples:

Example 7.4

Jennifer: 'I've really enjoyed being out with you this evening Gary, and that's why I want to explain something I've been uncomfortable about. When you put your hand on my breasts, in front of other people like earlier on, I feel really embarrassed. I wanted to say then, but couldn't think how to explain it.' (I message)

Gary: 'Hey; I was only joking around. Nobody was watching anyway!'

Jennifer: 'You don't think anyone could see, and you were just kidding.' (Reflective listening) Gary nods. 'But I did feel uncomfortable.' (I message) 'It may seem silly,' (Reflective listening), 'but I find it embarrassing.' (I message)

Gary: 'Okay, I'll remember. No problem.'

Jennifer: 'Thanks.'

Example 7.5

Father: 'Tim, I get tired of picking up people's clothes so I can walk through the main room. Your shoes and socks are on the floor there now.' (I message)

Tim: 'Oh, dad!'

Father: 'It just seems a nuisance to get up right now huh.' (Reflective listening)

Tim: 'Yeah. I'll do it later.'

Father: 'I believe you mean to do it later, but I also know you forgot before' (Reflective listening — confrontation), 'and I want to make sure I don't have to step round them again.' (I message)

Tim: 'But I'm tired *now*.'

Father: 'You think I should have told you before.' (Reflective listening) Tim nods. 'But I only came across them just now. I'm also really tired, and I don't want to end up doing your work as well as mine.' (I message)

Tim: 'Well . . . Okay.'

Father: 'Great. Thanks, Tim.'

In each case, the person who is told the I message doesn't have a really strong reason to disagree (*that* would be a conflict, see next chapter). They just have an initial problem accepting the I message. When the other person listens to them, it makes it easier for them to listen as well. The assertive person has shown them the basic assumption of assertiveness: My feelings and opinions are important, and so are yours.

Using reflective listening in this way kind of 'takes the wind out of the other person's sails'. Instead of wasting your energy arguing with their feelings, you can accept them *and* still express your own concern. This works a lot better than sending a second I message about their complaint. Imagine that difficulty . . .

Father: 'Tim, I get tired of picking up people's clothes so I can walk through the main room. Your shoes and socks are on the floor there now.' (I message A)

Tim: 'Oh, dad!'
Father: 'And another thing I don't like is when I tell you about something like this and you don't listen to me. I end up wasting five minutes to get you to do a 10-second job.' (I message B)

Now this father has sent two different I messages. He's trying to solve two problems at once, and Tim is twice as upset. The chances are he'll lose at least *one* argument by being sidetracked. Reflective listening helps keep your I messages concentrated on solving the problem you wanted to solve.

What if they leave?
If the person's reaction to your I message was to leave the room, of course you won't be able to send a reflection of their feelings (which may be along the lines of 'You don't want to hear about this'). There's no magic way to stop someone leaving the room. You need to choose then: Will you try and resolve the issue later on? Will you bring up the issue of leaving the room during conflicts, later on? Or will you find some way to change your relationship with this person to protect you from their non-communication (like seeing less of them; getting help from a counsellor)?

Other Assertive Uses of Listening Skills

Because assertion means respecting others' feelings and opinions as well as your own, listening skills also have an important place in general assertive speech. If you want another person to listen to *your* problem, it makes sense to 'show them how it's done' by attending and listening when they disagree with or criticise you. In this situation, *questioning* may include checking what specifically they disagree with, as in the following examples:

Example 7.6
Employer: 'Lisa, your work just isn't up to standard.'
Lisa: 'What things do I need to improve on?'

Example 7.7
Jan: 'I didn't like those creeps you invited round the other day.'
Phillip: 'What were the things that annoyed you about them?'

The reflective listening skill of *sorting issues* may help select one issue at a time to discuss. Sometimes, when someone is upset, they offload a whole collection of problems at once, as in the following examples:

Example 7.8

Sylvia: 'Why do you always have to take the car when you go uptown? It wastes petrol. And you can bet it's me who ends up having to refill the tank when it gets low. I always end up being the one who checks on it: just like with putting out the rubbish bags.'

Bob: 'So, there are two things we need to sort out: the use of the car, and my remembering to check for the petrol, rubbish bags, and so on. Can we discuss the car use first, then come back to the other?'

Example 7.9

Mother: 'Gail I wish you'd tell me where you're going when you leave the house. Honestly! Last night you had two phone calls I had to answer. And the first time, I didn't even know you'd gone out! I went into your room looking for you. Not that I'd be able to find you if you were in there, piled high with mess like it is!'

Gail: 'Well, I know you'd like the room tidy, but the main problem is telling you where I am; Right?'

When someone criticises you, *they* own the problem. These listening skills will work best if you use them gently and with a genuine interest in understanding what that problem is. If you simply can't put aside your own feelings in response to their criticism (if *you* own a problem too) it may be more helpful to explain that in an I message.

ANGER AS A SIGNAL

When I teach groups to use I messages, I often check what words they are using to describe the *feeling* they have. In over half of all cases, their word will be 'angry' or a word meaning angry ('enraged', 'furious', 'mad', 'pissed off', 'annoyed', etc.).

Obviously anger is a very common response when someone owns a problem. In fact, Harriet Goldhor Lernor (author of *The Dance of Anger*) describes anger as '. . . a signal, and one worth listening to. Our anger may be a message that we are being hurt, that our rights are being violated, that our needs or wants are not being adequately met, or simply that something is not right.' She suggests that it is particularly important for *women* to give themselves permission to recognise and feel their anger. The force of anger, she points out, 'can motivate us to say "no" to the ways in which we are defined by others and "yes" to the dictates of our inner self.'

While feeling angry alerts us to the fact that we own a problem, and gives us the energy to do something, it does not *in itself* explain what the problem is. This is why Lerner suggests that, rather than giving vent to anger, we need to feel it and discover what the problems that cause it are.

Anger and Men

A very similar description of the importance of anger for *men* comes from two Christchurch men, Tim Williams and Ken McMaster, in their article 'Anger Management: A Course For Aggressive Men'.

They say of their courses for men that, 'The primary principle underlying many aspects of the course is that many of the outbursts of violence reported by men in our group related to them not recognising anger when it builds up, or trying to ignore anger. This latter course occurs as they have usually had violence modelled to them as the only appropriate expression of anger.'

The extra power conferred on men in our society (check the numbers of men and women in Parliament, for example) often seems to give permission to violence as a male expression of anger.

The Feelings Underneath Anger

Like Lerner, Williams and McMaster encourage their course participants to discover the feelings which underlie their anger, for example: 'Almost all the men in the group reported being particularly angry and prone to violence at times when they felt rejected.'

While rejection may underlie much of these men's anger, Lerner finds that feeling as if their individuality is denied underlies much of women's anger. Recognising the feelings which produce the anger signal means you can send even clearer, more concrete I messages.

Let's say you've arrived late for your class or course. The tutor sends you an I message: 'I feel really angry when you arrive so late.' The message tells you about the *force* of her feeling, but it doesn't actually tell you *what* she feels. Compare it with an I message explaining 'I feel really worried about whether I'm going to get through the material when we start so late' or 'I'm getting very frustrated with having to stop and start so often'. It's easier to want to help someone who is 'worried' or 'frustrated' than someone who is 'angry' because (a) you know more about what's causing their problem, (b) you can hear the feelings as inside them rather than 'about' you.

A father who has trouble with his kids running round the supermarket while he's shopping will get a better response by explaining 'I feel embarrassed about the people staring at me', rather than 'I feel angry at your running'.

The Volcano Model

Christchurch counsellor Bryan Royds suggests that anger can be thought of as the top hole in a volcano. Usually the volcano has side vents and when pressure builds up lava runs out these side holes — holes like frustration (the feeling of being blocked), fear, embarrassment, resentment (the feeling of doing more than a fair share), pressure, rejection, and powerlessness. When these feelings aren't permitted (when your upbringing closes off those vents), the force which was behind those feelings doesn't just go away. It builds up and finally explodes out the top. Someone who is constantly angry needs to re-open the other vents so more appropriate feelings can be expressed. This is what I messages do. They take the pressure off the system, leaving more time to *enjoy* life.

▶ *Healthy system*

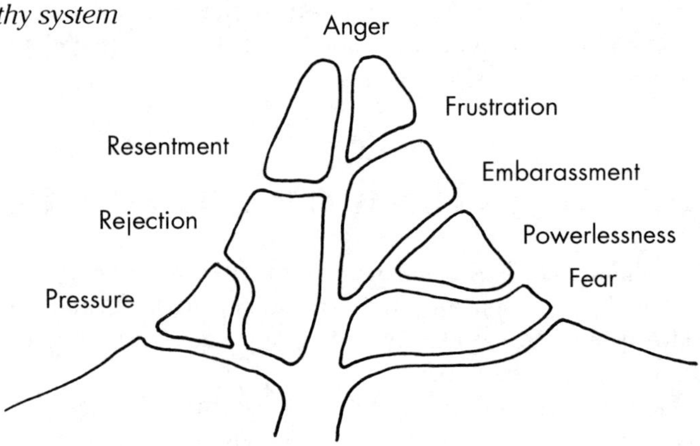

▶ *Blocked system*

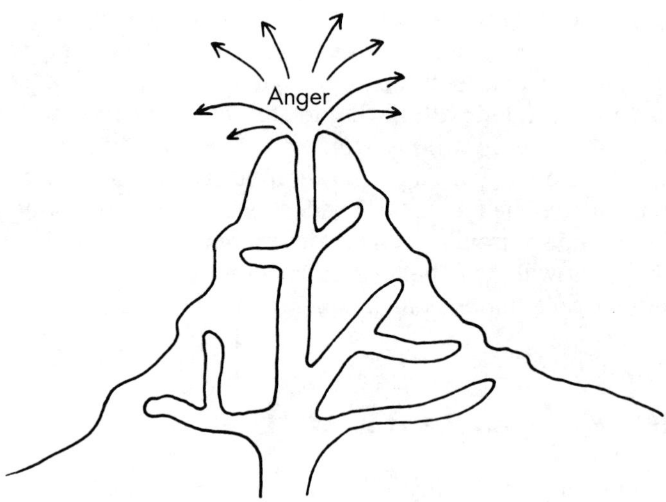

Agreeing and Other 'Protective' Skills

There is a difference of opinion between assertiveness training instructors about some skills. These skills are referred to as 'protective' skills by Marjorie Manthei — who recommends their use in situations where your aim is not to express your opinion but to protect yourself from someone else. They include:

— agreeing with the other person's criticism verbally or saying that they may be correct, when you actually disagree.

— repeating your I message continuously without listening to the other person's concern. This is *sometimes* the result of using the 'broken record' skill, though in Marjorie Manthei's own examples (see Manthei 1981, p. 54) she uses reflective listening, as we described above.

— selective ignoring of issues you don't want to discuss.

While these skills *may* at times protect people, my own experience is that the anger they generate may just as easily endanger people. It is for this reason that other sources (such as Arthur Lange and Patricia Jakubowski) do not recommend their use.

Using I Messages to Compliment Others

So far, we've talked about I messages as a skill to use when you own a problem, or think you may soon own a problem. Expressing yourself in an I message is also an excellent way to tell someone what you appreciate about them. This makes your praise or compliment easier for the other person to accept, and so reduces the chance of the following confusion:

Nurse: 'You're doing really well with those crutches Mr Smith.'

Mr Smith: 'Not really. I can't seem to do it the way the physiotherapist showed us.'

Nurse: 'No, you are. You've only just started. You're going great!'

Mr Smith: 'Rubbish. I've never been any good at these sorts of things. It's no use pretending.'

Nurse: 'Don't be so negative.'

Mr Smith: 'Don't be so bloody pushy!'

Lets try it again using *I* messages and reflective listening, instead of *you* messages.

Nurse: 'I'm impressed with how quickly you're getting around the ward on those crutches Mr Smith.' (I message)

Mr Smith: 'Well, I get around, but not the way the physiotherapist showed us.'
Nurse: 'You think you're doing it the wrong way?' (Reflective listening)
Mr Smith: 'Well, I think I'm doing it correctly, but I'm a bit clumsy with them. The physio made it look rather easier.'
Nurse: 'Compared with her you're not so fluent, eh.' (Reflective listening) 'Well, as I say, *I'm* impressed.' (I message)
Mr Smith: 'Oh well. Maybe I'm not doing so bad then.'

The Power of I Messages

A good I message is difficult to argue with. Mr Smith is able to hear the nurse's comment as a fact about her. It becomes easier for him to feel good about himself when her compliment isn't a you-message judgement. Every parent who has tried to praise a child's painting can understand how much safer it would be to say 'I love the blues and greens in your picture' than 'What a good painter you are'. I messages are powerful. It's more powerful to say 'I love you' than to say 'You're loveable'. 'You're loveable' is a mere judgement. 'I love you' is a personal revelation. Positive I messages can be written using the same format as ones about a problem: Behaviour, concrete effects and feelings. For example:
— 'When you do the dishes without being asked, I feel really cared about. It means I can relax for the evening.'
— 'Thanks for getting your work in to me on time. It meant I was able to finish my part of the job without any rush. I enjoyed doing it more and I think I did better work.'
— 'I really appreciated the way you listened to me when we had that argument. It felt like our friendship was safe, even though we disagreed.'

Whether you use them to express your appreciation, to tell someone a problem you are experiencing, or to explain a problem which you want to avoid, I messages are an ideal first step in assertiveness. An I message may have three parts:
— a non-blameful description of the *behaviours* and events involved
— an explanation of any real concrete *effects* on you
— a naming of the *feeling* you have about these behaviours, events, or effects. If this feeling is anger, it can help to identify the other feelings which underlie this anger.

When another person has a problem as a result of what you do or say (for example, when someone criticises you, or when a person 'resists' your I message) listening skills can be used. The person's feelings can be acknowledged using reflective listening, before you restate your I message. At times you may use the reflective skill of sorting issues, or ask a question, to clarify the other person's problem.

EXERCISE 7.3

Aim — to practise writing I messages.

Write an I message you could send in each of the following situations. Check your answers in pairs and ensure they fit the definition of an I message, given in the previous pages. Discuss what the other person's likely reaction to your I message would be. Write a reflective listening response you could make to that reaction.
Report back to the group.

1 Your flatmate has the stereo up loud enough so that you find it hard to concentrate on the study you're doing in your room.

2 Your 8-year-old daughter borrows your hammer and leaves it out in the rain. When you eventually find it a week later it is already rusty.

3 You are a nurse and observe a fellow nurse changing a patient's dressing without washing her hands before, thus risking infection. (Note that there may be no concrete effects on you in this situation.)

4 You are working in a psychiatric unit and one of the clients there has been interrupting your staff meeting every five minutes, to ask about their medication, check whether their relatives have rung, and find out if you've finished yet.

5 A client of yours arranges an appointment for 4 pm, the time you usually leave work. You wait for half an hour and then realise he's not coming. The next day he rings to ask for another 4 pm appointment, without mentioning the previous day.

6 Your family has one car and you are hoping to be able to use it this Saturday evening to go out to a friend's place for the evening. You want to tell your spouse, to ensure he/she doesn't have other plans.

7 You plan to watch live TV coverage of a sport's game at 3.30 pm today and want to advise the rest of the household so others don't interrupt you.

8 When you arrive home from work you find that one of the others in your household has rescued all the clothes you had out on the clothesline, from an afternoon downpour. She/he has folded them ready to be put away. You plan to thank him/her.

9 You are writing to thank a work colleague of yours. She wrote excellent notes explaining what phonecalls you received during your two days off work earlier this week.

EXERCISE 7.4

Aim — to practise saying I messages.

1 Think of a recent situation where you owned a problem about someone else's behaviour (e.g. a friend, a relative, someone you met in the course of your work.). Work out a non-blameful description of the behaviour, the concrete effects on you (if any) and the feelings you had. Write an I message you could send if that situation occurred again.
2 Check your I messages in pairs, and ensure they fit the earlier definition of an I message. Discuss what the other person's likely reaction to your I message would be (assume for now that they stay in the room). Write down a reflective listening response you could make to that. Check your responses in pairs to ensure you have used reflective listening and not a roadblock (see this chapter p. 158 for the definition of a roadblock).
3 Practise, in your pair, sending the I message, hearing the other person's response, and using reflective listening. Continue using *only* these two types of response for a few minutes and check how it goes. Initially, have your partner role play the person you're sending the I message to, while you act as yourself. If you find your partner's role playing less convincing, reverse the roles so that your partner plays you, and you act as the person you have the concern with.
4 Discuss in a group how these roleplays went. You should have reached one of three conclusions:
   a agreement that the person will change.
   b a conflict of values: the person doesn't believe their behaviour has any concrete effect on you. They think it's 'not your business'.
   c a conflict of needs: each of you has a problem. They don't want to change because it creates a new problem for them.

EXERCISE 7.5

Aim — to rediscover the side vents on your 'Anger volcano'.

1 Individually write answers to the following questions:
   a What situations do you most often get angry in?
   b Who do you most often get angry at?
   c What body feelings do you have when you are angry?
   d What do you say to yourself when you are angry?
   e What images flash through your mind when you're angry?
   f What ways do you act when you're angry?
   g Considering all your answers to the above questions, what *other* feelings is your anger related to, further down in the 'volcano'.
2 Discuss in pairs the answer to question (g) and check what else you learned doing this exercise.

SUMMARY

It's exciting to realise that you can express your own feeling and opinions in ways that don't put down either others *or* yourself. In this chapter you've learned the skills that go with this *assertive attitude.* They begin with acknowledging your own assertive rights and learning to love yourself. This includes recognising inside yourself the *feelings that underlie anger* (such as hurt, fear, frustration, and powerlessness), so they can be more directly expressed. It includes giving up the *codependent* concern entirely with others' happiness and the *addictive* compulsion for only one's own 'fix'. The concrete expression of the assertive attitude is the use of non-blaming I messages to express your opinions and feelings. In dealing with others who own a problem about your behaviour (such as people who are upset by an I message you've sent), the most useful assertive response is to *use listening skills.* Reflective listening and open questions not only help the other person feel understood in the assertive situation, they also make it easier for them to listen to you and change.

Bibliography & Further Reading

Bolton, R. (1979) *People Skills*, Prentice-Hall, Englewood Cliffs, New Jersey.

Cameron-Bandler, L. (1985) *Solutions*, Futurepace, San Rafael, California.

Kasl, C.D. (1990) *Women, Sex and Addiction*, Mandarin, London.

Kasl, C.D. (in press) *Many Roads, One Journey: Moving Beyond The Twelve Steps*, Harper and Row, San Fransisco.

Lange, A.J. and Jakubowski, P. (1978) *Responsible Assertive Behaviour*, Research Press, Champaign, Illinois.

Lerner, H.G. (1985) *The Dance of Anger*, Harper & Row, New York.

Manthei, M. (1981) *Positively Me*, Methuen, Auckland.

Metge, J. (1986) *In and Out of Touch*, Victoria University Press, Wellington.

Schaef, A.W. (1988) When *Society Becomes An Addict*, Harper and Row, San Fransisco.

Williams, T. and McMaster, M. (1984) 'Anger Management: A Course for Aggressive Men', in *New Zealand Social Work Journal*, vol. 9, no 2, pp. 2–7.

CHAPTER 8
Resolving Conflict

KEY CONCEPTS:

Recognising three types of conflict

Conflict prevention: environment and communication style

Effects of using power over others

Win-win conflict resolution skills

Resolving internal conflicts

What is Conflict?

Objective: to be able to distinguish conflicts of needs from conflicts of values, and identify two main methods of preventing conflicts.

CONFLICT

Whenever I ask people why they've come to one of our communication skill courses, 90 per cent of the answers will concern conflict. You don't have to look far internationally to realise that resolving conflict is the single most important *social* challenge of our age. For me, teaching conflict resolution is a delight. The skills that help people resolve conflicts are easy to understand and learning them always produces a kind of 'aha' experience. 'So that's how it all fits together' is a common comment, as people realise that the skills we've studied so far (especially reflective listening, I messages, and problem solving) are the *ingredients* for this next process. Once you've learned to use those skills as taught in Chapters 4, 5, and 7, this chapter will give you the most crucial step to successful relationships.

Simply stated, a conflict is a situation where two or more people each 'own a problem' about the same situation. Usually, as one of them tries to solve their problem, it creates a problem for the other, so each resists accepting the other's solution. You want to go shopping but your 3-year-old daughter wants to stay and watch TV. You want to wear some new shoes up town and your best friend says she won't be seen in public with someone wearing that colour. You're trying to study and the people in the house next door are having a party. You think your spouse should spend more time with you but he or she wants more space to be alone. You and a friend want to watch different TV channels and there's only one TV set.

Types of Conflict

Interestingly, all conflicts fit into one of the three following categories:
— closed communication loops
— conflicts of needs
— conflicts of values.

The simplest to resolve are closed communication loops, which are 'misunderstandings' that result when people forget to use I messages and reflective listening. We'll discuss them later in this very section. Sometimes, even though you've sent a clear I message and listened fully to the other person's response, there is still a disagreement.

That could be because the other person doesn't believe your complaint is any of your business. They don't think you have a 'real' problem at all. An example would be if you told your partner you wanted him or her to change hair styles. Probably your partner would suspect that their hairstyle really had *no concrete effect* on you and was 'none of your business'. This situation is a conflict of values. At least one of the people in a conflict of values does not believe the other person is concretely affected (even though you may be convinced that your partner's hairstyle gives you serious headaches, if *they* don't believe it, it's a values issue). Such conflicts include disagreements about religion, sexual activity, clothing styles, use of language, and standards of behaviour. We will discuss conflicts of values in Chapter 9.

The other kind of conflict — conflict of needs — happens more often and is usually easier to solve. In a conflict of needs, each person can understand that the other is affected by the situation. But it seems as if when one of them gets their way, the other will lose out. You and your partner each wanting to watch a different channel on the one TV is a conflict of needs.

The following examples are likely to fit in each category:

Conflict of needs	**Conflict of values**
You want to go shopping but your 3-year-old wants to watch TV.	You think your spouse should spend more time with you, but he or she wants more space.
You're trying to study and the people next door are having a party.	You think one of your work colleagues needs to be more polite with clients: they disagree.
Both you and your best friend are wanting to use the same library text book to study for an exam.	You don't want your children to swear but they enjoy it.

Conflicts of needs are the main subject of this chapter and will be fully discussed, in the section 'Conflict Resolution' (see p. 197).

Preventing Conflict — the Environment

Most people would agree that the very best way to sort out *any* conflict is not to create it. In fact, there are two main ways we can prevent conflicts. We can change the environment, or we can change our communication. Thomas Gordon and Linda Adams have developed a very simple way of thinking up new ideas for changing the environment. They say that conflicts can be prevented by:

— *adding* things to the environment
— *removing* things from the environment
— *reorganising* the environment
— *planning* better use of time in the environment.

Take the average home. Depending on what the common sources of conflict there have been: *Adding* might include inviting people to tea, doing a project together, adding a room, or getting foldaway furniture to create more space. *Removing* means things such as agreeing on rooms where food won't be eaten, turning off radios and TV, using headphones to listen to music, and giving away unused furniture. *Reorganising* could involve rearranging furniture to provide useful room areas, changing tea time to fit in with people's other interests, keeping a list of phone numbers by the phone, sorting the books on the bookshelf. *Planning* may include writing important dates on the calendar, precooking some meals and keeping them in the freezer for emergencies, and prewarning others when you are planning to go out for the evening.

All these ideas reduce the chance that people will have conflicts of needs. When a group begins its time together by working out a contract (discussed in Chapter 1) it is changing the environment to reduce conflicts. Understandings about confidentiality, starting times, and so on are important ways of planning ahead to prevent disagreement.

A Communication Model

So far, all the communication skills we've discussed in this book are important ways of preventing conflicts. Many disagreements are the result of people not expressing themselves in assertive *I messages*, or not listening fully to others and checking their understanding with *reflective listening*. The following diagram was developed by Claude Shannon and Warren Weaver to explain how such misunderstandings happen.

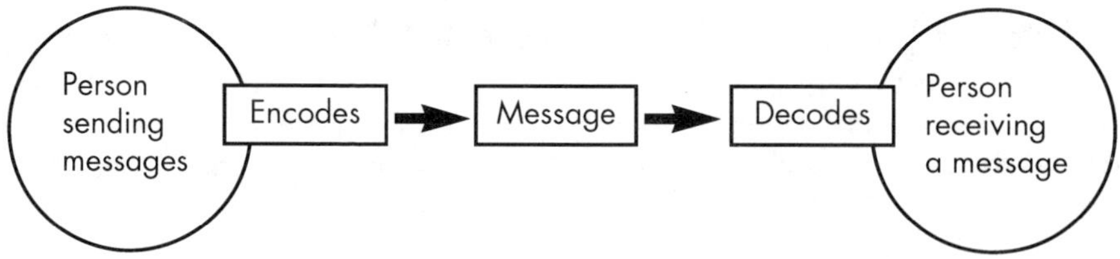

When one person sends a message to another, as this diagram shows, the person sending the message (represented as the circle on the left) has to 'encode' their thoughts and feelings. They have to find some *words* or actions that will be a *code* for their meaning. The person receiving the message (in the circle on the right) can't read their mind; they have to 'decode' the words or actions to understand what was meant. In the following example, a person who feels hungry asks the person cooking, 'When is tea?' The words are their code. The receiver has to decode this to understand what was meant.

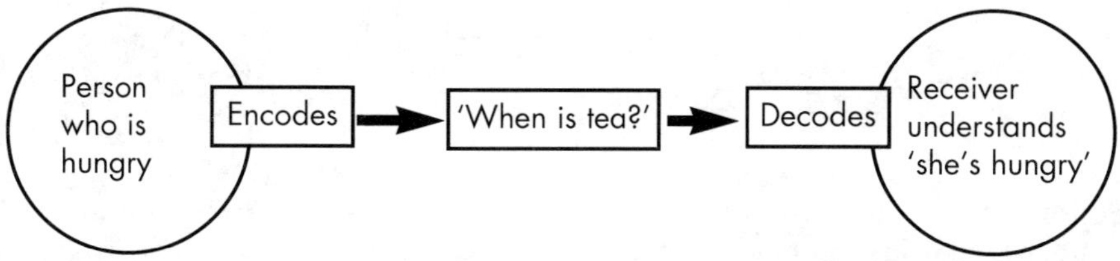

But what if the receiver decodes wrongly? Perhaps this receiver can remember another time when someone asked 'When is tea' and *that* person was angry about tea being late. The receiver might well now decode *this* message as meaning that the sender is angry. After all, 'When is tea' is not a very clear code for this message. 'I'm hungry' (an *I message*) is a clearer code. A smart receiver could also check that they got the right message, by using *reflective listening*, for example:

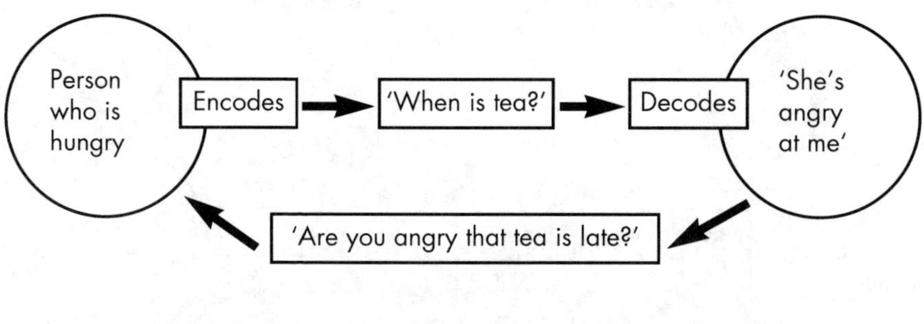

This will help the sender know whether they've been understood. The sender's next coded message will then be a clearer 'I message' code (e.g. 'No, I'm just hungry, and that sure smells good!'). Reflective listening encourages clear I messages.

Closed Communication Loops

What happens when nobody bothers to send clear I messages and nobody checks their understanding using reflective listening? Messages go back and forward, and each person *thinks* they know what is happening.

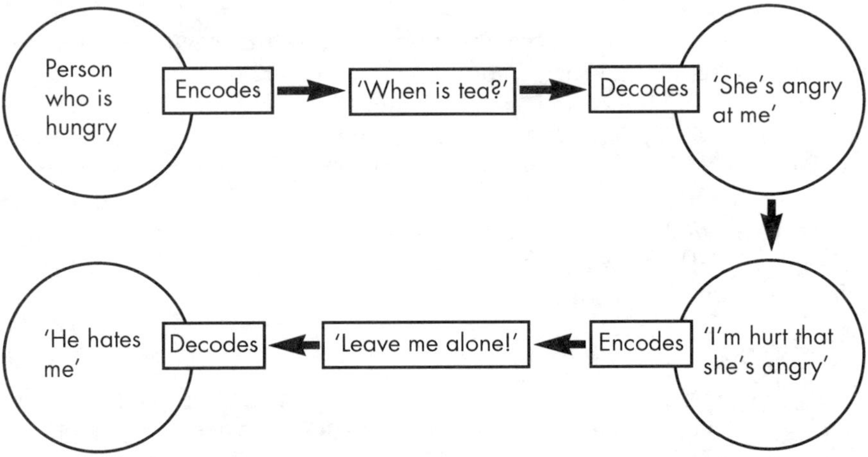

Following the diagram above, the person who was only hungry ends up believing that the other hates them. She might well then storm out of the kitchen slamming the door. This will 'prove' to the cook that she *was* angry all the time. When the cook avoids the other person later that evening, this will 'prove' to the questioner that the cook really *does* hate her.

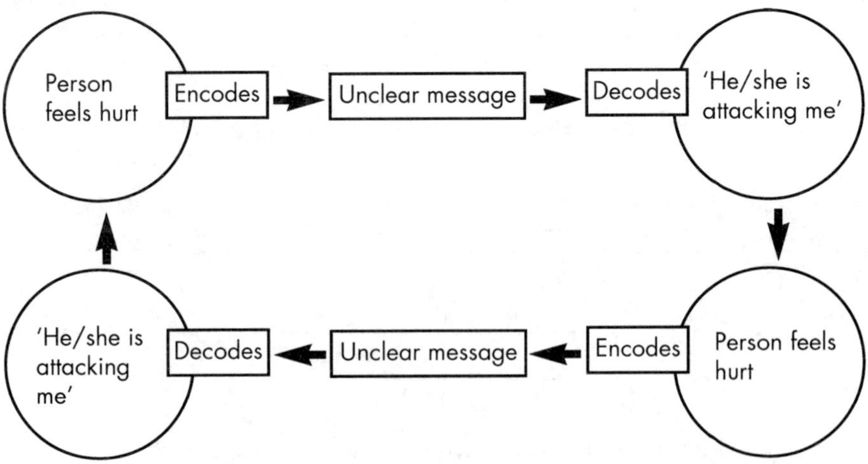

This is a closed communication loop. Sometimes the unclear message is not even sent in words. It may be just the way the person raises their eyebrows, looks away, frowns, or sighs that is decoded 'he/she is attacking me'. In Chapter 3, we discussed several examples of closed communication loops based on body language. Probably, if you think carefully over your own relationships, you can recognise this sort of misunderstanding. When I counsel couples, most of what I do involves helping them identify such loops. The solutions are very simple. Whenever a person feels hurt or 'under attack' they need to check carefully what the message was, in sensory specific terms (what did they *see, hear,* or *touch* that they decoded as an attack). They can then use reflective listening and I messages to 'open up' the communication loop.

EXERCISE 8.1

Aim — to use Gordon and Adams' model for Modifying the Environment to Prevent Conflicts.

1 Choose an environment all group members are familiar with (e.g. a workplace they all will work in, the environment the group meets in).
2 Each person individually lists ideas for ways to modify that environment, under the headings (a) Adding, (b) Removing, (c) Reorganising, (d) Planning.
3 Collect the ideas on a whiteboard or newsprint sheet.

A conflict occurs when two or more people 'own a problem' about the same situation. This may be:
1 A closed communication loop, where reflective listening and I messages will clarify the situation.
2 A conflict of needs, where each person can understand that the other owns a problem, but fears that if one gets their way, the other will lose.
3 A conflict of values, where one person doesn't believe their behaviour concretely affects the other.

Conflicts can be prevented by:
1 Changing the environment (adding, removing, reorganising, and planning)
2 Using I messages and reflective listening.

Power Over Others

Objective: to be able to describe the three basic effects of solving conflicts by using power over others.

OBEDIENCE

A psychology experiment is taking place in a central city building (this could be in a New Zealand city: the experiment has been repeated in several western countries).

In one room a man sits strapped to a chair, with an electric wire attached to his wrist. He is memorising a list of words and has been told that when he makes a mistake he will be given an electric shock. In the next room sits the 'teacher' at a control panel. He/she (the experiment has been done with both men and women) has come to these rooms in response to a newspaper advertisement. The teacher has been told that this is a study in the use of punishment. Beside her/him stands a lab technician psychologist in a grey technician's coat, who says when to give the electric shocks.

They can see the man strapped to the chair through a one-way mirror. As the experiment goes on, the psychologist instructs the hired teacher to give heavier and heavier electric shocks. They turn up the dial to a level which is marked 'Danger — Severe Shock, 330 Volts'. As the shocks become more severe the man strapped to the chair says he wants to stop. He begins to beg to be let out. He explains that he has a heart condition. Finally, he appears capable only of emitting agonised screams, and then he is silent.

The psychologist does not threaten the teacher in any way, but he calmly insists that 'It is absolutely essential that you continue the experiment . . .'.

Obedience Is *Not* A Virtue

Actually, the person strapped to the chair is a trained actor, and he is not receiving any shocks. The real aim of this disturbing experiment is to find out how long the hired teacher will continue giving what he/she believes are severe shocks. How many people, in this situation, would obey the psychologist's orders and 'murder' the man in the chair? Stanley Milgram, who ran this experiment, asked psychiatrists how many people they thought would obediently kill in this way. 'One in a thousand', they told him. The true answer was always over 60 per cent. *Most* people in our society are obedient enough to make excellent Nazi concentration camp commanders. The horrific behaviour we witness in war could be done by most 'normal' human beings. Milgram's teachers often told the psychologist they wanted to stop, trembled, stuttered, laughed nervously or groaned . . . but they went right on pressing the button. One said afterwards 'I believe I conducted myself behaving obediently, and carried on instructions as I always do. So I said to my wife "Well, here we are. And I think I did a good job." She said "Suppose the man was dead?"' (the man replied) . . . 'So he's dead. I did my job!' (from Milgram, 1974).

Obedience is *not* a virtue. Obedience means giving over to someone else's control every virtue you might otherwise have. Obedience is the death of virtue.

EFFECTS OF POWER OVER OTHERS

The word power can be used to refer to energy or 'personal power'. In that sense *everyone* can become powerful without endangering anyone else. But power over others is a different matter. Power over others refers to the *ability* to reward and punish, to meet someone's needs, or not to meet them. It is the ability to create obedience. We all have a certain amount of this power too. Most of us know ways we could reward or punish our friends if we really wanted to. When we choose to *use* that power, though, the risks are horrendous.

Power over others is what Anne Wilson Schaeff calls a key part of the White Male System. In many of our organisations power over others is routinely used as a way of dealing with conflicts. It so happens that most of these power holders are white and male. They are also often middle-aged, wealthy, able bodied, and heterosexual. But power over others can be, and is, used by people of every description. What happens when a person with power over you uses that power to get you to do what they want? Some people have a belief that being ordered around 'never did me any harm!' However, it's different when, in our communication classes, we ask people to remember a *specific* time when someone else coerced them by using rewards or punishment. They may recall a time when a teacher, police officer, parent, government official, boss, spouse, or friend used power over them. As they think back over exactly what they heard and saw, remember how they felt, and check what they did in response to this situation (e.g. how they behaved with that powerful person in following situations) . . .

they remember that needs and feelings don't simply disappear because someone else won the battle. Their reactions fit into three categories:

1 *Fight reactions*: such as arguing, paying back later on, taking it out on others, ganging up with others, and feeling angry.
2 *Flight reactions*: such as lying, hiding feelings, cheating, and withdrawing into themselves.
3 *Obedience*: which includes conforming to the rules without thinking about it any more, avoiding taking the initiative, and 'greasing up' or 'crawling' to the person in power to try and get in their good books.

Punishment

When they want to stop someone doing something, one obvious and 'easy' way that occurs to people is to punish. At times this achieves the result, and certainly it often makes the punisher feel better because they got their feelings out (though more often the punisher feels guilty that they have caused pain). But what results does it have for the person who is punished?

Since the 1940s an enormous number of studies have checked the actual effect of punishment. The most important fact, confirmed again and again, is that punishment produces feelings of anger (although these feelings may be hidden), and this anger is often expressed as aggression. Increased violence is the most guaranteed effect of *physical* punishments in particular. Research also shows that people who are punished will do everything possible to avoid contact with the person whom they see as punishing — everything from avoiding answering questions, or sulking, to running away physically. The 'lesson' that punishment teaches most effectively is that others are powerful and can hurt us (Ritchie and Ritchie 1981, p. 54.5).

Rewards

We know from research, of course, that rewards are more successful in achieving obedience than punishment. But people who use such rewards need to be aware of how limited the success of even this method is. Research shows that people who are paid for playing with enjoyable puzzles soon play *less* with the puzzles than people who play without being paid. Children promised a reward for using a particular toy find they want to use it less. Social psychologist David Myers (1983, p. 66) explains that when rewards are overused 'as happens in classrooms where teachers dictate behaviour and use rewards to control the children — child-driven learning may diminish .... My younger son eagerly consumed six or eight library books a week — until our library started a reading club which promised a party to those who read ten books in three months. Three weeks later he began checking out only one or two books during our weekly visit. Why? "Because you only need to read ten books, you know".'

This doesn't mean it's wrong to praise people or give presents; simply that using this as a technique to control them will — at best — produce obedience, *not* enthusiasm.

THE POWER USER

Power is not even very pleasant for the person who uses it. We have worked with hundreds of men, parents, teachers, bosses, and others who use power in their relationships. *All* of them come to recognise the fact that their use of power is building resentment in others. They often feel guilty about the threats and punishments they use, and resent the constant struggle to stay on top. 'But what can I do,' they explain, 'I can't just let the other person win. I *have* to use power.' This may be true. Even recognising the damage which using power over others causes, you may decide it's worth it. We'll discuss that situation in a moment.

The saddest thing about the use of power over others is that usually it simply isn't necessary. In most conflicts you can use the skills we explain in this chapter and the next to resolve your conflicts so both you *and* the other person win. Neither the authoritarian 'I win — you lose' style, nor the permissive 'you win — I lose' method is worth making a way of life.

When Is Power Necessary?

In the real world there *are* some situations where you will try and control another person's behaviour by using power. Thomas Gordon suggests that these situations could include:

- Situations where you don't have the say over what the rule is. If you work for a company you won't be able to negotiate solutions that give away their property. If you are a teacher you won't be able to arrange for someone to break a school rule. (You can, of course, work to change such rules.)
- Situations where your own need is overriding. You don't, for instance, have to put up with a child repeatedly hitting you; forcibly preventing them may well be worth their response of frustration or resentment.
- Situations where it seems to you that another person is obviously in danger. It wouldn't make sense to calmly watch someone walk in front of a speeding car, while sending the clear I message 'I'm really worried that that car will hit you!' Mostly their initial annoyance, at being grabbed and pulled off the road, will be worth coping with.

— Situations where there is no time to discuss the matter. If you have a conflict arise ten minutes before your plane is due to take off, you may decide it's worth temporarily refusing to sort it out.
— Situations where talking with the person is impossible. This will include many conflicts involving children less than two years old, and conflicts with people who are drunk or fully unconnected to reality.

Minimising the Effects

Even in these cases, it's worth remembering the damage power over others causes. You can reduce the damage to your relationship by:
— Only using the minimum force to solve your problem. A child who is hitting you may need to be held, or even confined to a space away from you, until they can agree not to hit you; but they don't need to be hit themselves (which is much the same behaviour you're trying to stop), yelled insults at, shut in their room for the afternoon, and so on. Doing these extra things is increasing their resentment and making more work for yourself.
— Explaining, afterwards, how you came to use power, and assuring the other person that this is not your usual intention.
— Using reflective listening to acknowledge their resentment, and spending time rebuilding your relationship.
— Planning how to avoid that situation in future.
These last three steps could be done quite simply, as in this example: 'I'd like to talk about what happened before. I don't mean to push you around, and only did that because I couldn't find a way to safely sort it out at the time. I guess you felt pretty annoyed, and I'd like to try and sort out some agreement, so we don't get into that situation again.'

When you use power over others, that is, your ability to reward or punish them, they will respond either by fighting back, flight and avoidance, or the shutting down we call obedience. You yourself are likely to feel resented by them and frustrated with the constant struggle.

It may be necessary to use power over others, when:
— there is a rule outside your control
— your own need is overriding
— the other person is clearly in danger
— there is no time for discussion
— talking with the person is impossible.
In such cases you can use the minimum force necessary, and discuss the event afterwards using I messages and reflective listening.

EXERCISE 8.2

Aim — to recognise our personal style of responding to the use of power.

1 Use the relaxation exercise (Exercise 2.3) or some similar process to enable course participants to relax.
2 Have them recall an incident from their adult life where someone used power (the ability to reward or punish) to get them to do what that person wanted. This could be a teacher, a parent, a boss, a spouse, a friend, or a person in a position of authority in some agency. Such events come in big as well as small sizes, so remind group members that they can choose an incident which feels safe to remember, and that, if some other incident intrudes, they will be able to 'place' the unwanted incident in a box beside them, lock it in, and move the box far enough away so they can feel comfortable and find a more useful example.
3 Have people recall in detail the events of this incident, what time of day, what the air temperature was, what surroundings they were in, whether they were sitting or standing as events happened. They can rerun the story like a video film, listening to how they and others talk, and watching what happens.

Then (after about a two-minute pause) have them check how they felt about these events . . . and what things they did then or later as a result.
4 Remind people to return to the room they are in, aware of their surroundings and able to recall the effects of the use of power on them. Have people discuss these in pairs.
5 Report back to the group. The group leader could list people's responses under the three headings 'Fight', 'Flight', and 'Obedience'.

EXERCISE 8.3

Aim — to experience non-verbally our own reaction to the use of power.

1 Clear the room of desks and chairs, so that two opposite walls are also free of obstructions.
2 Group members get into pairs and stand along one of the clear walls. One person is going to be the power user, while the other is to be pushed. Once pairs have chosen their roles, check if the power user is obviously physically stronger. If so, go on to step 3. If not, the pushed person will need to 'handicap' themselves by holding one or two hands behind their back (or even by hopping on one leg if the power user is considerably weaker).
3 The power user now uses their strength to physically push the pushed person to the other side of the room. The pushed person should resist this as strongly as they can (but, because of the handicapping or their lesser strength, will be pushed across the room).
4 Reverse roles and repeat steps 2 and 3.
5 Discuss in pairs what it felt like to be in each role:
   — did you find it difficult to force someone else?
   — did you find it difficult to accept being pushed?
   — was one or other of the roles an enjoyable one for you?
   — is this similar to, or different from your usual way of behaving?
6 Report back to the group.

Conflict Resolution

Objective: to be able to resolve internal and interpersonal conflicts of needs, using win-win problem solving.

WIN-WIN SOLUTIONS

Conflicts of needs are inevitable in any relationship. They happen between people who work together, between workers and their clients, between friends, between relatives, between lovers. But it *isn't* inevitable that someone will lose in such conflicts. Here you'll learn the key to creating caring relationships where everyone wins. In a conflict of needs, two people have each developed a plan to meet their need or solve some problem, and the plans don't fit together. Let's say I plan to use our family car this Saturday night, to go out to a sports club meeting. When I tell my partner, my partner says he or she also planned to use the car this Saturday night (to go over and visit a friend). Obviously we can't *both* use the car for the whole evening.

In such a situation, most people don't despair. They realise that what really counts is that I get to my sports club meeting, and my partner gets to visit their friend. Using the car for the night is just the particular plan, the particular solution each of us thought up to achieve these more basic goals (or meet these more basic needs, to use other words: the word 'need' here simply means a *basic* 'want', or goal).

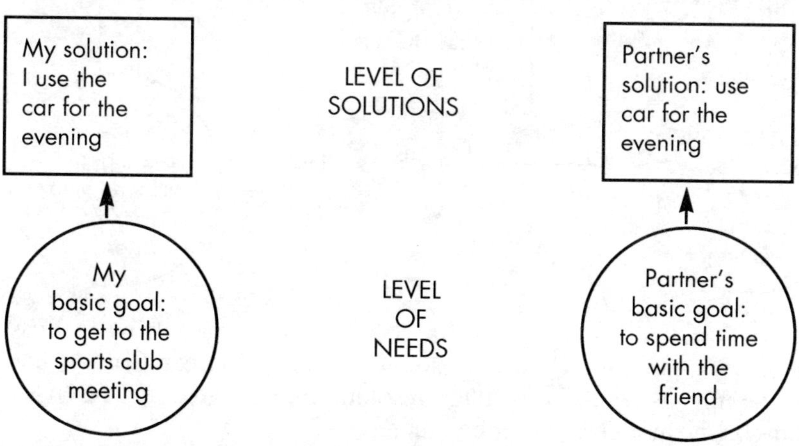

Once we realise this, we can invent several solutions which will fully meet *both* our basic goals. For example:

1. I drive my partner to the friends and pick them up after the meeting.
2. My partner drives me to the meeting and picks me up after their visit.
3. I use the car and my partner's friend visits at our place.
4. My partner uses the car and we arrange the meeting at our place.
5. Someone else picks me up on the way to the meeting and my partner uses the car.
6. My partner's friend picks them up and I use the car.
7. One of us gets a taxi and we share the taxi fare, while the other uses the car.

No Compromising

None of these solutions is a compromise, in the sense that none of them results in one of us giving up any of our basic goal. And none of these solutions is a win-lose solution where one of us uses our power to win at the other's expense. (A compromise might be: I go to the first half of the meeting, and my partner goes for the last half of the evening — we both give up a little. Compromises are the result of talking at the level of *solutions*. Win-win conflict resolution results from talking at the level of needs.)

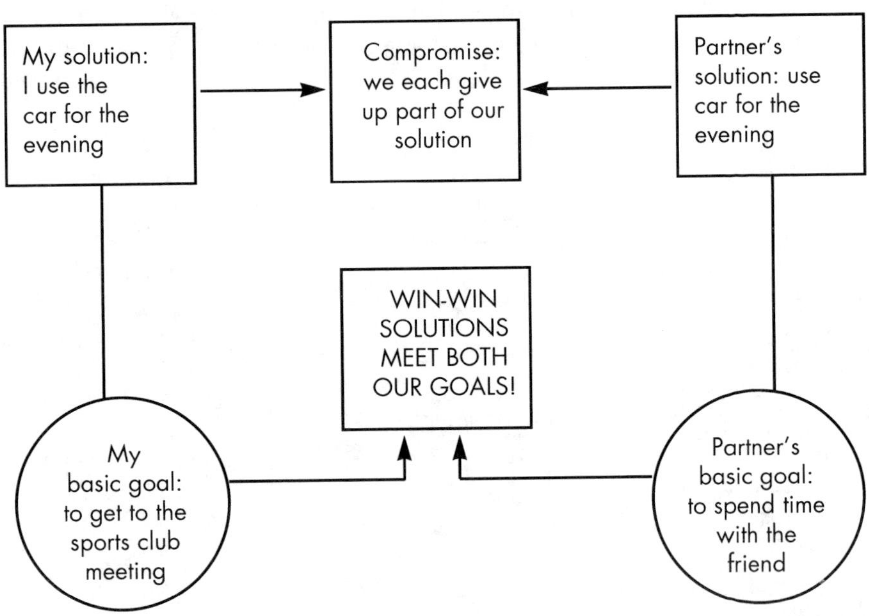

This win-win method is really a variation of the problem-solving process, discussed in Chapter 4. Here are the steps which Thomas Gordon and others identify as win-win conflict resolution, compared to the basic problem-solving model we described then:

Win-win process

1 Define the conflict in terms of goals or needs, not solutions.
2 Brainstorm possible solutions to meet both sets of needs.
3 Check how well these meet both sets of needs.
4 Choose the best solution/s.
5 Act.
6 Evaluate how well it worked.

Basic problem solving

1 Define the problem.
2 Set a goal.
3 Planning actions.

(Planning actions, continued)

(Planning actions, continued)

4 Act.
5 Evaluate how well it worked.

An example

I used the win-win method to resolve conflicts with my son Francis from when he was 3½ years old, so by the time he was six he understood it fairly well (even though he couldn't have listed the steps, he knew 'intuitively' how it worked).

Like everyone, I'm not perfect, and sometimes I forget how easily conflicts can be solved to suit *everyone*. One evening, when Francis was six, he reminded me of this very skilfully.

We were out visiting a friend of mine, and it was later than the bedtime Francis and I had arranged for him (we'd arranged this using the win-win method. Francis liked to be read a short story to help him relax at bedtime; I didn't want to be reading or entertaining him after 8 o'clock. Having a regular 8 o'clock bedtime suited us both). On this occasion, I'd chosen to visit the friend as she was upset — I planned to use my listening skills. I figured I'd be willing for Francis to stay up later this one night, so I suggested he watched TV while we talked.

Unfortunately, he seemed to want to climb over me as I listened to the friend (being climbed on is an occupational hazard of early parenthood). I sent him a strong 'I–you' message. 'You can go and sleep in my friend's spare bed, or you can watch TV, but I'm trying to listen here and I can't do it when you climb over me.' 'Well,' he said 'I'd really like to sort this out so we both get what we want.'

Now, I'd been all set to order him out of the room (after all, there are some times when maybe you have to use power, I figured). But this statement of his really hooked me. It's a very good way to start win-win conflict resolution. If he'd said 'Well I want to get *my* way' I'd have simply said 'Forget it!' Instead, he began by saying he wanted to meet my needs too.

Francis' Solution

This was a bit embarrassing, in front of my friend, but I knew there weren't any other solutions so I told Francis:
'Yeah, I like to sort things out that way too, usually, but there isn't any other way this time.'

'Well, I'd like us each to say what the problem is', he suggested. (step one of the win-win process)
'Okay', I agreed thinking I'd quickly prove to him that the win-win method couldn't work, and get back to listening to my friend. 'My problem is I want to be able to listen to my friend, and yours is you want to play with me. Right?' (This was my attempt at an I message and reflective listening.)
'No,' he replied, 'I'm really tired. I'd like to go to sleep but I don't want to sleep in the spare bed because it's a strange room and it scares me. But I don't want to watch TV.'
Wow. This stunned me! It reminded me how easily I *assume* I know what others want, when I haven't really listened at all.
'Fair enough,' I countered, 'but even so, we still can't solve it. Either you watch TV or sleep in there.'
'Do you have any other ideas for solutions?' he asked.
'No', I replied, annoyed at such a silly question.
'Well, I have a few', he offered, and then listed five possible solutions, each of which would solve both our concerns. (step two of the win-win process)
I was now even more embarrassed.
He was right. There are always more ideas (see Exercise 4.4).
'Okay, do any of those', I agreed.
'Well, I think we should check which one will work best', he suggested. (step three of the process)
So we did. The solution we chose (steps four and five) was for him to wrap up in a blanket and lie down on the floor by my feet. In five minutes he was asleep, safe and rested; therefore, perfectly meeting his need *and* mine. Naturally, the next day I checked how the arrangement went. (step six of the win-win process)
'Well I guess I solved that problem last night pretty well, eh Francis?' There was an amused smile.

How to Start

The way to get people from talking about their particular solution to thinking about basic goals or needs is simple. To define my own needs I use *I messages*. To define their needs I use *reflective listening*. Like Francis' statement 'I'd really like to sort this out so we both get what we want' invites the other person to begin. And a second invitation 'Do you have any ideas how we could solve this for both of us' can be used to move on to step two, once feelings are aired and the problem defined for each of us.

Sometimes having people unload their feelings in step one is the most important part of the whole process. Often, at the start, people in a conflict are so upset they don't believe things can ever be sorted out. When they realise they're being listened to, they begin to remember that their 'opponent' is only another human being, who may also have needs and goals of their own. Win-win conflict resolution cannot be fully used until you have understood its building blocks: *I messages* and *reflective listening*. Once you have those skills, it's child's play, as Francis proved.

In the Family

Conflict resolution can be used in every area of your life. We use it routinely to solve problems in my family. I've heard people theorise that 'women like to know who's boss' or 'kids like to have limits set', but I've never yet *met* a person of any sex or age who prefers to have their needs overridden. Its certainly true that some people are wiser, more knowledgeable and more experienced than others. But no amount of experience means you know more about how someone else feels, or what *their* problem is, than they do. On that subject, they are always the expert. You get better decisions by understanding everyone's actual needs than you will by using only your own knowledge. Remember, win-win conflict resolution doesn't mean you have to compromise or give in. If you feel like you've lost something, then you don't yet have a *real* win-win solution, and it would be best to sort it out again.

Even with a child too young to discuss their needs (say younger than three years old) you can still use the win-win *attitude* when in a conflict. This means asking yourself 'What was this child's more basic need or goal, and how could I help them meet that in a way that suits me too?' Here are examples of using this win-win attitude (discussed in Solter 1984, pp. 160–209) with younger children:

Situation	**Parents' need**	**Child's need**	**A possible solution**
1 Child pulls things off supermarket shelves while shopping.	Not to have to put things back on the shelf.	To feel he is involved and helping	Point out one or two things he can get down for you.
2 Child refuses to let parent put clothes on her. Parent in hurry.	To get out as soon as possible.	To put on her own clothes.	Find one or two items of clothing she can easily put on herself.

Situation	Parents' need	Child's need	A possible solution
3 Child draws on the wall with crayons.	Not to have to repaint the wall.	To enjoy drawing on a large surface.	Get some cheap newsprint (from a newspaper) and pin some up over an area of bedroom wall, for her to use.

This simplified approach could also be useful in relating to anyone with intellectual impairment.

In Work Situations

'Excuse me, Richard, can we talk to you?' Three students from one of my nursing classes peered in through my office door.
'Sure, come in.'
'We're wondering if you'd be able to cancel our class tomorrow. It's the only class we've got all day, so if you cancel it we can use the day to study for Friday's test.'
I nodded, getting out my diary. 'Hmm. Well, I see the problem.
It's a nuisance to have a class from one to three in the middle of the day.'
'Yes,' one of them added, 'and some people have to bus in to town just for that session, so it virtually wipes out their day.'
'The problem is,' I continued, 'that it's the only time I have to go over the instructions for next week's fieldwork visit. I really need that two hours this week.'
'Oh well.' Looks of disappointment. 'It was worth a try.' They turned to go.
'Well, hold on. Maybe we can sort it out though. What other time do you have free this week? If it's a time when I don't have another class to teach, I don't mind doing the session then.'
One of them got out her timetable. 'How about tomorrow from three to five? We've got Psychology then, but I know we're going to get a study guide to do, so maybe we could use that time.'
'Suits me,' I agreed, 'providing you check it out with your Psychology tutor first, and get back to me with her "okay".'
'Great! We'll be back in a few minutes.' They left hastily.

Situations like this arise continually in work relationships. Technically, it seemed as if either the students had to put up with a 'wasted' day, or I had to ruin my fieldwork plans. But once we recognise our basic goals, many more solutions are possible. In my experience, my willingness to use win-win processes creates a sense of co-operativeness which I can rely on when I need my students or workmates help.

The Results

Notice that win-win conflict resolution doesn't produce standard solutions. Each agreement is specifically designed for those people at that time. What suits one person perfectly may be a plan which another person would feel compromised by. What counts is that you find the best solution *for you*.

Win-win solutions don't need policing. That's their beauty. People are motivated to keep up their end of the bargain when they know it meets their own needs perfectly. This is a very old principle, on which all human societies depend. It is summed up by the English saying 'You scratch my back and I'll scratch yours', and the Maori proverb 'He kai, he kai' ('Some food for some food' — said by the chief Rakai-paka when messengers came from his coastal Whakatane relative, Tamatea-rehe, asking for forest delicacies). Therefore, the win-win method will end up saving you time. When my son was three, we had an argument every meal-time about how much he would eat. It not only took up a lot of time every day, but it spoiled my own meals to have to supervise, hassle, and bribe him into eating. Sure, it took us about a quarter of an hour to sort out the conflict . . . but that time was well invested. We *never* had another fight over his eating the meals.

Earlier in this chapter we discussed the side effects of using power to resolve conflicts. Are there any side effects to the use of the win-win method? There certainly are. Increasingly people become more creative in thinking up solutions, and take more responsibility for helping everyone have their needs met. The feeling of mutual respect and love grows deeper with every conflict resolved. Those are the kind of side effects worth having!

People in Power

When you try to use this method with someone who has more power (to reward or punish) than you do, it will help to get well prepared.

1 Work out a clear I message to explain your own needs; and make a few guesses as to what the other person's basic goals are (so you're ready to use reflective listening with them).

2 Always *reframe* the other person's behaviour as 'the best way they can understand right now to meet their needs'. (See Chapter 6 for a fuller explanation of reframing.) No matter how aggressive their words or actions may seem, when you reflectively listen to them, restate their basic intention as being *to solve their own problem*, rather than believe their aim is to cause *you* problems. For example:

   A supervisor tells you, 'There's no other way. You have to work at least one-and-half times as fast next month as you usually do. We *must* get that work contract completed. You slobs only work half speed anyway!' You respond, 'It's vital to you that we get the work done on time. I'm happy to work with you to find ways to make sure we all keep our jobs, and I see how telling us to speed up has been the most obvious solution to you. I think we can come up with even better ways to solve the problems you've had, by bearing in mind some of the things we cope with at our end.'

3 Protect yourself from being pushed into an agreement you don't want to live with. To do this ask yourself 'What would I do if I couldn't reach a satisfactory agreement?' In the example above, the worker's answer might be:
 — stay at this job but immediately begin looking for a better one
 — leave the job
 — organise a strike, or other industrial action
 — stay on the job, continue working at a comfortable level and accept the possibility of being fired.

Once you know what your *best* option outside the conflict discussion would be, compare any of the possible solutions to this 'best outside option'. In so doing, you can tell whether it's worth continuing to work with the person in power, to create solutions you both accept. Knowing your other choice, you are less likely to start giving up on your own needs, or accepting the other person's way of defining the issues. You can help give yourself more equal power by strengthening the 'best outside option' (the worker in our example might contact the union to plan for a strike, or check out other job possibilities while the issue is still not resolved).

Internal Win-Win Solutions

The win-win method also works for conflicts between different needs inside yourself. Ever wanted to go on a diet but also craved for cream cakes? Or intended to study each night but ended up watching TV? Perhaps you've had to choose between two courses of study, or two jobs, both of which interested you. What about times when one part of you is determined to push you into extra work, and you find you've got the flu and end up *having* to rest?

In all these situations, one part of you wants one thing, while another part wants something contradictory. These are conflicts of needs. Some people deal with them by using rewards and punishments to force obedience from themself. You now have a better choice. Discover what the basic need or goal is for each part, and you can find solutions that work for all of you. For example:

Situation	Part 'A' needs	Part 'B' needs	Possible solutions
1 John wants to go on a diet (part A), but overeats on creamcakes when he gets home from work (part B).	— to feel attractive when in company. — to feel energetic and 'healthy'.	— to feel nurtured and rewarded after a hard day at work.	— keep to the diet and build in lots of extra rewards: videos, visits to friends, massages, good music, etc., for the evenings. — eat the creamcakes, and arrange a regular exercise class as well. — find a low calorie alternative to creamcakes.
2 Cynthia works 50 hours a week to save for her university course. She gets the flu and has to take a week off.	– to raise the money for the university course.	— to sleep in at least once a week and 'recharge'. — spend time socially one night a week.	— keep the job, put aside non-essential work round the house for the year, and get both the sleep and the social night. — put back the start time of the university course by a year and reduce work hours. — keep the job, have friends come round for social evenings weekly, plan hours to allow sleep-in. — find a better paying job.

Wider Uses

How far can you go with the win-win method? Would it work in large institutions? In communities? Could it one day replace much of what we now call government?

Amory Lovins (reported in Robbins 1988, p. 1344) is director of research at the Rocky Mountain Institute, in Snowmass, Colorado. His particular political interest is promoting environmentally safe energy projects. He achieves this with the use of, what he calls, 'Aikido politics'. He finds out the basic goals of the electricity companies and the public and works to prove to them that things such as nuclear power aren't very good ways to meet any of their needs. In one case he spoke at a hearing where a local council was planning a huge nuclear power plant. The company had already spent US$300 million (twice that in NZ dollars) on this plant, but Lovins convinced them that smaller, alternative energy sources would work better for them and the public. The company accepted its $300 million loss and took up his suggestions. Since then he has been hired as a consultant by other electricity companies. In another case, a local council decided to start a drive for fuel conservation and weather-proofing houses. This cut their use of electricity drastically, so they paid off their debts and made three rate cuts over the next two years. Meanwhile customers saved $1.6 million in fuel costs each year.

Lovins and others like him are literally creating the basis of a new culture. The world desperately needs new models for resolving conflict. If you can solve the disagreements between yourself and your friends using the win-win method, then you have already added to the chances that humanity will survive into the twenty-first century. Humanity, by the way, means you, your children, and your friends' children.

In Chapter 10 we will consider the use of win-win conflict resolution in groups.

The win-win process of conflict resolution has six steps:

1 Define the conflict in terms of basic needs or goals, not solutions.
2 Brainstorm possible solutions to meet both sets of needs.
3 Check how well these solutions meet both sets of needs.
4 Choose the best solution/s.
5 Act.
6 Evaluate how well the solution/s worked.

I messages and reflective listening are the tools which help you to clarify each person's needs, but the same *attitude* can be used to find win-win solutions when someone is too young to use these skills with or has an intellectual impairment.

When you use the method with someone who has power over you, reframe their intention as meeting their own needs, and work out your 'best outside option' to compare possible solutions against. The win-win method can also be used to find solutions to internal conflicts of needs.

EXERCISE 8.4

Aim — to develop the win-win way of thinking about conflict.

For each of the following situations, describe each of the two conflicting sets of *needs* and then list at least three possible solutions which would meet these needs.

1 Each night Rosanne cooks the family meal so that it's ready at 6 pm when her husband Jacob gets home from work. Rosanne likes spending this time together with her family, but their 6-year-old son Tom has a favourite TV programme beginning at 6 pm each night. As a result Tom hardly eats his meal and rushes in to watch TV.

2 Rick has been looking forward to his accounting course for a while. It runs on Thursday evenings and he hopes to learn a lot that will help him in his new job. Unfortunately, the first night the teacher is rushing through the material too quickly for him to make good notes. 'Sorry,' the teacher explains, 'I've had the course hours reduced by a quarter, so I need to speed up. You'll just have to write faster.'

3 Sandra wanted to make sure that in her second marriage she would share the housework with her husband. Soon after their wedding she told Mike 'It's very important to me that you pitch in and do your share of the housework on Saturday mornings'. 'But my weekend is really important to me,' he complained, 'I like to keep it free so I can recover from the week.' Sandra shrugged. 'That may be, but in my experience doing the tidying up together is the only way to be sure we're both doing an equal amount.'

4 Susan definitely intended to do the ten hours study a week which she thought her course needed. She set aside two hours after tea each week night and was careful not to arrange any other engagements for that time. Unfortunately, after tea she found she was often quite tired. As a result, she'd sit down in front of the TV to have a rest, and slip into a sort of half asleep (or even fully asleep) state. By the time she remembered her study plan, it was often too late to concentrate, and she'd just give it up as a lost cause (carrying on watching TV till near closedown).

5 Choose a recent example of a conflict you have been involved in and write it up in this way.

SUMMARY

By using the communication skills described in Chapters 1–7, and by *changing the environment* you live or work in, an enormous number of potential conflicts simply won't happen. This is particularly so of *closed communication loops:* misunderstandings that I messages and reflective listening will solve. However, *conficts of needs* and *conflicts of values* will still occur at times. In this chapter a remarkably successful model for resolving conflicts of needs was explained.

In a conflict of needs you will occasionally have specific reasons why you are unable to discuss the issue and find a solution which meets both your needs and the other person's. However, the effects of one person winning while the other loses are not worth it. For the person who loses, these *effects of power* include resentment, fighting back, and avoidance of the winner. *The win-win process* is considerably easier to live with. It involves defining each person's basic needs (using I messages and reflective listening) and generating new solutions to meet both sets of needs. This same win-win approach can be used to *resolve internal conflicts* where you seem to have a difference of opinion with yourself.

Conflict resolution brings together the skills of several previous chapters (particularly Chapters 4, 5, and 7.)

Bibliography & Further Reading

Adams, L. (1979) *Effectiveness Training for Women E.T.W.*, Putnam, New York.

Bandler, R., Grinder, J., Satir V. (1976) *Changing With Families*, Science and Behaviour Books, Palo Alto, California.

Bolton, R. (1979) *People Skills*, Prentice-Hall, Englewood Cliffs, New Jersey.

Cameron-Bandler, L. (1985) *Solutions*, Futurepace, San Rafael, California.

Fisher, R. and Ury. W. (1981) *Getting to Yes*, Hutchinson Business, London.

Gaulke, E.H. (1975) *You Can Have A Family Where Everyone Wins*, Lutheran Publishing House, Adelaide.

Gordon, T. (1974) *T.E.T. Teacher Effectiveness Training*, Peter H. Wyden, New York.

Milgram, S. (1974) *Obedience to Authority*, Harper and Row, New York.

Myers, D. (1983) *Social Psychology*, McGraw-Hill, Auckland.

Ritchie, J. and Ritchie, J. (1981) *Spare the Rod*, Allen and Unwin, Sydney.

Robbins, A. (1988) *Unlimited Power*, Simon & Schuster, London.

Shannon, C.E. and Weaver, W. (1949) *The Mathematical Theory of Communication*, University of Illinois Press, Urbana, Illinois.

Solter, A.J. (1990) *The Aware Baby*, Shining Star, Goleta, California.

CHAPTER 9

Values

KEY CONCEPTS:

Clarifying values

Influencing others' values: consulting

Modelling your values

Values

Objective: to be able to define values and describe the processes of (a) identifying shared values, (b) modelling values, and (c) values based consultation.

WHAT ARE VALUES?

Imagine a situation where a friend buys a new set of clothes that you think look terrible on them. They ask you for your opinion. Is it the right thing for you to be truthful to your friend, or to make sure they don't feel hurt?

How about the situation where you and your best friend are graduating from nursing training and both looking for jobs in the same area of nursing. By chance you learn of an ideal job opportunity in that field. Do you tell your friend about the job? Is friendship or a career more important? These are questions about values.

Values are your personal ideas about what is important or not important, what is right and what is wrong, what is good and what is bad.

The Importance of Values

In this book you're learning a great many skills. Such skills have the potential to make your life rich and fulfilling, to increase your happiness a hundred-fold. But only if you use them in the service of things you really value. People who have the power to make their wishes come true must be careful what they wish (as several stories about magic wish-granting genies remind us). Use these skills to achieve wealth and power, when you really value friendship and the quiet life, and the skills won't bring you happiness at all.

Unfortunately, a lot of our values are unconscious — we don't think about them, we just act on them. Sometimes it's only when we meet someone with different values that we realise what *is* important to us.

A Values Hierarchy

What's important may change from area to area in your life. Let's take friendship. What's important to you about your friendships? Try listing at least six things right now; for example, love, fun, support, challenge, shared goals, honesty, respect, time together, loyalty, freedom to be yourself.

Once you have a list, try comparing the items, two by two, so you can discover which are your highest values. To compare love and fun, for instance, you'd ask 'If I had to give up one of these two things in a friendship, which would be the most difficult to give up?' Imagine yourself in each of those situations and check which value feels most essential. Then go down your list and compare the next one to each of those first two.

Once you have a hierarchy listing your values from most important down to less important, you know a lot about why you act like you do. Think about what you've discovered. Does this tell you why you make friends with certain people and not with others? In Chapter 3 we discussed the concept of rapport. Rapport happens on the level of values as well. A group of people who share at least one major value can achieve amazing things. Especially if they agree about the sensory specific ways to express that value. (You and I might both agree that fun is very important in our friendship, but if I'm thinking of the fun we get from talking together while you're planning skiing trips, our rapport will be short lived.)

IDENTIFYING SHARED VALUES

If you are interested in building a relationship with someone, one of the most powerful things is to find at least one value which you *and* they share. Once you know what that is, you can plan together ways to express that value. I'm sure you've used this principle before. Say, you're going over to a friend's place. This friend has a 6-year-old son and you really want to get on well with this kid. What would you do? Probably you'd find out what he's interested in — what he values. Perhaps it's computer games, chewing gum, and musical instruments. You may not like chewing gum or music, but you've played a few video games in your time and enjoyed that. Video/computer games are a shared value. If you want to get on with your friend's son, you'd plan a way to spend time together expressing that value.

In 1990, in New Zealand, Reckitt and Coleman put out a new group of household cleaners called 'Down To Earth'. Although these cleaners were sold in non-returnable plastic bottles, they were advertised as 'taking good care of the environment'. Their contents were biodegradable and not tested on animals. Why did this major company put out a whole new range of cleaners? Because they recognised the growing power of a new value — 'care for the environment'. All advertising appeals to shared values. 'Coke adds life, and *everybody* wants a little life.' 'Good time, great taste ... of McDonalds.'

Using Shared Values

If you're trying to befriend, or even to persuade someone, you can use this same principle. Say you want to convince a 14-year-old not to smoke cigarettes. Will it work to discuss the risk of her getting a heart attack in her thirties? Probably not. You'd be better talking about how the smell of cigarettes can turn off potential friends. You need to find a shared value. In their book *Reframing*, Richard Bandler and John Grinder give an interesting example of their use of shared values to resolve a conflict over non-shared values. A father has just told his daughter 'If you don't listen to me and don't come home by 10 o'clock, I'll ground you for a week . . .'. After checking that this message (a 'You message' and 'a threat to use power') doesn't get a very good response from the daughter, Bandler and Grinder ask the father what the *value* is behind his command.

He replies 'Well, I care. I don't want her hanging out with hoods. I don't want her out in the street. There's dope out there. I want her to be in the house, safe and sound. She's my girl, and I want to make sure that she has the kind of experiences that she needs to grow up like I want her to grow up.' The daughter explains her values: 'But it's *my* life!'

Bandler and Grinder then point out a value that both of these people share. 'OK, Sam. Is part of that image that you have of your daughter growing up for her to be independent? Do you want her to be a woman who knows her own mind, who can stand on her own two feet and make decisions for herself based on the realities of the world? Or do you want her to be pushed around by other people's opinions?'

Once these two people realise that they *share* the value of 'independence', they will probably find more useful ways to behave. In a sense, they want the same thing, only their methods differ. The father may now be willing to alter his way of discussing the matter, the daughter may be willing to alter her evening pattern. They may, in fact, be prepared to resolve the problem using the win-win method discussed in Chapter 8.

WHEN VALUES DIFFER

However, in most conflicts over values issues, at least one person will not be prepared to negotiate a win-win solution. This is because they do not believe it's the other person's business to discuss this issue. As Sam's daughter (above) said, 'But it's *my* life'. In this case the person does not believe that their behaviour has any concrete effect on the other person. Sam may send his daughter a nice clear I message ('When you arrive home after 10 o'clock I get really worried that you've been hurt') and she just says 'You worry too much dad. Perhaps you could talk to a counsellor about it'. What can he do?

The real questions are, 'How important is this relationship to him?' and 'How important is it to him that he actually change his daughter's value?' If his relationship is not as important as stopping her going out, he could use power. The use of power over her (e.g. 'grounding' her) will damage their relationship, as we saw in the last chapter. The use of power also has very little effect on her values. Sure, it stops her going out. But it doesn't stop her *wanting* to go out. Power only changes what people do, not what they value. Nonetheless, the danger may seem serious enough to make it worth using power.

A nurse who forbids patients to smoke in the hospital grounds, a boss who orders employees not to listen to the radio while working, or a teacher who insists her students wear 'no more than one item of jewellery' are all achieving the behaviour they want without affecting the others' value in the slightest. The most predictable result is resentment.

What could they do if they *really* wanted to influence these people?

Consulting

A consultant is a person hired to offer their expert skills and knowledge. There are business consultants, educational consultants, health consultants (everyone from chemists to the Avon salesperson), and so on. You can use the consultant model to influence others' values. Effective consultants:

1 Get prepared — they know the information about their subject. Don't bother trying to convince your kids about the dangers of drugs if they know more than you.
2 Don't start trying to influence until the other person has agreed to listen (in other words, get yourself hired first). The first statement of every good salesperson is a request to talk to you.
3 Explain opinions using I messages in as brief a way as possible.
4 Listen to the other person's opinions using reflective listening.
5 Leave the other person to make their own decision.

For example:
Imagine a nurse trying to be a health consultant to a patient who smokes, and failing to use these principles.

Nurse: 'Mr Smith, you shouldn't be smoking.'
Mr Smith: 'Why not: what's it to you?'
Nurse: 'You know very well why not; don't be silly.'
Mr Smith: 'I don't see why I should stop now. It's one of the few pleasures I have.'
Nurse: 'I'm only telling you this for your own good Mr Smith. Do you want to be in here forever?'
Mr Smith: 'No, I don't. Just leave me alone.'

Nurse: 'You'll be sorry. Mark my words. I know a lot more about this than you.'

Mr Smith: (Stony silence)

In this brief exchange, the Nurse has been 'fired' as a consultant. By trying to use increasing force, she has lost any ability to influence. Mr Smith begins to experience her as using her power over him, and his anger will prevent him co-operating in other areas of their relationship. It's by 'consulting' like this that many parents get fired by their teenagers. Here's how it could have been handled more effectively.

Nurse: 'Mr Smith I'm really concerned about your smoking. Do you mind if we talk about it briefly.'

Mr Smith: 'I suppose not . . . What does it matter?'

Nurse: 'We find that men who quit smoking at your stage of coronary disease have a much lower rate of recurrence than those who carry on. I believe it's one of the most important things you could do to give yourself a long and enjoyable life.'

Mr Smith: 'But smoking is one of the few pleasures I have, especially if I have to be on this damn diet.'

Nurse 'I guess it does seem like a lot of restrictions happening all at once. I think of this as a time when people need to discover a new range of things to enjoy. Everyone needs treats, that's for sure.'

Mr Smith: 'Hmm. Well, I'm going to finish this one anyway. I'll think about it, Okay?'

Nurse: 'Okay. See you inside later.'

Mr Smith: (smiles) 'Right'.

This time, the result is quite different. Most important of all, the relationship between the nurse and Mr Smith is still intact. You can only influence someone who is willing to relate with you. Also, Mr Smith may well be about to change his value and stop smoking. Very few people change their values *as* you talk to them. Mostly, they need time to go away and think about it, imagine what the new value would be like, check how it feels and talk it over with themselves. If you leave them while they still feel good about *you*, they have a head start to feeling good about what you said.

Modelling

The second powerful skill for influencing someone's values is modelling. Modelling simply means demonstrating, by your own actions, that your value works. 'Practise what you preach' may be a well-known saying, but it's fascinating how many people ignore this truth in their daily life. Teachers who routinely smoke in their staff room give out detentions to students caught smoking in the school toilets. Parents who make a practice of lying about their motives ('I'd like to give you a donation, but I have to go to the bank,' 'Sorry we can't come over to visit this Saturday, we have relatives coming,' and so on) tell their kids not to lie. The very country which has defied United Nations resolutions and invaded Granada, Panama, and Nicaragua is most eager a year later to punish another country for invading Kuwait. A man who ends family arguments by punching his wife tells his kids to control their temper.

If your values really work for *you*, others will adopt them. This is particularly so if you have a good relationship with those people. People tend to copy the values of those they admire. Notice how often a husband and wife end up with similar opinions, or a group of friends all wear the same style clothes. When a collection of much admired rock musicians runs a concert to aid famine victims, hundreds of thousands of their fans donate money. If you remember a teacher you really admired from earlier in your life, you can probably recall right now some of the ways you used that teacher as a model.

Why Influence?

The main reason people try to influence others' values is to help those others. That is, they are motivated by love. *Consulting* and *modelling* give you ways to share your values with *love*, instead of creating conflict with the very person you care for. If, after time, your attempts to influence someone are not working, you might ask yourself 'Is that so terrible? Can I not live my values and allow them to live theirs?'

In some cases you may need to accept that changing your relationship to allow for this difference is the best solution that can be achieved.

What does 'changing your relationship' mean?

For a non-smoker and a smoker it might mean agreeing on a separate area where the smoker can continue their habit. For two people with strongly opposed political beliefs it may mean agreeing not to discuss certain topics. For a wife who cannot accept her husband's active alcoholism it may mean living separately.

In other cases, you may discover that it is possible to continue your relationship and accept the difference. Is any of us so absolutely certain of our map of the world that we can insist all others follow?

Are You Sure?

Robert Fulghum tells of a friend of his who has some very alternative beliefs:
'Its all crap,' says he 'All lies. Your senses lie to you, the president lies to you, the more you search the less you find, the more you try the worse it gets. Ignorance is bliss. Just *be*, man. Don't think or do — just *be*. The *world* is coming to an *end*!' The day before he left, he jumped off a lakeside dock with his clothes on to help a kid who appeared to be in danger of drowning in the deep water. And he confessed to being in town for the National Lawyers Guild Convention, since he's a member of its social justice committee. 'So, if it's all lies and crap — and ignorance is the ultimate trip — then how come . . .?' I say. 'Well,' says he, '*I might be wrong*.'

Our values are those things we consider important, right and good. Part of building rapport is finding and working with the values we *share*.

In a conflict of values, using your power over others can change their behaviour, but not their values. To change someone's values, it's important to keep a relationship of mutual respect. You can then influence them using modelling and consulting. Good consultants (a) get prepared, (b) get hired, (c) use I messages, (d) use reflective listening, and (e) leave the other person to make their decision.

When you are unable to influence someone's values, you may choose to accept the difference, or change your relationship.

EXERCISE 9.1

Aim — to find shared values for your group.

1 Identify the main subject being studied by your group (e.g. 'communication', 'nursing', 'relationships').
2 Each person individually lists six values important to them when considering this subject, and ranks them from most to least important.
3 Collect all the values group members have listed, on a central list (e.g. on the whiteboard or on newsprint).
4 Clear a floor space in the room and declare one end 'important' and the other end 'not important'. For each of the values on your central list, have group members stand along this 'continuum' space. You are searching for the most strongly shared value.
5 When you have identified this most strongly shared value, brainstorm ways in which the group could more fully *express* this quality in their interaction.

EXERCISE 9.2

Aim — to discover the qualities of good influencers.

1 Use a relaxation process such as in Exercise 2.3.
2 Invite group members to think back through their adult life to a time when someone else influenced them (that is, when they changed the way they behaved, or their opinions, as a result of someone else's actions) and they accepted that influence, welcomed the influence. The person may have been a relative, a teacher, a friend, even someone they read about or saw on a film ... Have them *see* that person in front of them, *hear* the kind of thing that person would usually say in their tone of voice, and *feel* what it would be like to have that person beside them now ... Once they can recall this person fully, have them find words for the qualities that this person had, which enabled them to influence people. What was it about this person, what did they do, that caused others to accept their influence ... Having done this, have group members thank this person, in their mind, because this person was probably someone very special to them. They may not have realised how much this person meant.

Invite group members to gently put that person out of their mind, remembering the qualities they had.

3 Repeat step (2) with a person who influenced the group members earlier in their life.
4 Have group members share their experience in pairs. Then collect the list of qualities these influencers had, and discuss:

— do we have these qualities?
— are these the qualities we usually call upon when trying to influence others?

EXERCISE 9.3

Aim — to practise consulting about a values' issue with a partner who has different values about the issue you discuss.

1 Clear a space on the floor and declare one end 'yes', the middle 'don't know', and the other end 'no'. Read out each of the statements (listed (a) to (p) below) in turn, and have group members place themselves according to their own response. Ask people to use their own interpretation of the statements.

Do *not* clarify or discuss the statements at this stage. As soon as you have people on opposite sides for any issue, pair those people up: one 'yes' with one 'no'. These pairs should move out of the floor space, and not participate in the rest of the yes–no voting.

2 Each pair will find a space to sit next to each other, and elect one person *A* and the other person *B*. The sequence of their discussion should *strictly* follow this procedure (to prevent a loss of safety):

— Person *A* describes their opinion about the statement, using an I message.
— Person *B* listens reflectively to this, until person *A* agrees that their main point has been understood.
— Person *B* describes their opinion with an I message.
— Person *A* listens reflectively to person *B*'s satisfaction.

Repeat the process at *least* twice.

3 Collect the group together again and check how it went. Did people discover they actually agreed? Did people shift their positions? Did people become more accepting of their difference?

Statements

a Men's and women's emotional response is naturally different.
b All employers of five or more people should be required to hire an equal number of men and women.
c Employers should be required to hire a percentage of Maori staff which matches the percentage in the population.
d Members of parliament should be allowed to speak to parliament in Maori or in English.
e The Treaty of Waitangi should be the basis of all New Zealand law.
f Abortion is a woman's right to decide.
g Corporal punishment should be used in schools.
h Capital punishment should be reintroduced for some cases of murder.
i New Zealand should be a neutral country.
j Children over the age of 12 should have the vote.
k Parents have the right to choose their children's high school.
l All factories should be run by a system of community control.
m The Bible should be the basis of all New Zealand law.
n Racism is a more basic form of oppression than sexism.
o Some people are born good and some are born evil.
p Nudity in public should not be allowed.

EXERCISE 9.4

Aim — to clarify values based decisions.

1 Play the game 'A Question of Scruples', from Milton Bradley Co. (1986).
2 Each group member selects a question card from this game for discussion. (Alternatively, the group leader could select a few cards she or he considers relevant for that group.)
For each card chosen:
a Read out the card.
b Discuss what you *expect* the group members responses to this card will be.
c Disclose your own response to the card and invite others to share theirs. (Remember to use I messages.)

SUMMARY

Partially, this short chapter continues the discussion of conflict discussed in Chapter 8. In a conflict of values, the use of power will at best change the behaviour of the other person, but not their values. Better ways to influence their values include *modelling* your values and *consulting*. A good consultant (a) gets prepared, (b) gets hired, (c) uses I messages, (d) listens reflectively, and (e) leaves the other to decide.

However, this chapter not only discusses conflict situations, it is also an encouragement to clarify your own values (what's important to you), and to find out what values you share with the others in your life. When you know these values you can use the other skills in this book to create a truly fulfilling lifestyle.

Bibliography & Further Reading

Bandler, R. and Grinder, J. (1981) *Reframing*, Real People Press, Moab, Utah.
Fulghum, R. (1990) *All I Really Need To Know I Learned In Kindergarten*, Grafton Books, London.
Gordon, T. (1974) *T.E.T. Teacher Effectiveness Training*, Peter H. Wyden, New York.
James, T. and Woodsmall, W. (1988) *Time Line Therapy and the Basis of Personality*, Meta Publications, Copertino, California.

CHAPTER 10
Group Communication

KEY CONCEPTS:

Group development

Task and maintenance needs

Group facilitation

Meeting structuring

Consensus

What Happens in Groups

Objective: to be able to list three main group functions related to the task dimension and three related to the maintenance dimension, and describe the three stages of group development according to W.C. Schutz.

WHAT IS A GROUP

In the world of communication, two's company and three is usually a group. You probably belong to several groups — family, friends, workplaces, neighbourhoods, clubs, and classes of students are among the common examples.

Human beings spend a lot of their time in groups. Not every collection of three or more people is a group though — the people waiting at the busstop aren't really a group, even though they happen to be near each other. To be a group, people need to have some recognition of who does and does not belong, as well as what needs are met by the group existing.

When groups are so important in our lives, what's fascinating is how little thought we give them. In this chapter we'll explain how to use communication skills in a group setting, but first I want to mention two very important facts about groups themselves:

- groups have a series of stages they go through
- the interaction between people in a group happens on two levels (task and process).

Cohesive Groups

The morning before I wrote this section was the first day for 160 new nursing students at Christchurch Polytechnic. They filed uncertainly into the lecture theatre, not quite sure what to expect. By and large they were a quiet group, speaking — when they did — mainly in response to questions from staff or second-year students. No one person stood out, or expressed any strong opinions. In contrast, the group of second-year students who welcomed these newcomers was talkative and relaxed. People spoke loudly and confidently, chatting and laughing amongst themselves. Several second-year students described their closeness to the others in their own classes and to their tutors. They spoke of the friendships that the first-year students could expect the coming year. Looking at them I had the impression of people who had known each other for a long time. They discussed their different experiences of nursing in an easy manner, joking about the dissimilarities within their own group (e.g. who was old, who was young, who had more children than the national average, etc).

Next year, of course, the scene will repeat itself. The quiet, reserved, homogenous group of first-year students will have become a vocal, outgoing, affection-expressing, and difference-filled group of second-year students. A group like these second years can be described as *cohesive* (meaning they 'stick together') although it's interesting that people in a cohesive group are *more* able to express their differences as well as their similarities.

Stages of Group Life

A cohesive group doesn't just 'happen'. It *develops*, and that development occurs in fairly predictable steps. William Schutz divides the development of group cohesion into three stages:

— The Inclusion Phase
— The Control Phase
— The Intimacy Phase.

The new students described above were experiencing the inclusion stage of their group's life. At this stage, the main questions people are asking themselves are: whether they 'belong' here, whether they are included by others, and so on. Therefore, members may make a lot of statements about what a good group it is, but don't refer to any *particular* people they like or dislike, any particular issues they agree or disagree on. People tend to 'go with the flow' to show they belong. If you're planning activities for a group at this stage, you'll get better results by giving them opportunities to introduce themselves to each other, and to feel a part of the activity.

For our nursing students the control phase is usually in full swing about halfway through their first year. Having assured themselves they belong (or having left) people now start thinking about how much control they have, whether they can get their needs and values respected , and so on. There may be conflicts with the person/s who 'run/s' the group, and disagreements over who has more say. Some members will react to these conflicts with a fear that the group is 'breaking up' (because they are still not sure about their inclusion).

Indeed, some groups don't survive this challenge. Exercises and activities which increase people's active participation, as well as opportunities to renegotiate ground rules, are helpful at this time.

The second-year students I described above are in the intimacy stage of their group. Knowing that their needs will be respected, group members are now able to express their different feelings towards other members, and face the risks of both closeness and rejection. Although this is sometimes painful, it also brings some extraordinary moments of real human contact. Free to be different, people meet each other as they really are, instead of as the carefully presented image offered earlier on. Such a group will respond to a wide variety of different activities, especially enjoying those where affection can be shared.

Group and Individual Development

According to several group theorists the stages a group goes through (development) are very similar to the stages an individual person grows through. For example, Erik Erikson suggests that people pass through eight life stages as they grow: his model of 'psychosocial' development. Each stage has its own central issue. If a person does not resolve that issue successfully, later stages will cause difficulty. It's as if the stages were building blocks piled one on top of the other — if an early block is faulty, later blocks may fall down.

Erikson's stages, with the qualities which he says are the result of completing each stage successfully or not, can be compared to Schutz stages of group development on the right.

Erikson's Stages of Psychosocial Development		**Schutz's Stages of Group Life**
Birth – 18 mths (Infancy)	*Trust* or Mistrust	*Inclusion* Phase
18 mths – 3 yrs (Early childhood)	*Autonomy* or Shame & Doubt	
3 yrs – 5 yrs (Middle childhood)	*Initiative* or Guilt	*Control* Phase
6 yrs – 12 yrs (School age)	*Industry* or Inferiority	
12 yrs – 18 yrs (Adolescence)	*Identity* or Role confusion	
18 yrs – 30 yrs (Young adulthood)	*Intimacy* or Isolation	
30 yrs – 60 yrs (Middle adulthood)	*Generativity* or Stagnation	*Intimacy* Phase
60 yrs – Death (Old age)	*Integrity* or Despair	

It's as if the group has its own infancy (inclusion phase), childhood (control phase) and adulthood (intimacy phase).

TASK/MAINTENANCE

Mostly, when people think about groups they think about the *task* the group has to achieve. As we said, to qualify as a 'group', a collection of people need to have a common purpose (learning about communication, raising children, making money, playing tennis, etc.) and this is the group task.

But a group is much more than just a machine doing a task. It is a collection of human beings. How these people get on together, and how they get their own needs met, make up the other side of what a group does. This other side is often called the 'group process', and you could think of it as the ways the group looks after or *maintains* itself.

The task is the stuff that gets written down in the minutes, if you keep minutes. When someone brings in a cup of tea it probably isn't worth writing in the minutes — but it sure is worth doing! Sharing a cup of tea maintains the group.

When people only pay attention to the task, the group will eventually break up, because the needs of individual members and of their relationships are being ignored. An example is a very boring lecture. There may be lots of important content in such a lecture, but this is wasted if people are asleep. Several members being asleep is part of the group process.

On the other hand, when people only pay attention to group maintenance, the group fails to get its job done, and again it tends to collapse. Think of a student 'study evening' which turns into an all-night party. Everyone's individual needs are cared for, people co-operate really well, and no one remembers what the task was.

A successful group is one which balances task and maintenance needs. Keeping yourself aware of the balance is the single most important contribution you can make to any group you belong in.

Task and Maintenance Functions

What do you *do* in a group to help keep this balance between getting the task done and supporting the group of people who do the task? Comments group members make which support the task are called *task functions* and include:

1 Giving information or opinions about the task discussed, e.g. 'I think we should have our next meeting on Monday the fifteenth.'

2 Asking others for information or opinions about the task being discussed, e.g. 'Who else is available on that Monday?'
3 Using the problem-solving model (see Chapter 4) to discuss the task (i.e. starting the discussion, summarising information collected, defining the problem, suggesting a method of finding solutions, checking solutions, and evaluating decisions), e.g. 'Okay, so far we have two possible dates. Shall we just take the one which most people can come to?'

Other comments focus on the group itself, and are known as *maintenance functions*. They include:

1 Expressing your own needs and feelings, using I messages, humour, and so on, e.g. 'I'm starting to feel overwhelmed with information. Let's take a five-minute break.'
2 Encouraging others to express their own needs and feelings, using reflective listening skills, e.g. 'You're still frowning. Are you unhappy about us making a decision in this way?'
3 Using the problem-solving model to discuss the group (i.e. saying what you've observed of the group process, acknowledging interpersonal problems, suggesting solutions to better meet everyone's needs in the group, and evaluating how the group 'contract' is working), e.g. 'I'm aware that in the last ten minutes only the men have been talking. I think it would be good if we listened to what some of the women's responses are.'

These are the six key functions which any group needs to succeed. Together, they make up what has in the past been called 'leadership'. In this way of understanding it, leadership is a set of functions which someone in the group needs to perform. You could let one person do them all, but in a well-developed group (one that has worked through the *control* phase) these functions are shared by the whole group.

The more members who contribute to these functions, the more your group is using its full talent, and the better decisions you'll make.

All these functions can be learned — in fact, they are all described in other chapters of this book.

A group is a collection of people who have a sense of belonging and purpose together. As groups develop they tend to go through an *Inclusion Phase*, a *Control Phase*, and an *Intimacy Phase*, which are analogous to the infancy, childhood, and adulthood of a person's life.

A group has a content which is being discussed, and a process by which the discussion occurs. '*Leadership*' can be thought of as the set of functions which keep a balance between the group task and group maintenance, and they are:

Task functions:

— giving information or opinions
— receiving information or opinions
— problem solving the task.

Maintenance functions:
— expressing needs or feelings
— encouraging others to express needs or feelings
— problem solving the group process.

EXERCISE 10.1

Aim — to develop skills in group observation. Assign each group member a session of the group for them to observe, and have them take notes using the headings below. At the end of the session, or at a later date, have the observer report back to the group and enable the group to discuss their comments.

Group observation

Posture

a How close are people sitting?
b Who leans towards the group and who leans away?
c Who has an open body position and who has a closed position?
d Who seems physically tense, and who is relaxed?
e Who sits still and who moves? What types of movement do they make?

Facial expression

f Who looks away from the group and who looks towards others?
g Who smiles or laughs?
h Who frowns?
i Who yawns?
j What other body language are you aware of?

Speech

k Who speaks and who is silent?
l Who is able to finish what they say? Who interrupts?
m Who changes the subject?
n Who makes jokes or uses humour?
o Who criticises, blames, judges, or insults others?

Leadership functions

p Who offers information or opinions?
q Who asks for information or opinions from others?
r Who suggests moving to the next step of problem solving/working on the group task?
s Who expresses their feelings or needs in an I message?
t Who uses reflective listening skills?
u Who invites the group to discuss or problem solve their *process*?

Summary

v What was the task of this group in this particular session?

w How would you generally describe the group process, based on all the previous questions? (e.g. is the group friendly, withdrawn, tired, energetic, tense, relaxed, co-operative, resistant?)
x Did you think a good balance was kept between task and maintenance needs in the group? If so, what helped? If not, what would have helped?

EXERCISE 10.2

Aim — to explore levels of intimacy in the group.

1 Using a copy of the following (circular) diagram, write in the names of all the other members of your group, showing by where you place them who are:
— best friends you talk to or spend time with a lot.
— close friends you talk to or spend time with fairly often.
— friends/acquaintances you spend time with less frequently.
2 Get into pairs and discuss (a) what it was like to fill in this form, and (b) anything you feel comfortable sharing of what you wrote down.
3 If the group is sufficiently trusting, each person could be invited to set out their diagram using the actual people in the room, and an imaginary large size diagram on the floor.

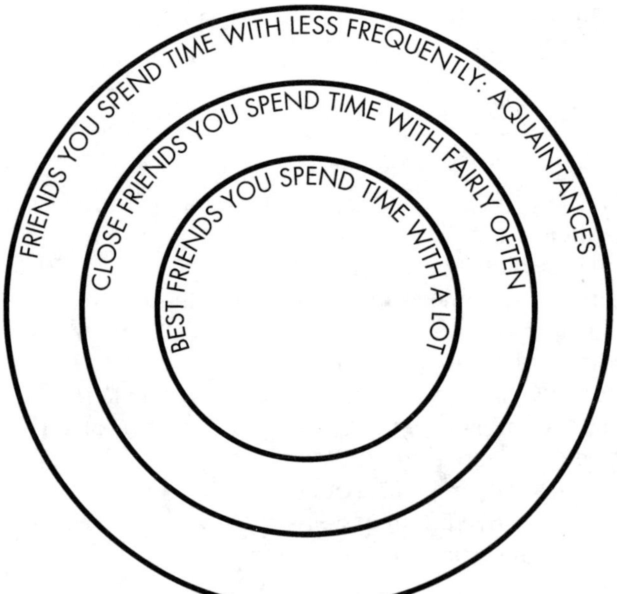

Helping a Group Reach Agreement

Objective: to be able to help a group create consensus decisions, by using the skills of (a) meeting structuring and (b) win-win conflict resolution.

FACILITATION

Psychotherapist Milton Erickson told a simple story which clarifies his method of helping. He explained that, when he was a child, he found a horse wandering aimlessly down a country lane. Realising it had escaped from some nearby farm, he climbed on and rode it five miles up the road. At this point the horse turned off the road and walked up a drive, where they met its astonished owner. 'How did you know he should come here?', the farmer asked. Erickson explained, 'I didn't know... The horse knew. All I did was keep his attention on the road.'

Helping a group make decisions (or an individual for that matter is like that. Everytime the group 'wanders off the road to eat the grass' you lead them back, and eventually they will find their own way. This model of running a group is often called *facilitation*.

Chairperson *v* Facilitator

The facilitator's job is to make it easy (from the Latin word 'facilis' meaning 'easy') for the group to find solutions. Being a facilitator can be contrasted with being a chairperson in a more traditional 'meeting'. The role of the chairperson includes making decisions for the group at times. People are expected to speak 'to the chairperson' rather than directly to each other. On the other hand, the job of the facilitator is to ensure that people speak as directly as possible to each other.

The chairperson is expected to know and perform the key group functions, whereas the facilitator encourages others to perform these functions. Does this mean that facilitating is easier than chairing a meeting? I don't think so.

Being an effective facilitator requires an ability to use *all* the communication skills we have studied in this book. It takes an awareness of body language, and an ability to help people alter their state of mind (relaxing if they are too tense, or energising if they are tired, for example). It is first and foremost a helping role, in that the facilitator's aim is to help others sort out what they want, rather than to persuade them to choose the facilitator's solutions. And yet the facilitator needs to be able to explain her or his own intentions in clear I messages, and to use the skills of modelling clear communication and consulting — skills aimed at offering group members new values. Most of all, the facilitator needs to have a very clear idea of who owns which problems, and of how to use the problem-solving, win-win process. She or he needs to know this process well enough to teach and assist others to use it too. And finally, the facilitator needs to know how to structure the group time, so as to provide a beginning (warm-up) and an ending (closure).

POWER USE IN GROUPS

Resolving conflicts in a group is similar to resolving conflicts between two people. There are several methods of making decisions in a group, where one or more people use their power over others to win at the others' expense. These include the following:

— Autocratic: one person makes decisions for the group.
— Minority rule: a few people make decisions for the group.
— Autocratic or minority rule with consultation: as above; but before making the decision, the decision makers check what other people think, and may (or may not) take their views into consideration.
— Majority rule: everyone in the group discusses the decision, and the decision is made by whoever has the largest number of people supporting their proposal.

Problems With Power

In all of these methods, some people's needs are not met. This is more obvious in the first two cases, where people's needs are not even listened to (the situation in most workplaces, in many schools, and in political dictatorships). In the last two cases, people can explain their concerns. However, there is an incentive for people to argue *against* each other rather than co-operate, because whoever is the least persuasive could lose totally. Often in a majority rule system, one party of like-minded people always votes together; therefore, minorities end up having next to no influence on group decisions (the situation in the New Zealand parliament: only the party in government can make decisions). Adolf Hitler's Nazi party was voted in by majority, and was able to 'democratically' override the needs of such minorities as psychiatric patients, Gypsies, and Jews.

As with conflicts between two people, the use of power may be worth the resentment it can create in certain circumstances — for example, when there is no time for discussion (see 'Power over Others' in Chapter 8). Also, many groups accept that minor decisions will be made by one of these methods, but major decisions are sorted out using the win-win method.

CONSENSUS

Consensus is the name given to the use of win-win conflict resolution in a group. The goal of consensus is a decision consented to by all group members. This doesn't have to mean that everyone thinks this is the very best solution (a unanimous decision). It just means that everyone can live with the decision and will agree to support the group in choosing it. This goal encourages people to work together to find solutions acceptable for everyone, instead of competing.

As with all win-win decision making, the big advantages of consensus are that:

— everyone's creativity is used to generate good solutions, and
— people tend to be very committed to making decisions work.

The disadvantages are that

— it takes time (remember, though, that time enforcing unwanted solutions will be saved), and
— at least some people in the group need good communication skills to make it work (hence the advantage of having one person designated 'facilitator').

Amongst groups who use consensus are the Religious Society of Friends (Quakers), a large number of Maori Marae, co-operatives such as Women's Refuges, and many workplace groups (including mine). We also use consensus in our family.

A great deal of research has been done by such groups into how to best create consensus (see, for example, the book *Building United Judgement: A Handbook for Consensus Decisionmaking*). The suggestions which follow come out of this experience.

MAKING A START

Henare, a community worker, was invited to help sort out a disagreement between the four workers at a community creche. He arranged a two-hour time slot (from 5–7 pm one Thursday) and suggested they begin by sitting in a circle so they could all see and hear clearly. Henare began by telling them that he was pleased to be with them and that he planned to help them find solutions they could all live with. He emphasised that he wasn't there to tell them the *rules*, but he had a couple of ideas about how they could find their own *agreements*. He invited them to take three minutes of silence to collect their thoughts and relax into the meeting.

After this Henare suggested each person briefly introduce themselves and say how their day had been. He started.

'I had a hectic day today, and it's actually nice to be concentrating on one task for these two hours.'

A woman to his left continued, 'My name is Miriam; I'm the person who phoned you, and I'm just hoping we can sort this out soon and have a better year. I suppose I'm feeling quite anxious.'

'Me too,' agreed the man beside her, 'I'm Roy. I wasn't working today so I've just come in for this meeting. I'd rather be sleeping . . .'

'My name is Leslie,' the woman next to Roy put in, 'I've been working here two years now, and I'm not really sure if I plan to carry on . . . I feel quite tense.'

'Moana is my name,' the fourth person finished, 'I've only been here a few weeks and I feel like I've sort of walked into all this conflict. I had a good day, no problems.'

Henare continued by checking that the 7 pm ending time was okay for everyone. 'What things led to the decision to invite me here this evening?' he prompted.

Roy began. 'Well, last year we had a couple of really unpleasant situations here, where conflicts happened between staff. There was a lot of backbiting, and eventually one person got so upset she left. I want to make sure it doesn't get to that again, so I suggested we have an agreement about not talking behind people's backs.'

'Yeah,' Miriam nodded, 'I agree with Roy. People have got to be honest with each other for it to work. I think, last year, we ended up all grizzling about things to the wrong people.'

'Well . . . there was a lot of aggro . . .' Leslie paused. 'But it's just not as simple as you make it sound Miriam. Sometimes people get upset about something and they don't really know what it is till they've talked to someone else. Sandy — that's the woman who left, Henare — she . . . it just took her a long time to be able to . . .'

'Yeah. And in the meantime she started telling all the parents who came here that I was some sort of ogre!' interrupted Miriam. Leslie was about to reply, but Henare intervened. 'I know this is important to both of you, and I want to make sure you each get a chance to say your bit. I think it will help if we wait for each person to finish their comment . . . is that agreeable?' There were nods.

'That was all, anyway,' Leslie concluded, 'I don't think it's that simple.'

'I suppose,' contributed Moana, 'that I'd have to go along with Roy and Miriam. But one thing I find is that *they're* really used to all this communication stuff. And I can see that I'd find it intimidating to be in that situation. So I don't know . . .'
'Okay.' Henare checked everyone was ready to go on. 'So the main thing you'd all like to sort out is what happens when someone is unhappy with a situation. Sounds like Miriam, you, and Roy both want an understanding about no talking behind people's backs. You'd go along with that Moana, but you can also understand what Leslie says: which is that in real life it seems not so simple. Is that right?' General nods. 'And that's the main thing we need to sort out?' Again, nods.

Meeting Structuring

Already, Henare has structured this meeting to make sure that several important group processes occur, in a useful order. These include:

1 *Starting on time and clarifying the arrangements about ending*
It may be that the meeting will carry on hui style till things are resolved, or it may be that people have other commitments (e.g. needing to get back for babysitters) and will appreciate an agreed on ending time.

2 *Sitting in a circle*
Seating arrangements set the tone of any get together. Ensuring a circle gives a sense of equal power. No one is 'in front' of anyone else.

3 *Checking how people are*
Providing an opportunity to say briefly how everyone is helps people learn who is here. It creates a sense of group *cohesion*.

4 *Working out what the task is and how we will achieve it*
This really creates a sense of *contract*. Henare has requested agreement about two processes already. One is that his role as a facilitator will be to assist them to reach consensus. The other is that people will allow each speaker to finish their statement. He has also checked the agenda, which in this case has only one item. A more formal process might include:
   a Collecting people's suggestions for group guidelines (such as no interrupting, confidentiality) and listing those agreed to on a sheet of newsprint.
   b Listing agenda items, estimating how much time each item will take, and deciding which order to discuss the items in. If there are too many items for your time, some will need to be put off till the next meeting.

5 *Leaving time for evaluation*
Someone needs to keep track of time if there is a set agenda and an agreed ending. The facilitator may do this or a separate timekeeper could be appointed. At the end, a space for people to each say how they found

the meeting will help give a sense of *closure* to the meeting. (*Cohesion* and *contract*, the two key elements in warmup to the beginning of a meeting, are discussed in more detail in Chapter 1. *Closure* is commented on in Chapter 11.)

The Facilitator's Comments

If you check back what Henare actually said in the first few minutes of this meeting you'll realise that he uses all the communication skills described in Chapters 5–9. Particularly important is his use of:

1 *I messages* (e.g. 'I want to make sure you each get a chance to say your bit. I think it will help if we wait for each person to finish their comment'): These are used to share his feelings, and to offer his opinions as a consultant.

2 *Reflective listening* (e.g. '. . . this is important to both of you. So the main thing you'd all like to sort out is what happens when someone is unhappy with a situation.'): Notice that Henare not only reflects what individuals say, but also restates what is happening to the group or to couples in the group. This might be called 'summarising' or 'sorting issues'.

3 *Reframing*: at the same time, Henare skillfully reframes the significance of what is occurring. His reflections draw attention to *similarities* and areas of *agreement* between those in the conflict. (Even when the only similarity is that both people are angry or upset, or that both people want a solution!) As a facilitator he asks himself 'Which are the areas of disagreement here, and where are the areas of agreement?', and 'Can the conflict be narrowed down by agreeing about part of it, and *then* considering the remaining area of disagreement?'

Finding Agreement

Henare realised, near the start of the meeting, that in a majority vote Miriam, Roy, and Moana would all vote for Roy's proposal. Probably both Moana and Leslie would end up unhappy with the result. He understood Miriam's need to avoid people talking behind her back. She gave a more detailed account of what had happened when Sandy had done this the previous year, and everyone (including Leslie) agreed that this wasn't acceptable. But he wasn't quite clear about Leslie's concern.

'Could you tell me some more about what your concern is Leslie? Maybe: "what would an agreement need to do, for it to work for you?" '
'Well, I don't know.' She frowned. 'I just know that some people find it

really hard to do what Roy's asking. Because they don't exactly *know* what they're upset about.'

Henare nodded. 'And you think in that case, they can't go and tell the person they're annoyed with until they've worked that out.'

Miriam sighed. 'But that's just being unassertive.'

'Maybe it is,' Henare accepted, 'but it's also a genuine difficulty which you, Leslie, are acknowledging someone might have. Are there any ways to support people with that difficulty, which don't involve talking behind people's back either?'

'Getting assertiveness training.' urged Miriam.

'Or having a person like you available to help them work it out', suggested Moana. 'I mean, what you're doing with us is, like, listening so we can sort this out. You could do that with someone who is annoyed, instead of them talking to the parents or anyone off the street who wants to hear.'

'Why can't *we* do that for each other?' Leslie asked.

'Because that's talking behind each other's back.'

Leslie nodded. 'Yes, but if it was only once to sort out the thing you wanted to say . . .'

Roy considered. 'Well, I suppose I could live with that *if* it was very clear how it happened.'

Henare wrote quickly on a sheet of newsprint. 'Okay. We've got three ideas here. Assertiveness training, use a facilitator, talking once with someone to clarify ideas. Any other ideas?'

As they explored further, a solution which combined the first and third suggestion developed. Ideally, people would discuss any unhappiness with the person they had concerns about. If they couldn't work out what to say though, they could talk it over once only with another person on the staff. That person's job would be to help them go back to the one they were unhappy with, and discuss the problem in an assertive way.

Henare checked a couple of times to see how well the solution was meeting each person's need. 'Let's just find out how we're going here. On a continuum where this . . .' he held his arms wide apart, palms facing each other '. . . represents a perfect solution which meets all your needs, and this . . .' he held his hands with palms together '. . . represents a disaster; how would you rate the agreement we've got written down here?' People held their arms with palms at varying distances apart, and had a look around to see the result.

CAN WE REACH CONSENSUS?

You'll recognise, from Chapter 8, the win-win conflict resolution method Henare used here. Working with a group, he also needed to find a way to test for 'consensus' which didn't take several minutes of talking. One example is the 'sociometric' method he used above. Another technique would be a 'straw vote', where a vote is taken purely to check how close to total agreement the group is (rather than to find a majority for a win-lose decision). With a long list of possible solutions, one of these methods could be used to assess the initial feeling about each solution.

What about when it just doesn't seem to be possible? Groups that use consensus have evolved many different answers to this question. They include:

— Voting on whether to revert to majority rule. If the vote is 'yes', then a second vote decides the issue. If the vote is 'no', the issue is postponed till next meeting.
— Representatives of each main 'faction' within the group hold a smaller meeting where they seek a consensus.
— A break in the discussion is called. People may use this time to play group-building games, to release their feelings about the issue, to relax, or to imagine this situation from the other points of view, and think up new solutions.

Attitude

The attitude a facilitator has is as important as her or his skills. Science Fiction writer Theodore Sturgeon tells a story about this attitude (much as I like Sturgeon's fiction, this story happens to be true). One time during Sturgeon's youth, he was at a family gathering with his grandparents and his uncle. His grandfather was a retired English church Rector whose 'brains were beginning to melt just a little', while his grandmother was still very much present and 'in charge'. During the gathering, a ferocious argument erupted between uncle Ernest and the grandmother, about her attempts to make the decisions for the family. The uncle stormed off in a huff, and took an overdose of the adrenaline which he used to counter his asthma. When he came back, he had pinpoint pupils, his cheeks were fiery red, and he held a .38 automatic pistol in his hand. In fury he screamed that he was going to kill himself and burn down the house.

Frantically working out how best to leap into the fray, and simultaneously wondering how his uncle could burn the house down *after* killing himself, Sturgeon sat on the edge of his chair. Then suddenly, '. . . my grandfather came back from Out There, set his teacup down on the low table, got up and stood nose to nose with the wild man. "I say, Ernest", he said in that soft oboe voice of his, "Why can't we all be chums?" '

Why Can't We?

The effect was dramatic. Uncle Ernest burst into laughter, started coughing, and collapsed into a chair, dropping his gun in the process. The humour in this story is, of course, based on the fact that we all recognise the grandfather's out-of-touch naivety. But Sturgeon offers a dramatic reframe. Who, he asks, is really out of touch with reality? The old man with his simple question 'Why can't we all be chums?', or those of us who sit powerlessly by as a man plans murder? It is a question which Sturgeon says haunts him, every time he watches a couple of cats fighting . . . or a flight of B52 bombers taking off for some middle east village. He concludes 'So really — why can't we all be chums? Why can't we? Why?'

It is precisely this question which the group facilitator asks at each moment, to create consensus.

The process of helping a group develop win-win solutions that all can live with is called facilitating consensus. A facilitator's skills must combine meeting structuring and conflict resolution. Meeting structuring includes:
— keeping to arranged start and finish times
— sitting in a circle
— checking how people are, and enabling them to meet as people (building *cohesion*)
— clarifying the task: (a) defining group guidelines and (b) listing, timing, and prioritising an agenda (building *contract*)
— evaluating at the end (building *closure*).

To assist the creation of consensus, facilitators use:
— I messages
— reflective listening both individuals and group
— reframing to find similarities and agreement
— testing for consensus
— using alternative strategies such as representative consensus, voting, and time out, when consensus is not achieved.

EXERCISE 10.3

Aim — to develop group members' consensus building skills.

Following are tasks which require the group to reach consensus. These can best be used by the group leader explaining the task and then sitting back and leaving the group to their own devices. Another option is to divide the group in half and have half the group complete the task while the other half observe (one person sitting behind each person in the task group). The observers could use a form listing the six group functions; placing a tick beside one of the functions each time the task group member they observe speaks. These functions are:
a Giving information/opinions
b Seeking information/opinions
c Problem solving the task

d Expressing needs/feelings
e Encouraging others to express needs/feelings
f Problem solving the group process.

1 Design an advertising campaign, with a slogan, a poster and a TV ad, to attract people into your group.
2 Rank the following jobs, from those which have the highest percentage of women employed in them to those which have the lowest percentage (answers, from the NZ Ministry of Women's Affairs Newsletter Panui No.2, 1986, are given on p. 265.)

Members of parliament
Lawyers
Accountants
Practising doctors
Managers
University professors
University lecturers
Secondary principals
Secondary teachers
Primary principals
Primary teachers
Kindergarten teachers

3 New Zealanders were asked 'What attracted you to Your Spouse?' in a survey which collected separate results for men and for women. Here are the results (in a random order) of the ten most valued qualities listed by each sex. Rank them as you would expect the actual results, from (1) = most highly rated to (10) = least highly rated.

A class could choose one list to work on with one half observing the task group, then use the other half observing while the second list is used. Lists are from Colgan, Dr A. and McGregor, J. *Sexual Secrets*, Alister Taylor Publishers (1981). (For answers see p. 265.)

Women Value	*Men Value*
entertaining ability	entertaining ability
erotic ability	erotic ability
social ability	social ability
looks, physical attraction	looks, physical attraction
general personality	general personality
way he relates to me	way she relates to me
good communication	good communication
affection	intelligence
sense of humour	similar interests/activities
quiet and shy	purely sexual attraction

SUMMARY

Working successfully with a group draws on the skills discussed in every chapter in this book. Now you've learned two models for understanding groups. The first was a simple *model of group development* as having an inclusion phase, a control phase, and an intimacy phase. The second was our division of group needs into two areas: *task needs* and *maintenance needs*. Being aware of the balance between these two areas is crucial for any group's success.

The chapter also explained the specific skills of a *group facilitator* (person assisting a group to make its decisions). These skills include *structuring the meeting* so it has a beginning and an end, including time to meet task and maintenance needs. They also include such previously explained skills as I messages, reflective listening, reframing, and conflict resolution. The creation of win-win solutions in a group is called *consensus*.

Bibliography & Further Reading

Avery, M., Auvine, B., Streibel, B., Weiss, L. (1981) *Building United Judgement*, The Centre for Conflict Resolution, Madison, Wisconsin.

Erikson, E. (1968) *Childhood and Society*, W.W. Norton, New York.

Haley, J. (1973) *Uncommon Therapy: The Psychiatric Techniques of Milton H. Erickson*, W.W. Norton, New York.

Johnson, D.W. and Johnson, F. (1975) *Joining Together: Group Theory and Group Skills*, Prentice-Hall, Englewood Cliffs, New Jersey.

Shaffer, J.B.P. and Galinsky, M.D. (1974) *Models of Group Therapy and Sensitivity Training*, Prentice-Hall, Englewood Cliffs, New Jersey.

Sturgeon, T. (1989) *The Golden Helix*, Carroll & Graf Publishers, New York.

CHAPTER 11
Conclusions

KEY CONCEPTS:

Stages of grief

Tangihanga

Closure, in groups and helping

Chunking: from specifics to concepts

Saying Goodbye

Objective: to be able to discuss closure in human relationships as including grieving, evaluation, referral, and futurepacing.

ENDING A RELATIONSHIP

At some time in our life, most of us have had the experience of an important relationship coming to an end. It may have been a marriage ending in a divorce, a love affair ending in separation, a friendship terminated by conflict or by distance apart, or the death of a close relative.

As you can remember, those situations bring up powerful feelings. Feelings like sadness and grief, but also at times ones like regret, guilt, confusion, fear, loneliness, relief, depression, or anger. It's not always easy to understand where these emotions come from.

Confusing Feelings

The most important goodbye in my childhood was the death of my grandmother. Throughout my childhood she had played with me, told me stories, indulged my interest in comics, and provided me with a home away from home. It was she who first suggested — when I was four years old — that 'the way I talk' I should be a teacher. On the day she died, it shocked me to realise I could not cry for her. Even more mysterious, on the day of her funeral I completely forgot the whole situation, and went to a friend's place to play. When I arrived home late, my parents were furious. I couldn't understand the incredible anger they unleashed. It's not just when someone dies that people react in such unpredictable ways. In some, perhaps smaller way, *any* 'goodbye' brings up the range of feelings we describe as *grief.* Here we'll identify the main 'ingredients' of grief, and think about how to assist people to deal with the ending of a relationship.

GRIEVING

Swiss doctor Elisabeth Kubler-Ross has spent much of her life living with those most of us prefer not to think about: the dying. She suggests that those who face a loss tend to work their way through a simple five-step process. They don't always move systematically from step one to step five, but may wander back and forth as they deal with each stage at another level. Here are the stages as she observes them:

1 *Denial and Isolation*: This is the 'It can't be true . . . No, not me' stage. The person who realises separation is coming may forget all about it, or talk as if it isn't happening. Others can help them, not by arguing, but by letting them know 'When you want to talk, I'm available.'
2 *Anger*: The 'Why me?' stage of anger, envy, and blaming others is often the first obvious emotional response. This anger has its basis in a terrific sense of powerlessness. Rather than criticise them or try to smooth the anger over, others can help the person most by reflective listening to their rage ('Makes you want to scream eh!') and finding safe places to vent it.
3 *Bargaining*: At this stage the person accepts the separation, provided that life allows them certain conditions. 'If I live, I'll give my life to God' and 'If the group splits up, we must go on meeting for social contact' are examples. Bargaining is a temporary truce, and most people don't actually keep the deals they make in this state. Nonetheless, this is a good time to make plans which allow for the reality of separation.
4 *Depression*: A temporary 'shutdown' at this stage gives the person time to allow their deeper feelings to emerge slowly. These feelings may include regrets, guilt, anger, sadness, or even love. Others can assist the grieving person to release such feelings (see 'Catharsis' in Chapter 6).
5 *Acceptance*: A quiet, at peace, 'It's Okay' stage gradually flowers out of grief. The person's energy is now more fully withdrawn from the relationship which is ending, and directed towards the new.

THE TANGIHANGA

The Maori tangi or funeral acknowledges a grief cycle, and involves all five stages suggested by Elisabeth Kubler-Ross. Throughout its stages, there is a fundamental belief expressed in another form of life. The dead have passed on to the next plane of existence, referred to as Hawaiki nui, Hawaiki roa, Hawaiki pamamao.

At the tangihanga, unfinished business is dealt with. Time is given for people to vent anger, frustration, excitement, happy memories, or whatever, openly. The event also provides a platform that allows and welcomes people 'dumping off' their own personal grievances apart from that of the death of the person for whom the tangi is being held. The processes of haakari and whakangaahau (i.e. celebration with food and entertainment) coupled with 'takahi o te whare' (tramping the house to ensure the dead's soul or spirit has departed and has no need to delay its journey back to Hawaiki) allows mourners time (generally three days and nights after the burial; sometimes shorter, but never longer) to refocus on real life again. Closure occurs through a group process (i.e. whanaungatanga, relationship).

The poroporoaki (farewell), as held at other hui, allows people time to detach from the gathering and refocus their attention on departing for home.

CLOSURE IN A GROUP

In a group, this goodbye could be called 'closure'. The whole group may weave its way through Kubler-Ross' stages, stages which are the reverse of Schutz' group development model.

Schutz says that towards the end of its life, the issues of *inclusion*, *control* and *intimacy* re-emerge in a group in reverse order, thus:

— *Intimacy* (Kubler Ross' Denial and Isolation stage). People daydream, arrive late or forget to come more, and withdraw from closeness.

— *Control* (Kubler Ross' Anger and Bargaining stages). People may bring up old issues, and re-evaluate the group leader. They may also attempt to bargain for the group to continue.

— *Inclusion* (Kubler Ross' Depression and Acceptance stages). People begin to look forward to a life without the group, no longer thinking of themselves as group members. This may not occur till some time after the actual separation.

CLOSURE IN HELPING

It's important for helpers to be aware that the same process occurs for both them and their clients. When I was nursing, my very first patient under my individual care was an elderly man. A day before I left, I explained that tomorrow was my last day on his ward. 'I suppose I won't see you again then', he said sadly. 'Oh no', I reassured him, overwhelmed by my *own* sadness. 'I'll be able to come back in and check how you are, on my way to the next ward.'

A week later I realised, with a little maths, that within six months I might be 'checking in' on about 24 people a day. It was important that I begin to acknowledge closure. Helpers can set aside time to assist the closure process, whether they are working with individuals or with groups. During this time, their tasks include evaluation, referral and futurepacing.

Evaluation

Evaluation means checking (a) How the process of the relationship was for each person, and (b) whether any specific goals were achieved. At the end of a group session, time could be provided for people to say one thing they liked and one thing they'd change about the session. A counsellor might use one or more sessions to review the story of their counselling, compare the original goals, and discuss what the person's next step will be.

Referral

This next step may well include referring the person on to another helper or group. If you want your referral to work, remember that it has three parts: (a) the person you are referring. Discussing the suggestion fully with them, and the advantages you believe referral will have, is crucial. After all, it is *their* feelings that will determine whether referral works. They deserve to know what, if any information you intend to give their new helper, (b) the person/s you are referring them to. Ensuring you understand what service they offer, and *how* they like people to be referred, will enable them to feel more positive about their new client. They may have special information they need from you, or other help they'd like to be able to get from you, and (c) the linking process. This includes ensuring the person you refer knows when and where they will meet up with their next helper. It may even involve you assisting at this meeting.

Futurepacing

'Futurepacing' means referral back to real life. It is the process of ensuring that personal changes don't stay 'anchored' to the relationship with the helper, but are anchored to the real-life situations where they are needed.

My friend Annette and I shared an office. Each time Annette came to work and saw my biscuits, she remembered that it was nice to have a snack available for morning tea. She was committed to buying some to share, but in the meantime she shared mine. After some weeks, we realised that this was a problem of futurepacing. Annette's good intentions were anchored to the office (where they were utterly useless; our office did not have a biscuit vending machine).

I had Annette imagine herself coming into her local dairy. I told her to see the things she would see as she came in the door and look over to the shelf where the biscuits were. I suggested she feel herself (in her imagination) walking over to the shelf and picking up a packet. In this way, her good intention would be likely to be anchored to the naturally occurring sights and feelings of Annette's real life, the exact moment before they were needed. Sure enough, the next time Annette came into the office, she reported success. She had walked into the diary to buy milk, seen the biscuit shelf, walked over to it . . . and realised she had no money in her pocket to buy biscuits!

Using futurepacing

Anyway, you get the hang of it from my story. If you want people to do the things they learn, *in their real life*, simply have them roleplay, or imagine themselves in the situations, doing the things they have learned. This is the natural way people use to remember things. If you decide you are going to compliment your friends more, you imagine seeing your friend in front of you, you hear her or his voice, you feel your mouth forming the words, and you listen to the sound as it will sound in real life. People who rehearse new skills in this way are likely to use them. That's futurepacing.

At the end of a course, a group session, or a counselling process, futurepacing is the natural link to a new way of life. Imagine how your memory will improve when you use it. See yourself in your mind's eye, right now, as you rehearse your way through all those things that in the past you've forgotten. Hear the words you'd say if you were futurepacing and be aware of the self-assured feeling that a good memory will give you . . . .

Life and Death

Once we are more aware of closure, we actually value our time together. Elisabeth Kubler-Ross says that she considers our western culture has lost immeasurably by hiding death from view. When parents realise that their children *may* die, they tend to put a lot more energy into saying how they love them and a lot less into yelling at them. When a person knows they are going to die, they are far less likely to waste their life 'waiting for something to happen' or brooding over a past argument that they never bother to resolve. Their lives, Kubler-Ross suggests, often become richer, more real, more loving. N.L.P. developer Richard Bandler says that the thing that most struck him when he began working as a therapist was that people spend a lot of their time waiting. Waiting to relax, waiting to have fun, waiting to do the things they need to do. Their lives have no closure.

If you knew that today was the last day of your life, what things would you want to do? Who would you spend time with? What things would you want to say to those people? Now . . . what stops you from actually doing those things? Whatever it is, is it really so important that it's worth waiting your life through, day after day? Every moment that passes will never return. The sky above you will *never* again look just like it does at this moment. The sound of the birds outside, or the laughter of the children, or the rise and fall of the wind is for this second only. And the actual feeling of your body, of life flowing through your lungs and your heart, can only be experienced now. The memory is *not* the same.

Death is real, utterly, undeniably real. But only as real as the fact that you are alive right now. If all my wishes for you were one wish, it would be that you live each moment with the understanding this truth can bring.

Grieving tends to involve the five processes of (1) denial and isolation, (2) anger, (3) bargaining, (4) depression, and (5) acceptance. If you are bringing closure to a relationship, be aware that these feelings may occur. You could also plan opportunities to (a) evaluate how the relationship went, (b) assist linking up others to a new relationship, in referral, and (c) help the person anchor new learnings to the sensory experiences of real life — a process called futurepacing.

Being more aware of closure means living more fully each moment.

EXERCISE 11.1

Aim — to futurepace the learnings from your course.

1 Use the relaxation exercise described (Exercise 2.3) or some similar process.
2 The group leader then reads out the following instructions, using the same relaxed voice as previously; pausing briefly at each '. . .'

> 'Now I'd like you to remember how it was when you first began this course . . . the things you saw as you first came into this group and heard my voice and the voices of the others in the group . . . and the feeling of sitting in the chairs for the first time . . . and really wondering . . . what the course is going to be like . . . and whether you will *learn new things* . . . because there are many ways to *learn new things* . . . not only by listening to the things I explained and reading about communication skills . . . but also by really meeting the people in the group . . . and particularly those people in this group who have had special importance for you . . . at those specific times when you really enjoyed the fact that they were there . . . or learned from the things they said . . . and what you did together . . . as the course went on . . . learning new skills . . . and trying out the ways of talking that you discussed here . . . to see which were most *useful for you personally* . . . realising that some of the skills just clicked into place . . . and you could see right away what use you wanted to make . . . or feel the way that skill would fit for you . . . and thinking through the various topics we studied, all the way up to today . . . .

It's impressive how many things *you did learn* . . . not always what you expected . . . or even what the course planned . . . but what you needed . . . and now I'd like you to feel all that wisdom inside you . . . as you remember the place where, above all else you want to *use these skills in your life* . . . because if you could use these skills in that most important relationship . . . even enough to recognise that *you are behaving differently now* . . . and *you have changed subtly* . . . then you would know that *you can use these skills* in any situation you need them . . . at home . . . with friends . . . in your job . . . in this group . . . and with those people who are most challenging for you . . . or most precious to you . . . so let's take a situation where it's *most* important to use communication skills . . . and look at that situation . . . and see the place . . . and the person or people there . . . clearly enough so you can see the particular expression they have at the time *you can use your new skills* . . . and hear the very tone of voice which reminds you that now is the time to *find the words you need* . . . which is the very best time to *anchor that feeling of relaxation* again . . . and imagine yourself actually using the skills *you have learned*' (pause) 'listening as you surprise yourself with a new way of responding to whatever they say . . . and always knowing that in your collection of skills *you can find the right solutions* . . . now or in the future . . . so that you may be beginning to be aware of the sense of confidence that this will bring . . . and how these new skills can *create whole new ways to meet your needs* and the needs of those you love . . . which is a good understanding to bring back to the room . . . as you become aware of your surroundings here in the room . . . returning in your own time to being fully aware and awake and ready to talk again.'

EXERCISE 11.2

Aim — to create a sense of closure in life.

1 The group leader asks people to imagine that this is the last day of their life. They are taking pen and paper to write some final comments on their life, to leave for those they love. They will have 20 minutes to write answers to the following questions:

- a What have you valued most of all in your life?
- b What are the most important insights you have gained from life?
- c Who or what had the most influence on your life?
- d What has challenged you most in this life?
- e What are your life's most important achievements?
- f What are your biggest unfulfilled dreams or desires?
- g What would you do differently if you had the chance?
- h Who do you need to speak to today? What will you say?
- i What do you most want to do today?
- j What advice do you have for others in a similar life to yours?

2 Share in pairs:

- a What did you learn writing this?
- b What questions were most difficult to answer?
- c What questions were most useful to consider?

Putting the Pieces Together

Objective: to be able to use the process of chunking to assist learning.

The Shrine

Once upon a time a brave explorer travelled into the centre of a harsh, lifeless desert. There she discovered a mysterious group of people. In the only oasis in the desert wastes, these people were facing hard times. There was barely enough food for them to survive from one year to the next. In the cold winter nights the weaker of the people died from lack of adequate nourishment and covering. For many years, they had braved this terrible environment, but it did not seem likely that even those courageous souls who were left would last much longer . . . For the high priest of this people, a man named Ler-Na, had taken to demanding an ever increasing share of their food as offerings to his sacred shrine. The explorer was puzzled. Crossing the desert had been risky, but there *was* a way. Surely these people could have left their tiny oasis and found their way to the green pastures beyond the desert's end. Why had they never sent out scouts to search for the passage? Did not their ancestors know the way? Eventually, she confronted Ler-Na and asked him these questions. He smiled tolerantly, and beckoned her to follow him. 'I know you are puzzled,' he answered reassuringly, 'but our deliverance is at hand. We have the answer to all our problems right here in this oasis, and it was indeed passed on to us by those same ancestors who brought us here. If only we treat it with the reverence it deserves, it will end all the difficulties we face here. It can also help you and your people.'

He led her into a deep cave beside the village. At first she could not see in the darkness, but as the priest lit a lantern the explorer recognised what must surely be the sacred shrine itself. Around it she could see the ashes of the food offerings. And perched on top of a huge stone slab was the magical focus of this people's religion. 'You may touch it,' the priest encourages, 'it is for the benefit of all humanity. We are merely the caretakers of this powerful magic.' Slowly, she opened it. Perfect in every detail, it was a map of the region, clearly marking the way out to green pastures.

Maps and Actualities

The people of the oasis are starving because of a confusion about the purpose of maps. Everyone of us moves around in the world by the use of our maps, our internal models of reality. But maps are only of use if you are willing to put them aside, once you have studied them, and actually live.

This book gives you many new maps to understand communication: maps like 'problem ownership', 'problem solving', 'helping', and 'assertiveness'. Once you have learned these maps you will know 'where you are' in a relationship, and 'which road to take' to get to the places you want to be.

Like the explorer, you will understand that these maps are *not* sacred. It is life itself which is sacred. Where the map doesn't fit with your life, you will have the wisdom to redesign the map so it suits you. Maps are only useful when they help you get around in the world.

SIX MAIN MAPS

There are six main maps in this book. They are:

1 *States*: With this map you can recognise what state of mind you and others are in, and change your own state.
2 *Problem management*: This map enables you to recognise who owns a problem, and find useful solutions for them.
3 *Helping*: When someone else owns a problem, this map gives you specific skills to assist them in finding solutions that will work for them.
4 *Assertion*: This map provides specific skills to express your own feelings or opinions, and explain your own problems, without putting others down.
5 *Conflict management*: Combining the maps for problem management — helping and assertion — this map helps you to prevent, recognise, and resolve the three types of conflict.
6 *Groupwork*: With this last map, the skills of the other five maps can be used in the more complex environment of a group. Each of these six main maps has several sub-maps, as shown on p. 252.

Helping and assertiveness have a special relationship: a relationship of balance. Assertion is more active, ensuring *my* needs are met, and helping is more passive, enabling the other person to meet their needs. The diagram on p. 253 is used in China and Japan to express the way active and passive intertwine. As the diagram shows, in the middle of active (assertive) times, there is also a place for being passive. In the middle of passive (helping) times, there is an area where being active is useful. In conflict resolution and groupwork this balance between assertion and helping is emphasised even more.

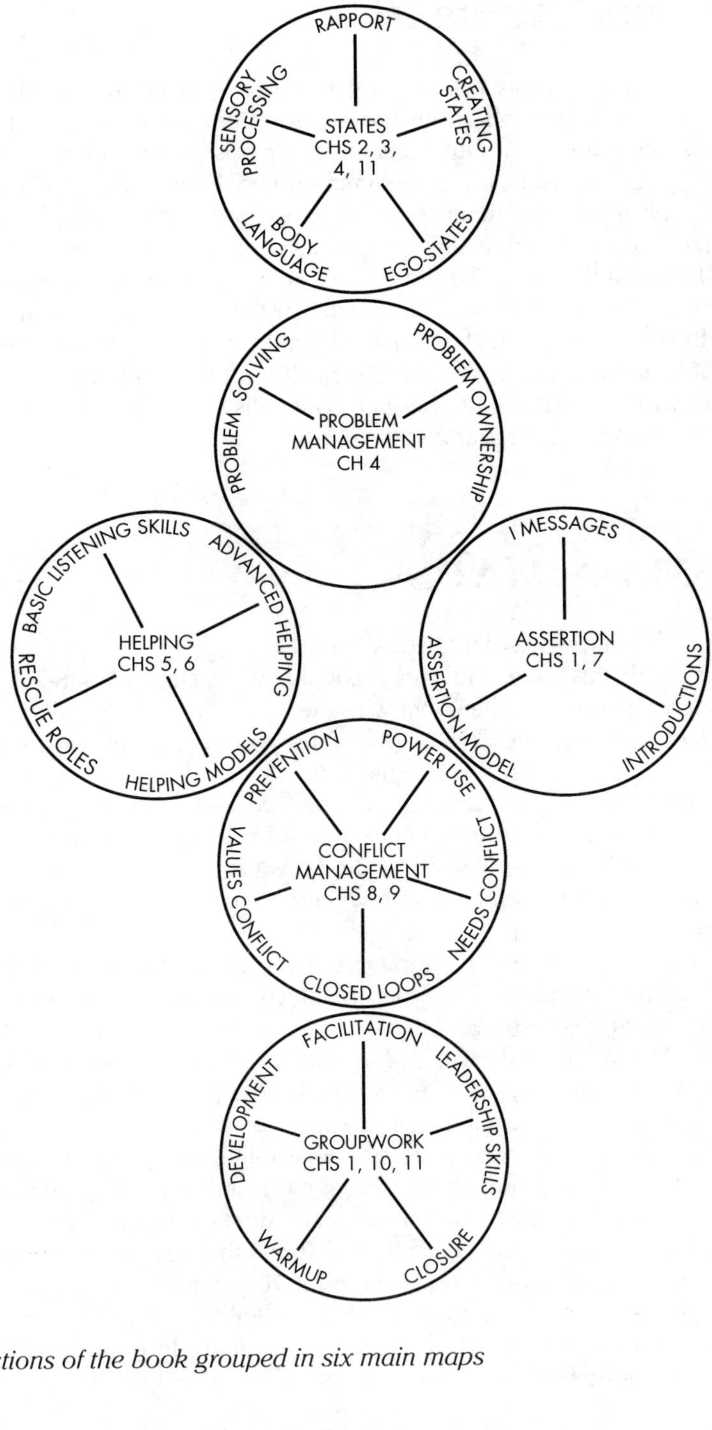

▶ *Sections of the book grouped in six main maps*

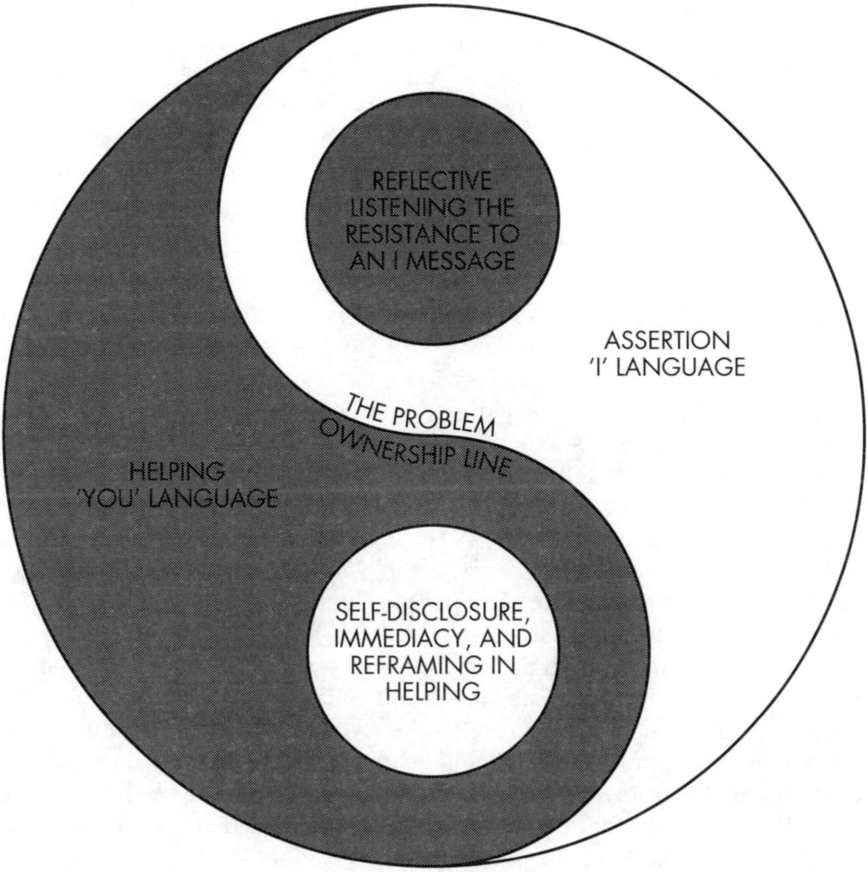

Chunking Down

The final skill which I want to explain to you is the skill of creating your *own* maps.

Try saying the alphabet to yourself for a moment . . . The alphabet has 26 bits of information (letters) in it, and to remember it you almost certainly said it in sections rather than in a continuous stream. These sections are called 'chunks', and the process of dividing something up into little bits is called chunking down. To learn a complex subject you need to chunk it down. Probably you remember people's telephone numbers the same way: in two chunks.

7±2

George Miller from Harvard University (reported in Rose 1985, p. 57) published a remarkable paper about chunking down. He showed that people can only hold between 5 and 9 (or '7 plus or minus 2' to use Miller's words) bits of information at one time. So if you want to remember something, break it into chunks that have around 7 facts each. Using lists of 10 or 20 things makes it difficult to remember. Incidentally, this principle is also used in this book. All 'unchunked' lists have six or less items. Look at the diagram on page 252, for example: there are six main maps — states, problem management, helping, assertion, conflict management, and group-work. Each of these is then chunked into five or less sections.

Chunking Up or Down

Knowing when to chunk down (get more detailed) and when to chunk up (get more general) is extremely important in communication. It's the secret behind many of the skills taught in this book. Whenever you are defining a problem (for example, telling someone in an I message what upsets you or helping a person clarify what upsets them), it's important to chunk *down* to details.

This means talking in a 'sensory specific' way — saying what you can see, hear, smell, taste, and touch. Most people (including most counsellors and therapists) tend to forget this. They talk about people being 'nice', or 'aggressive', or 'unsupportive', 'coping', 'not coping', 'in such and such a role', 'neurotic', 'psychotic','negative', and so on, without clarifying exactly what they saw or heard. As a result, others who are listening have to guess what actually happened, to 'hallucinate' the meaning. Usually they hallucinate differently from the speaker. Defining the problem as 'I felt really resentful when you started speaking halfway through my sentence' will need less hallucination than 'Your aggressive manner bothers me'.

On the other hand, when you are seeking new solutions to problems, it can help to chunk up, to get more general. Reframing is an example of chunking up. It involves making new and more useful generalisations about what is happening. When someone says 'I hate you', to say 'Thank you for being honest' is reframing; it makes a new generalisation ('being honest') about the three specific words 'I hate you'. To chunk up, ask yourself, 'What is this specifically an example of?'

Conflict resolution involves chunking up. When you define your basic *goals* or *needs* instead of your *solution*, you are describing things in a more general, less specific way. Instead of saying, 'I want the car this Saturday night' (a specific solution) you say 'I need to get to my meeting on Saturday' (a more general goal which could have several specific solutions).

LEARNING AS CHUNKING

All the models, the maps, the 'communication skills' in this book are generalisations from specific things that people said and did. Thomas

Gordon, for example, developed the six step process of win-win conflict resolution. When he taught it to parents, several came back to his classes saying it didn't work for their specific situations. These situations included a teenage daughter wanting to wear a miniskirt, an adolescent who preferred a group of friends his parent didn't like, an a youngster who refused to go to church.

From these specific situations, Gordon recognised a general principle: there were two different types of conflict (conflicts of needs and values collisions) and the win-win method was not the most effective skill for values conflicts. Here is the process Gordon used:

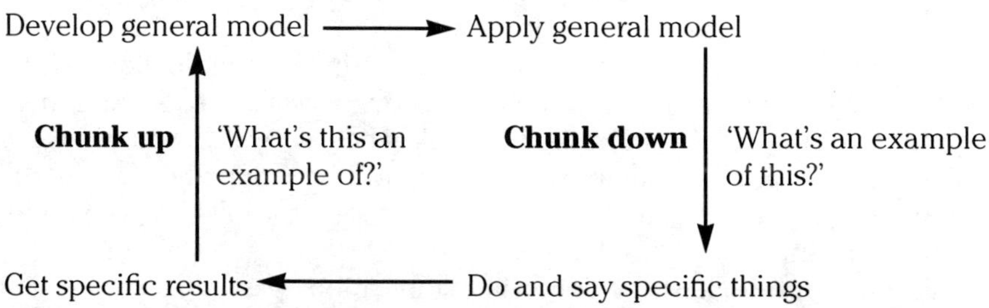

If you've been doing the exercises in this book, you've already been using this learning process. As you use communication skills in more and more specific situations, you're able to create generalisations which work for *you* (your own maps).

Love

The most useful generalisation I've been able to make about communication is that good communication is based in love. From the beginning, when my very survival depended on my mother and father's love, life has repeated this message again and again.

I thank my many teachers (people like George Sweet, Charlotte Daellenbach, Fred Grosse, and Vimala Thakar) for so clearly demonstrating and re-emphasising the importance of love. It seems to me that the writings of the great explorers in communication (I think of Carl Rogers, Thomas Gordon, Virginia Satir, Anthony Robbins, and the developers of N.L.P.) are also most of all about love. *And* love improves when you share it.

Whatever you've learned in this book will become clearer when you let it flow on to others. In Alcoholics Anonymous this is called 'The Twelfth Step'. When one alcoholic reaches sobriety, he or she finds another to help. I don't know whether you will teach, whether you will be a parent, a counsellor, a caregiver, or an artist, but I know you will find a time and place to reinforce your own learning by helping another learn whatever was precious here.

Gifts

No gift is too small that it cannot make a difference. You may be surprised where your assistance to another ends up. For example, when I was four years old, my mother bought me a young children's version of the 'Bambi' story. She must have read it to me a hundred times ... so many times that by the end I finally understood that the first five chunks of letters on page one were the first five words of the story. I had learned to read. Would I be writing a book now if not for that gift? Probably not.

When I was nine, my father told me how, during his own childhood, he used to spend hours lying on a tree branch overlooking a river. And there he dreamt of the future, and asked himself what life was. I could see the light in his eyes as he remembered this. Would I be writing here about the importance of love, if I never had that childhood permission to wonder about the meaning of it all? I doubt it.

Anthony Robbins tells the following story about passing on what you receive:

> *When I was a kid, our parents worked extremely hard to take good care of us. For various reasons we found ourselves in extremely tight financial situations. I remember one Thanksgiving when we had no money. Things were looking dim until someone arrived at the front door with a box full of canned goods and a turkey. The man who delivered it said it was from someone who knew we would not ask for anything and loved us and wanted us to have a great Thanksgiving. I never forgot that day. So every Thanksgiving, I do what someone did for me that day: I go out and buy about a week's worth of food and deliver it to a family in need. I deliver the food as the worker or delivery boy, never as the person actually providing the gift. I always leave a note that says 'This is from someone who cares about you and hopes someday you will take good enough care of yourself that you'll go out and return the favour for someone else in need.'*

That's the note I'd like to leave with this book too. I have no illusions about the world. The world can be a very brutal place, and good communication is rare. But you and I both know that it *can* change. Live long and prosper. And as you discover the secrets of living your life fully, may you pass them on to someone else in need.

Chunking

Example: the division of communication skills into (1) state, (2) problem management, (3) helping, (4) assertion, (5) conflict management, (6) groupwork. Chunk into 7 ± 2 pieces.

Chunking up
(Getting more generalised)
e.g. reframing, conflict resolution, developing your own maps to explain communication. Ask 'What is this an example of?'

Chunking down
(Getting more sensory specific)
e.g. to define the problem, to apply communication skills. Ask 'What is an example of this?'

EXERCISE 11.3

Aim — to practise the use of chunking and teaching design skills.

1 Reach a group consensus as to which are the five most important communication skills for a particular population (e.g. high school students, health care workers, parents, a particular work group).

2 Plan five two-hour sessions at which you will teach these five skills to a group of these people. Take 30 minutes. Decide:

— how well you expect the students to learn these skills
— what handouts with information, or worksheets, you'll need
— what exercises you will use to practise the skills.

SUMMARY

Mostly this chapter has been about endings. We examined *Kubler-Ross' grief process* (denial–anger–bargaining–depression–acceptance), and considered various situations where grief is expressed, including the Maori process of *tangihanga*. For those times when the ending of a relationship is planned, we can assist the process of *closure* by allowing for evaluation, referral, and futurepacing.

As part of the ending of this book, this chapter not only presents an overview of the concepts taught, but also an explanation of *chunking*. Chunking is the actual process of making generalisations from the details of our experience. With it you can design your own map of this book, and create your own concepts.

Bibliography & Further Reading

Cameron-Bandler, L. (1985) *Solutions*, Futurepace Books, San Rafael, California.

James, T. and Woodsmall, W. (1988) *Time Line Therapy and the Basis of Personality*, Meta Publications, Cupertino, California.

Kubler-Ross, Dr E. (1980) *On Death and Dying,* MacMillan, New York.

Munro, A., Manthei, B., Small, J. (1988) *Counselling: The Skills of Problem Solving*, Longman Paul, Auckland.

Robbins, A. (1988) *Unlimited Power*, Simon & Schuster, London.

Rose, C. (1985) *Accelerated Learning*, Accelerated Learning Systems Ltd, Aylesbury, Buckinghamshire, England.

Schutz, W. (1975) *Elements of Encounter*, Bantam, New York.

A FAREWELL

The first book I read about communication changed my life. I was 12 years old, and the book (it happened to be *Between Parent and Child* by Dr Haim Ginott) explained I messages and reflective listening. Right away I felt incredibly excited. I realised that these simple ideas would enable people to relate in an entirely different way.

If you've read this far, you have shared in that excitement. You will have learned some new ways of understanding what goes on in *your* life . . . you may have discovered some new skills, or looked at some old skills in a new light . . . and you may notice, even now, some changes in the way you're thinking about your relationships. And that's good, because it means that *your experience has already begun to shift at a deeper level*, hasn't it: moving towards the kind of choices you've wanted to make.

But you've done much more than reading a book, because this book is a journey through many of the things that are precious to me personally. In that very real sense, I believe you will have met *me*, and those who wrote this book with me (Margot, Jan, and Te Hata). And so you'll understand that I wish you well, as your conscious mind considers and makes sense of all these things, and as your unconscious mind creates opportunities for you to *put into practice those things that will work for you*.

If I could make one final suggestion it would be that you put this book somewhere easy for you to find when *you want to read it again*.

Best wishes as you return to your present and to your journey.

Index to Exercises

CHAPTER 1

Exercise 1.1 — to recognise the way beliefs (or 'maps') change the way we feel about and respond to situations (p. 6)

Exercise 1.2 — to investigate different ways of initiating conversations (p. 10)

Exercise 1.3 — to recognise how beliefs about people we meet affect our meeting (p. 11)

Exercise 1.4 — to learn each others' names and begin creating a sense of group cohesion (p. 13)

Exercise 1.5 — to create a sense of contract about how the group sessions are run (p. 15)

CHAPTER 2

Exercise 2.1 — to use postural change to create a state of trust (trust fall) (p. 31)

Exercise 2.2 — to use visual imagery to create state of raised self-esteem (visual swish) (p. 31)

Exercise 2.3 — to use tone of voice and anchoring to create a state of relaxation (p. 33)

Exercise 2.4 — to observe how your state of mind naturally changes (p. 34)

Exercise 2.5 — to affirm the significance of group members ancestry and sense of place (p. 43)

Exercise 2.6 — to affirm group members sense of gender identity (p. 44)

Exercise 2.7 — to help group members understand the social origins of body image, and affirm their own body (p. 45)

Exercise 2.8 — to identify student's individual parent, adult, and child ego states (p. 52)

Exercise 2.9 — to explore group members childhood 'life expectation patterns' (p. 53)

CHAPTER 3

Exercise 3.1 — to get used to the difference between intimate zone, personal zone, and social zone (p. 59)

Exercise 3.2 — to develop your skills in recognising the non-verbal expression of feelings (p. 63)
Exercise 3.3 — to consider how 'masculine' and 'feminine' postures relate to 'male' and 'female' social roles (p. 65)
Exercise 3.4 — to remind you of your ability to identify correctly states of attraction and dislike from non-verbal cues (p. 70)
Exercise 3.5 — to recognise sensory accessing cues in others(p. 76)
Exercise 3.6 — to discover which sensory system gives *you* the most important information about being loved (p. 77)
Exercise 3.7 — to develop your skills in pacing someone auditorally, visually, and kinesthetically (p. 80)

CHAPTER 4

Exercise 4.1 — to check understanding of the Problem Ownership Model (p. 87)
Exercise 4.2 — to give group members a supervised experience of the goal-setting and problem-solving process (p. 93)
Exercise 4.3 — to experience the value of goalsetting (p. 93)
Exercise 4.4 — to experience the value of creative brainstorming (p. 94)

CHAPTER 5

Exercise 5.1 — to provide practice identifying roadblocks and their effects (p. 108)
Exercise 5.2 — to experience the effect of attending (p. 111)
Exercise 5.3 — to practise forming open questions (p. 114)
Exercise 5.4 — to increase awareness of the different effect produced by open and closed questions (p. 114)
Exercise 5.5 — to practise developing reflective responses (p. 121)
Exercise 5.6 — to practise developing reflective listening in a group situation (p. 122)
Exercise 5.7 — to practise reflective listening in a one-to-one situation (p. 123)

CHAPTER 6

Exercise 6.1 — to feel human electrical energy 1–10 cm out from the body (p. 137)
Exercise 6.2 — to practise the use of touch as a helping process (shoulder massage) (p. 138)

Exercise 6.3 — to practise the use of helping skills and receive specific feedback (p. 149)

Exercise 6.4 — to practise the individual skills of metamodel questioning, matching sensory systems, confrontation, reframing, self-disclosure, and immediacy (p. 151)

CHAPTER 7

Exercise 7.1 — to assertively give and receive compliments (p. 164)

Exercise 7.2 — to experiment with different intensities of disagreement (p. 165)

Exercise 7.3 — to practise writing I messages (p. 179)

Exercise 7.4 — to practise saying I messages (p. 180)

Exercise 7.5 — to rediscover the side vents on your 'Anger volcano' (p. 180)

CHAPTER 8

Exercise 8.1 — to use Gordon and Adams' model for Modifying the Environment to Prevent Conflicts (p. 189)

Exercise 8.2 — to recognise our personal style of responding to the use of power (p. 195)

Exercise 8.3 — to experience non-verbally our own reaction to the use of power (p. 196)

Exercise 8.4 — to develop the win-win way of thinking about conflict (p. 207)

CHAPTER 9

Exercise 9.1 — to find shared values for your group (p. 216)

Exercise 9.2 — to discover the qualities of good influencers (p. 217)

Exercise 9.3 — to practise consulting about a values' issue with a partner who has different values about the issue you discuss (p. 217)

Exercise 9.4 — to clarify values based decisions (p. 219)

CHAPTER 10

Exercise 10.1 — to develop skills in group observation (p. 227)

Exercise 10.2 — to explore levels of intimacy in the group (p. 228)

Exercise 10.3 — to develop group members' consensus building skills (p. 237)

CHAPTER 11

Exercise 11.1 — to futurepace the learnings from your course (p. 247)
Exercise 11.2 — to create a sense of closure in life (p. 249)
Exercise 11.3 — to practise the use of chunking and teaching design skills (p. 257)

ANSWER TO EXERCISE 4.4

There are an infinite number of solutions. The most obvious are:

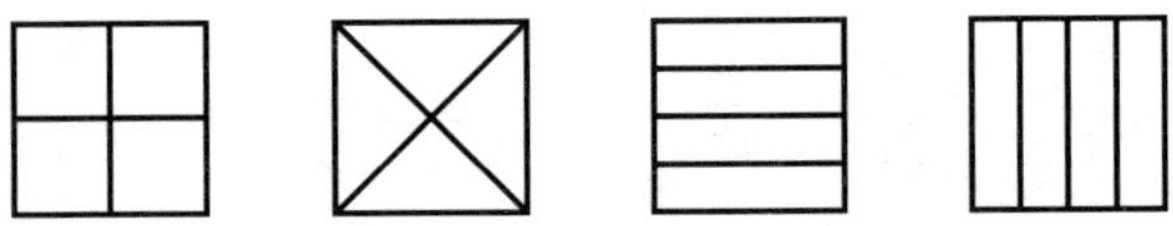

Any solution where the cake is cut in half first and then the halves are divided into an even half will also work, for example:

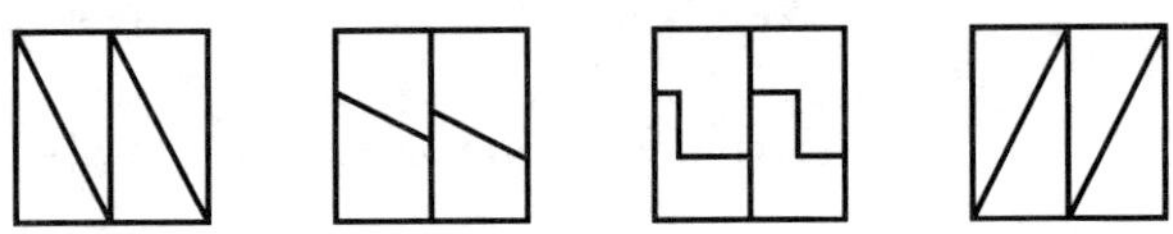

Any solution where two lines cross the centre at right angles will work, for example:

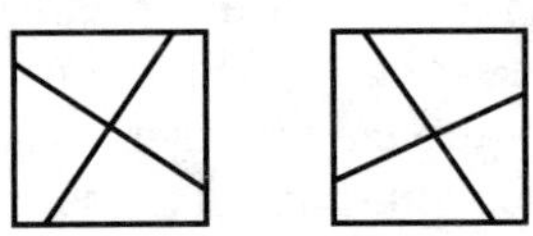

Solutions can be found by complex division of the square, or by using curved lines to vary any other solution, for example:

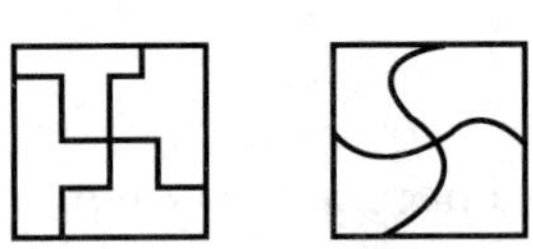

ANSWERS FOR EXERCISE 10.3

Percentage of Women Employed in NZ 1986

	%
Kindergarten teachers	99
Primary teachers	70
Secondary teachers	49
University lecturers	20.4
Practising doctors	20
Secondary principals	16
Primary principals	14
Lawyers	12
Members of parliament	13
Accountants	9.7
Managers	9.0
University professors	2.9

Most preferred characteristics in a spouse:

Women	*Men*
1 Looks, physical attraction	1 Looks, physical attraction
2 Way he relates to me	2 General personality
3 General personality	3 Way she relates to me
4 Good communication	4 Erotic ability
5 Sense of humour	5 Intelligence
6 Social ability	6 Similar interests/attitudes
7 Affection	7 Good communication
8 Erotic ability	8 Entertaining ability
9 Entertaining ability	9 Social ability
10 Quiet and shy	10 Purely sexual attraction

Index

Addiction 162
Aggressive behaviour 158–159
Anchoring 29–30, 148, 245–246
Anger 174–176
Anxiety 32–34, 67–68
Assertive behaviour 159–160
Assertiveness 155–182
Assertive rights 161
Attending 110–111
Attraction 66–67, 70–71
Auditory 72–77, 80, 141–142

Bandler, Richard 72, 139, 212, 246
Beliefs 5–6, 10–11
Berne, Eric 46–53
Body language 55–82
Breathing 28–29, 69, 74

Cameron-Bandler, Leslie 72, 139, 163
Catharsis 129–130
Children 199–202
Chunking 253–255
Codependence 162
Cohesion 12, 222–223
Closure 244
- in groups 244
- in helping 244

Compliments 164, 177–178
Confidence 68, 69
Confidentiality 131, 132
Conflict 73, 183–220
- of needs 197–208
- of values 212–218
- closed communication loops 188–189
- prevention 186–189

Confrontation 142–143
Consensus 231–239
Contract 12–17, 131
Culture 18–19, 37–40

Developmental stages 224
Doctor-Nurse Game 42
Durie, Mason 133–134

Ego states (T. A.) 46–50
- excluded 49
- contaminated 49–50

Erikson, Eric 224
Ethics 130–132
Eye movements 75–77
Facilitation 229–239
Feeling 119, 129–130, 169, 174–176
Futurepacing 245–246

Grief 242–244
Goalsetting 89–94
Gordon, Thomas 84–88, 186, 193, 198
Greenspan, Miriam 135–136
Grinder, John 72, 139, 212
Groups 12–17, 221–239, 244
- stages in groups 223–224, 244

Holism 132–138

I messages 166–181
Immediacy 146–147
Introductions 4–11, 20–21, 66

Karpman, Stephen 103, 105
Kasl, Charlotte Davis 162
Kinesthetic 72–77, 80, 141–142
Kubler-Ross, Elisabeth 242–244

Learning stages 95–97
Listening 109–114
Love 24–25, 66–67, 77, 139, 162–163, 255–256
Manthei, Marjorie 161, 177
Maintenance (of groups) 255–256
Maori 18–21, 37–39, 60–62, 133–134, 243–244
Maps 6, 10–11, 25, 250–252
Maslow, Abraham 95
McMaster, Ken 43, 175
Meetings 233–234
Memory 47–48
Men 41–43, 64, 73–74, 131
Metamodel 139–142
Mihi 20–21
Minimal encouragers 112
Mirroring 78–81, 115–124, 141–142
Modelling 214–215
Moreno, Jacob 104, 147

Now (speaking in the now) 147

Obedience 190–191

Pakeha 18–21, 39–40, 60–62, 73
Paraphrasing 119
Perception check 119–120
Perls, Fritz 132, 147
Posture 28, 61, 64–69
Power 190–196, 203–204, 230
Problem ownership 84–88, 157, 184
Problem solving 89–94, 128–130
Proxemics (closeness) 56–59
Punishment 192
Pupil size 57

Questions 112–114, 139–141, 173–174

Rapport 4, 78–81, 115–124
Referral 245
Reflecting feeling 119
Reflective listening 115–124, 141–142
Reframing 144–145, 212
Rescue triangle 103–105
Rewards 192–193
Roadblocks 105–108, 158
Robbins, Anthony 79, 256
Rogers, Carl 4, 9, 36, 79–80
Role theory 104, 105
Royds, Bryan 175–176

Schaef, Anne Wilson 42, 162
Schutz, William 223, 244
Self-affirmation 27, 161
Self-disclosure (helping) 146
State 24–35, 46–50
Summarising 120, 173–174
Sweet, George 118

Tangihanga 243, 244
Task needs (in groups) 255–256
Touch 62, 130–131, 137
Transactions (T. A.) 50–51

Unassertive behaviour 158
Uncertainty 68
Unemployment 36–37

Values 209–220
Visual 72–77, 80, 141–142
Visualising 26–27, 72

Warmup 12–17
Whakaiti 38, 160
Win-win 197, 208
Women 40–44, 64, 73–74, 131, 135–136